Disability and New Media

Routledge Studies in New Media and Cyberculture

Routledge Studies in New Media and Cyberculture is dedicated to furthering original research in new media and cyberculture studies. International in scope, the series places an emphasis on cutting edge scholarship and interdisciplinary methodology. Topics explored in the series will include comparative and cultural studies of video games, blogs, online communities, digital music, new media art, cyberactivism, open source, mobile communications technologies, new information technologies, and the myriad intersections of race, gender, ethnicity, nationality, class, and sexuality with cyberculture.

Series Titles

Disability and New Media

Katie Ellis and Mike Kent

Routledge
Taylor & Francis Group

LONDON AND NEW YORK

First published 2011
by Routledge

2 Park Square, Milton Park, Abingdon, Oxon OX14 4RN
52 Vanderbilt Avenue, New York, NY 10017

Routledge is an imprint of the Taylor & Francis Group, an informa business

Typeset in Sabon by EvS Communication Networx, Inc.

Library of Congress Cataloging in Publication Data
Ellis, Katie, 1978–
Disability and new media / Katie Ellis and Mike Kent.
p. cm. — (Routledge studies in new media and cyberculture ; 7)
Includes bibliographical references and index.
1. Assistive computer technology. 2. Accessible Web sites for people with disabilities. I. Kent, Mike, 1969- II. Title.
HV1569.5.E45 2011
025.04087—dc22
2010033036

ISBN13: 978-0-415-87135-8 (hbk)
ISBN13: 978-0-203-83191-5 (ebk)

This book is dedicated to our partners

Chris Pearce and Amanda Ellis.

Contents

Acknowledgments

There are many people who have supported us throughout the writing of this book; and we thank them for their interest and encouragement. In writing this book, we sought especially to build on Gerard Goggin and Christopher Newell's work in this area. It was with great sadness that we heard of Christopher's passing before having a chance to discuss our ideas with him. His contribution to this discipline was instrumental in shaping our desire to also work in this area. Gerard Goggin has been a true mentor, providing valuable feedback on the work and encouragement regarding its worth, especially in moments of doubt.

We feel indebted to and encouraged by the burgeoning discipline of critical disability studies in Australia and wish to thank members of this community for advancing this area from an "Australian" perspective including in particular Fiona Kumari Campbell, and Helen Meekosha. Web 2.0 platforms have also allowed us to join an international community of disability activists, academics, and technicians. We thank the vibrant disability and accessibility Facebook and Twitter communities we have been able to join and benefit from. Dennis Lembree, Angella Hooker, and Maria Strong have been the source of some excellent links, trending topics, and accessibility hints. We thank also Beth Haller for her insights on disability, Facebook and blogs, and her willingness to share them with us on Facebook. Along the way we've talked to numerous people with disability, both online and off and we thank you all for your insights about how you access the web.

We also wish to thank Tara Brabazon, Mick Broderick, Matthew Allen, and Debbie Rodan for their encouragement to pursue this project. We are also grateful to Amanda Ellis, David Cake, Kate Raynes-Goldie, Dave Aitcheson, Carleen Ellis, and Ceridwen Clocherty for their feedback on certain sections of the book. Leanne Ellis' insights on all things computer have also been greatly appreciated.

Finally, we thank especially our partners Chris and Amanda for putting up with us as we sometimes used (although legitimate) writing this book as an excuse from household chores and a reason to spend more time on Facebook, Twitter, and Second Life. We acknowledge also our pets, Fritz and Cameron who didn't do much but seem to deserve a mention!

Parts of Chapter 3 were first published in *Media Culture* and the sections on Twitter in Chapter 4 were first published in *Fast Capitalism*. We thank the editors of these journals for their support and encouragement and permission to republish here.

Abbreviations

3D	Three dimensional
ADA	Americans with Disabilities Act
AFB	American Foundation for the Blind
Ajax	Asynchronous JavaScript and XML
Alt Text	Alternative text
AOL	American Online
Apps	Application software
ARPANET	Advanced Research Projects Agency Network
Captcha	Completely automated public Turing test to tell computers and humans apart
CD	Compact disk
CERN	Conseil Européen pour la Recherche Nucléaire
CSUN	California State University, Northridge
DARPA	(US Defence Department's) Advanced Projects Research Agency
DBCDE	Department of Broadband, Communications and the Digital Economy
DDA	Disability Discrimination Act
DMCA	Digital Millennium Copyright Act
DRM	Digital rights management
DVD	Digital video disc (also digital versatile disk)
EFF	Electronic Frontier Foundation
FBI	Federal Bureau of Investigations
GB	Giga byte
GPS	Global positioning system
HCI	Human computer interaction
HREOC	Australian Human Rights and Equal Opportunity Commission
HTML	Hypertext markup language
HTML5	Hypertext markup language version 5
IBM	International Business Machines
ICT	Information and Communications Technology
IMDB	Internet movie database
IPO	International Program Office for the Web Accessibility Initiative

IRC	Internet Relay Chat
JAWS	Job access with speech
MACs	Macintosh Brand Computers manufactured by Apple Inc
MIRC	Internet Relay Chat for Microsoft Windows
MOGs	Massive online games
MOOs	MUD object orientated
MP3	MPEG-1 (Moving Picture Expert Group) Audio Layer 3
MUDs	Multi-user dungeons
NAD	National Association of the Deaf
NASDAQ	National Association of Securities Dealers Automated Quotations
NCSA	National Centre for Supercomputing Applications
NDC	National Disability Coordination Officer Program
NFB	National Federation of the Blind
NGN	Next generation network
NSF	National Science Foundation
NTIA	National Telecommunications and Information Administration
OCP	Omni Consumer Products
OS X	Mac OS X Leopard operating system
PBS	Public Broadcasting Service
PC	Personal computer
POUR	Perceivable, operable, understandable and robust
RNIB	Royal National Institute for the Blind
Section 508	Section 508 of the United States' Rehabilitation Act 1973
Section 504	Section 504 of the United States' Rehabilitation Act 1973
SL	Second Life
SMS	Short message service
SOCOG	Sydney Organising Committee for the Olympic Games
TEITAC	Telecommunications and Electronic and Information Technology Advisory Committee
THQ	Toy Head-Quarters
TTY	Telephone typewriters
UPIAS	Union of Physically Impaired against Segregation
US	United States
USSR	Union of Soviet Socialist Republics
UWA	University of Western Australia
W3C	World Wide Web Consortium
WAI	Web accessibility initiative
WCAG	Web Content Accessibility Guidelines
WCAG 1.0	Web Content Accessibility Guidelines (WCAG) 1.0
WCAG 2.0	Web Content Accessibility Guidelines (WCAG) 2.0

Introduction

The Great Potential of Digital Technology

"The dream behind the Web is of a common information space in which we communicate by sharing information.

The power of the Web is in its universality. Access by everyone regardless of disability is an essential aspect."

(Tim Berners-Lee, inventor of the World Wide Web, 1997)

In *Disability and New Media*, we explore how the early promise of the World Wide Web of access for all people regardless of disability has been hijacked by more recent developments in the online environment — from web 2.0 to virtual worlds. Many of the studies on disability and the web have focused on the early web, that is prior to the development of social networking applications such as Facebook, YouTube, and Second Life. This book discusses an array of such applications that have grown within and alongside web 2.0, and analyzes how they both prevent and embrace the inclusion of people with disability. The chapters that follow pursue the subject of disability from a number of directions — as integral to the future of the web, as in need of a theoretical revision, and as an opportunity to fully understand the diversity of the human experience.

Disability and New Media sets out its readings of disability within the domain of cultural and media studies; it is not intended to provide technical instructions on how to make websites accessible. Rather, it explores the significance and potential of the social construction of accessibility. In articulating his vision for a platform to share information, Berners-Lee believed that access for everyone regardless of disability was a crucial factor:

Worldwide, there are more than 750 million people with disabilities. As we move towards a highly connected world, it is critical that the Web be useable by anyone, regardless of individual capabilities and disabilities ... The W3C [World Wide Web Consortium] is committed to removing accessibility barriers for all people with disabilities — including the deaf, blind, physically challenged, and cognitively or visually impaired. We plan to work aggressively with government, industry, and community leaders to establish and attain Web accessibility goals. (Berners-Lee, 1997)

Web 2.0 platforms — with their focus on user-centred design, online collaboration, and user-generated content and participation — are generally seen as moving closer toward Berners-Lee's grand vision for a shared information space, where people can collaborate without barriers. However, it is becoming apparent that the increasing use of complex graphics and unstandardized user-generated content have resulted in a rejection of web standards, thereby taking Berners-Lee's vision of universality in a different direction (Craven, 2008). As Gerard Goggin and Christopher Newell argued in their seminal book on this topic, *Digital Disability*, the internet will not be fully accessible to all until disability is considered a cultural identity in the same way as class, gender, and sexuality. Goggin and Newell (2003) explain that although digital technologies such as the internet, broadband, and advanced telecommunications have the potential to revolutionize the lives of people with disability, this will not occur unless the trend to "build in" disabling features at the point of production is addressed. Since the time of their writing, there have been massive shifts in the way the web is used and developed. Yet accessibility, although more widely understood, is still generally ignored due to a continuation of the social prejudice that Goggin and Newell (2003) sought to expose.

The internet has been credited with "opening up the world" to people with disability, in particular those with an impaired capacity to use print media. The group of people with "print impairments" may include the following:

A person with blindness or low vision.
A person unable to hold or manipulate books or to focus or move their eyes.
A person with a perceptual disability. (National Disability Officer Coordination
    program, 2010)

Technology has the potential to assist this group to access text-based information — and indeed has in many instances. For example, social networking and online blogs have allowed this group to become more connected in public debate and interact socially with others in the community. Braille tablets and audio books likewise allow people with print impairments the possibility of participating in the workforce. New technology is a prominent component of social, cultural, and political change with the potential to allow a fuller inclusion for people with disability. Yet, as society collectively becomes more dependent on internet and computer technologies, people with disability face being left behind. Our concern is that historical analog social prejudice is reproduced in the digital world.

Technology is often presented as an automatic source of liberation; however, developments associated with web 2.0 show that this is not always the case. The uneven interface of the virtual and the analog indicates that inclusion is far from an inevitable consequence of development. Technological advancement does not occur as something separate from ideology and stigma, and web 2.0 has been developed in and by the same social world that routinely disables people with disability. However, a resistance has emerged in an attempt to reverse this trend in the form of critical disability studies, a discipline which seeks to reveal the workings of a disabling social world.

Critical Disability Studies

The discipline of critical disability studies seeks to develop new ways of understanding disability. An emerging discipline, it has developed from the now familiar base concepts of other investigations of the social construction of exclusion. In much the same way that other marginalized groups have exposed the ways that discriminatory environments have prevented their full inclusion, the disabled movement has rejected the generally-accepted notion that disability is a personal problem within an individual's damaged body. Just as we now recognize the complexities of ways of understanding race or gender that seem "natural", so too have we started to investigate more critically other bodily differences as identities (Garland-Thompson, 2000). This has led to the emergence of a social model of disability which redefines disability as something separate from the body:

> we define impairment as lacking part or all of a limb, or having a defective limb, organ or mechanism of the body; and disability as the disadvantage or restriction of activity caused by a contemporary social organisation which takes little or no account of people who have physical impairments and thus excludes them from participation in the mainstream of social activities. Physical disability is therefore a particular form of social oppression. (Oliver, 1996: 22)

According to this view, "disability" is socially created and is distinct from "impairment" which describes the physical attribute. This social theory argues that a limitation in a person's physical or mental functioning becomes disability because of the impact of the prevailing ableist social structures. This shift in emphasis situates disability in a cultural and political position and establishes a similar model to binary distinctions in other disciplines.

Throughout this book, we use words such as ableism, ableist, and disableist as a tool to organize ideas relating to a non-disabled view of the world. Ableism is an expectation of the primacy of a certain type of body and encompasses the practices that discriminate in favour of non-disabled people. Disablism describes the unwillingness to accommodate different needs (Miller *et al.*, 2004). Further, ableism describes the discrimination experienced by people with impairments; the concept is similar to sexism and racism. Campbell defines ableism as:

> A network of beliefs, processes and practices that produce a particular kind of self and body (the corporeal standard) that is projected as the perfect, species-typical and therefore essential and fully human. 'Disability' then, is a diminished state of being human. (Campbell, 2001)

However, whereas racism and sexism are easier to identify and define, ableism is not as widely understood (Linton, 1996). Critical investigations of disability seek to reveal the ideology and stigma around impairment, and problematize the way disabling attitudes and inaccessible environments influence social interaction and social policy. A consideration of disability as a cultural identity using a minority group model opens the possibility that technologies can be redesigned to eliminate rather than perpetuate ableist oppression.

In this book we also seek to rehabilitate the relevance of impairment to a social, cultural, and political investigation of disability, particularly within the context of digital technologies. While digital technologies have been held up as a way to eradicate socially constructed disability, different impairments do require differing adaptive technologies. As an example, curb cuts — the gaps in the curbing at the side of the road — demonstrate the benefits of the principles of universal design. Indisputably, they allow for improved wheelchair access and also, assist certain non-impaired users of the road and footpath. However, they also serve as a caution against regarding all impairments as the same. While curb cuts are of benefit to one group, they are a hazard to people with vision impairments who use the curbing to differentiate between the road and footpath. This phenomenon is mirrored in the digital environment — innovations that may aid one group of users may exclude another. Universal design, a process that seeks to include the broadest base of potential users, paradoxically is most effectively applied at the level of the individual.

Universal Design

Universal design seeks to accommodate the broadest potential number of users. Adopting this principle, conventional technology seeks to enable use by people with disability while also benefitting the population at large (Symington, 2004). For example, the location of the on/off button at the front of the computer or on the keyboard rather than at the back not only benefits people with disability but also provides convenience for the general population.

The Centre for Universal Design (1997) identified seven features of universal design. First, the design must be equitable by being useful to a number of different people with varying ability and disability. Second, the design must be flexible enough to be used in different ways by different people. Third, by being simple and intuitive, the design should be easy to understand and use regardless of the user's prior experience. The fourth feature of universal design relates to perceptible information which communicates effectively to the user regardless of ambient distractions or the user's sensory ability. The fifth point allows for a tolerance for error which minimizes the impact of potential mistakes and removes any hazardous consequences of these mistakes. The sixth requirement of low physical effort reduces the potential for fatigue and over-exertion. Finally, size and space for approach and use allows enough room for a user to navigate the technology regardless of their size, posture or mobility/ability, for example aids such as a wheelchair.

While the internet had its origins in military research during the 1960s, in 1989 Tim Berners-Lee proposed a more global sharing of information through an internet-based platform — the World Wide Web. He cited "universality" as crucial to the power of this communication across a shared information space:

> Its universality is essential: the fact that a hypertext link can point to anything, be it personal, local or global, be it draft or highly polished. There was a second part of the dream, too, dependent on the Web being so generally used that it became a realistic mirror (or in fact the primary embodiment) of the ways in which we work and play and socialize. That was that once the state of our interactions was on line, we could then use computers to help us analyse it, make sense of what we are doing, where we individually fit in, and how we can better work together. (Berners-Lee, 1998)

Accessibility is central to this universality. While at the CERN (Conseil Européen pour la Recherche Nucléaire) particle physics laboratory, Berners-Lee developed a set of open standards which were made available free to anyone who wished to use them. This freedom of access allowed the medium to develop into the dominant online platform that it is today — to become the embodiment of the way we work, play, and socialize. These agreed protocols also had the potential to benefit users with disability. Berners-Lee's grand vision rested on the theory that digital information is equitable and flexible as it can be accessed by users with different needs in different ways. Text size and color can be changed, and adaptive technology enables text-to-speech or output to a refreshable Braille device. However, technology is not neutral and digital technology has been both enabling and disabling for people with disability — a "realistic mirror" of disableism.

Adaptive technologies such as screenreaders and Braille outputs worked well in the early web environment which consisted largely of text and images. However, more recently, as bandwidth and processing power have grown, the environment has become much more complex. The web has come a long way since the 1990s and accessibility challenges have similarly intensified. The example of people with print impairments shows that the web does not allow "access for all." Developments in web design such as the increasing use of graphics, video, and user-generated content — coupled with conflicting or bypassed standards and the increased use of digital rights management (DRM) to "protect" online content — have created an increasingly complex environment that has a problematic relationship with assistive technology software. Video and animation now play a prominent role in the World Wide Web and new types of protocols have been developed to accommodate this increasing complexity.

As this has happened, the potential for individual users to control how the content is displayed has been diminished. Multimedia — which potentially allows different users with different impairments to communicate in ways that suit them — unfortunately means that each site is without consistency of standards. An unintended consequence of user-generated content is an increase in inaccessibility despite the early promise of universal design. For example, voluntary accessibility features in protocols such as Flash animations are unknown to most users, thereby limiting their potential for those who require different forms of access. These features should be built into the default settings to assist users without technical knowledge to make their user-generated content accessible. This would also help raise awareness of the importance of accessibility and including people with disability.

A number of common themes emerge across all the various aspects of internet-based new media addressed in this book. In many cases, technology starts out being relatively accessible. The early World Wide Web was a largely text-based environment with relatively simple links to other pages. This was very friendly toward screenreaders and other assistive technology. However, in many cases at this emerging level, there were very few people, normally only those with specialist knowledge of the technology, who were able to participate. Thus, ironically, in many cases this more simple technology provided maximum accessibility for people with disability at a time when it was least accessible to the broader population. The early text-based virtual worlds which preceded the more visual and immersive environments of World of Warcraft and Second Life are a prime example of this narrative.

Another theme is that in today's online digital world, technology has a much wider rate of participation amongst the whole population, but is designed in such a way that it excludes people with disability. An example is the social networking site, MySpace. This platform could be an ideal vehicle to improve the life of people with disability who may have mobility and other impairments that make it harder to interact socially in the analog world. They would gain great benefit from being able to use these technologies, yet are excluded by poor design decisions from doing so. As these different networks become more commonplace in the broader community, the societal cost of exclusion from them grows.

The final theme in this story is that these platforms, having achieved wide distribution and acceptance in the general population, belatedly turn their attention to access for people with disability. Access has been improved in a number of areas, from social networking to virtual worlds to iTunes, but we are also mindful that many areas of new media are yet to embrace the drive to accessibility for all. It is encouraging to see that even during the relatively brief period of writing this book, so many positive steps have been taken to make the digital world more accessible for people with disability. However, we argue that attitudes and approaches to these issues need to change more dramatically. The principles of universal design and a positive approach to access for people with disability need to evolve from being just ideas that are applied as a bandaid after a platform achieves success to being ones that are an integral part of the design process from the very beginning.

There is a fear that we are in the process of replicating online the analog environment of which the social model of disability has been so critical. While some positive steps have been taken, we also note the rise of DRM applications that are being implemented to protect digital content from copyright infringement on the internet. These applications often have the unintended, yet critical, side-effect of excluding people with disability from access to legitimate content by preventing assistive technologies from functioning correctly. Worse still is the rise of legislation that makes it illegal to circumvent these technologies in order to permit access.

Information and content stored digitally should be easily accessible in any number of ways to suit the user. Users should be able to choose from a range of different digital media — visually (as images, texts, and subtitles), as sound (both as spoken word, music, and a means of navigating objects in a real or virtual world), and also as touch (perhaps not yet as a fully-immersive replication of the feel and texture of the real world, but certainly through a Braille tablet).

At one level, providing access to different digital environments for people with disability is a commercial issue. There are numerous potential customers in the disability community and, as noted earlier, accessibility features stand to benefit all users, not just those with impairments. More importantly, however, it is a problem that should be framed in terms of equality and human rights. Digital designers, copyright legislators, and users putting up their own content to the internet all need to be aware of the consequences of their decisions on accessibility.

The best way to achieve this outcome is through political engagement and awareness-raising by people with disability and their allies. While this has occurred to a limited extent in some fields, new media and the internet seem to be somewhat neglected venues for this struggle. We hope that this book, and the debate it generates, is a step toward addressing this neglect.

Overview of the Book

This book questions the rhetoric that digital technologies are an automatic source of liberation and inclusion of people with disability, and demonstrates that disability is socially created and reproduced in digital technologies. The book is divided into three sections. *Part 1: At the crossroads* focuses on the current position of disability in relation to digital media. *Part 2: How Did we Get Here?* examines the developments that lead us to the current crossroad in digital universal design. The final section, *Part 3: Where to Next?* looks at future possibilities for the digital environment and disability.

The first chapter to follow the introduction, Universal Design in a Digital World, develops a critical understanding of three components that act to drive universal design online — government policy, organizations responsible for setting internet standards (e.g. W3C), and community expectations. We aim to rationalize how these groups are facilitating access to the web and promoting universal design principles. The chapter considers what is happening in practice and contends that the "real world" situation does not necessarily reflect these aspirations.

The next chapter, iAccessibility from iTunes 1.0 to iPad, tracks the development of Apple Inc's hardware and software underpinning the iTunes' online store, and the iPod, iPhone and, more recently, the iPad selection of portable digital devices. We explore Apple's successful, albeit belated, embrace of principles of accessibility and universal design for these products and in doing so, explore the broader environment of computer operating systems, mobile telephones, and media players that make up such a vital part of our new media landscape. We also explore how these elements come together in the delivery of higher education through both the Lectopia system for recording lectures and the delivery of material through iTunes U, the higher education channel of iTunes.

Chapter 3, Building Digital Stairways: Nice View, but what About my Wheelchair? considers the current web 2.0 environment, focusing in particular on user-generated content. These sites present particular challenges for universal design and people with disability. We also explore the premise that as the web becomes a more ubiquitous part of everyday life, the potential costs of being excluded from that environment grow. Throughout this chapter, we consider the ways people with disability are driving innovation on the web (for example, increased accessibility on platforms such as Twitter and YouTube) and we highlight the political importance of blogging.

In order to analyze the significance of disability to the development of the internet and World Wide Web, *Part 2: How Did we Get Here?* includes three chapters which offer new ways of investigating these communications technologies, the social problematizations of disability as they intersect with information communication technologies and the increasing importance of social networking platforms. Chapter 4, We Want you in our Network: Universal Design v Retrofitting the Web, turns to history to track the development of the World Wide Web from its not-for-profit origins through to its commercialization and the dot-com bubble at the turn of the century, to the more recent rise of what has come to be known as web 2.0. Each of these developments has implications for universal design and access for people with disability to the online environment. This chapter also draws on cultware (or culture-ware) — a cultural theory of the internet — to highlight the influence of disability and impairment at the intersection between hardware, software, wetware (computer knowledge), and access.

The fifth chapter, (Physical) Disability is a Form of Social Oppression? outlines our concern about the neglect of a theorization of impairment within hardline social models of disability. The social model of disability (re)defines disability as society's unwillingness to meet the needs of people who have impairments. Three clear stages of disability creation have been identified by Vic Finkelstein (1980) — the feudal era (no separation), the industrial revolution (a formation of able bodied normality), and a future third stage in which technological innovations will directly result in a change to institutions, practices, and ideas. While some argue that digital technologies have created an environment that in some respects supersedes the work of social modellists in the vein of Finkelstein, we do not believe that the social model has outlived its usefulness. Rather, we contend that the implicit focus on impairment that has always been present in the politicization of disability (Oliver, 1996; Finkelstein, 1980) must be foregrounded as we move forward into the Information Age. A focus on universal design would facilitate the realization of both Finkelstein's third phase of disability development (1980) and Berners-Lee's original vision for the web (1997).

In Chapter 6, Does That Face-"Book" Come in Braille? Social Networking Sites and Disability, we focus on the rapid growth within the online environment of social networking sites. In a world where one in four internet users has a Facebook account, we turn our attention to the accessibility of these sites. This chapter explores the notion of "doing production" suggested by Goggin and Newell (2003). In this context, we argue that the inaccessibility of many of these sites is a choice and we explore the histories of Facebook and MySpace to try to explain why these choices were made. This chapter also looks at how each of these sites has responded to criticisms of their accessibility and what changes have been made. We also explore how people with disability have been able to use social networking platforms as a place for both social interaction and political mobilization.

In *Part 3: Where to Next?*, we look toward online trends being heralded as the future of the web and seek to reveal the importance of mainstreaming accessibility in order to move to the next stage of the web's progression. Following on from the discussion of social networking in Chapter 6, Chapter 7 Avatars with Wheelchairs, but No Virtual Guide Dogs: Disability and Second Life, looks at persistent online virtual worlds. It examines the way people with disability are using virtual worlds, specifically Second Life from Linden Lab, and the broader exploration of disability issues within these environments. These environments allow for social interaction and have been much studied with regard to their use by those with mobility impairments. However, if this represents the three-dimensional future of the internet, then it will present a new set of challenges for those with perceptual and cognitive impairments. We also consider whether virtual worlds are simply mirroring pre-existing social prejudice and consider where they fit within the current discourse of the social model of disability.

Arguably, Second Life provides meaningful social identity; however, care must be taken not to present it, nor technology broadly, as a brave, new, unproblematic world when it brings older, analog world values with it.

In Chapter 8, Challenges and Opportunities: The Road Ahead for Disability in a Digital World, we return to the rhetoric of challenges and opportunities to chart the terrain ahead, looking at the potential developments that could both enable and inhibit the fulfilment of Berners-Lee's understanding of the power of the web. While forecasting the future of the internet is notoriously unreliable, this chapter seeks to touch on the key areas that will impact on disability in the near-future digital environment. These include the evolving regulatory framework that supports the internet and, related to this, the legal issues of copyright enforcement and DRM. It also follows evolving trends in digital design and online activity that will impact on this area.

In the concluding chapter, we look to the future with more hope than trepidation. While the online environment continues to evolve, it is the use of agreed standards that facilitated this growth and these in turn, if applied to universal design, will facilitate the participation in this environment for both people with disability and also those without who are turning to newer technologies such as mobile internet devices. The standards developed by the W3C in terms of internet accessibility for people with disability now form the basis of the standards being developed to optimize usability of the internet for mobile users. There is enormous potential for the online environment to mitigate for different impairments, although questions must be asked as to how much of this potential will be realized, and the danger that the existing position in relation to universal design will deteriorate further.

In this book we rewrite the history of the web through the lens of the history of people with disability. In some ways, disability has served as a narrative prosthesis (Mitchell and Snyder, 2000), rhetorically demonstrating the consequences of being excluded from such an all-pervasive aspect of modern life. Disability was central to Berners-Lee's grand vision of connecting the world. The pervasiveness of disability in much of the social history of the web reveals a fundamental aspect of contemporary internet culture. Disability has a narrative significance in the internet's history by operating as symbolic of wider cultural anxieties regarding a lack of access. The case studies examined in this book — from iTunes to Second Life to earlier web experiences including chat and ordering a pizza online — reveal the analytic insight of disability. However, we seek to reveal more about disability than its sidelined role in the way we discuss the web. Accessibility features will become increasingly mainstreamed as we move toward the next platform of the web. Likewise, as big corporations acknowledge the need to improve accessibility, the importance of including people with disability will be emphasized in a broader social sense.

Part I

At the Crossroads

1

Universal Design in a Digital World

"Web accessibility enables everyone to utilize websites, regardless of personal capability or technology used."

(Glenda Watson Hyatt, 2009)

"In the Maguire case we now have a firm worldwide precedent that inaccessible Web sites can be and are illegal."

(Joe Clark, 2002)

When Russian programmer Dmitry Sklyarov, an employee of Moscow-based ElcomSoft, travelled to the United States in 2001 to demonstrate the Advanced eBook Processor at the Def Con hacker show in Las Vegas, he was arrested by the FBI (Federal Bureau of Investigation) under the United States' Digital Millennium Copyright Act (DMCA). The DMCA criminalizes technologies which circumvent a program's access controls (such as DRM) with regard to their copyright — Sklyarov's software was designed to remove such restrictions on Adobe eBook format files, thereby allowing them to be accessed on other platforms. Sklyarov's arrest attracted considerable media attention and an international internet movement — freeSklyarov — swept the blogosphere. When Sklyarov was found not guilty — in large part due to the complicated nature of the DMCA — the extent of control that publishers could expect when releasing their content digitally became tenuous. The disability community likewise became concerned about the implications these legal measures would have on the development and use of such assistive technologies — although not their primary motivation, and not referred to in court documents nor in ElcomSoft's (Katalov, 2001) press release, the Advanced eBook Processor benefited people with disability as it enabled the copying of Adobe eBooks into more accessible formats.

The legal ramifications of manipulating data in order to access it are of significance to many people with disability. Wilkinson feared that the case represented a precedent:

developers of screen readers or other access software who find ways to access data may face prosecution themselves if the methods they use or the access they provide is deemed to constitute an infringement of the intellectual property rights of the companies that develop and own major operating systems. (Wilkinson, 2001)

The ElcomSoft case highlighted the way that corporations seek to maximize their profits by trying to force consumers to buy their products — even though these may not be in a format appropriate to their needs. The ability to access Adobe eBooks on different platforms is an example of universal design and a recognition of consumer demand; the Advanced eBook Processor benefited both people with disability and those without. Universal design is a core tenet of accessibility for people with disability, both within and outside the digital arena. While guidelines should be established to benefit as many people as possible, universal design is a broad concept which allows for accessibility on an individual level through adaptation. As Greg Vanderheiden suggests:

> if you want to talk about accessibility, you have to talk about a single person. You can never talk about something being accessible to all people ... So, you can't create a one page fits all. But you can create a one page that can be adapted to fit a very, very wide variety. (quoted in Ellcessor, 2010)

Accessibility and usability are important features of universal design. While accessibility enables people with disability to access the web, usability refers to simple and straightforward web content that can be used by all with minimal specialized knowledge (Ellcessor, 2010). This book seeks to explore accessibility and usability in the context of web 2.0 platforms and connections, and to question the ways disability is reproduced and created in them. Before considering specific case studies and the ways in which they relate to a cultural construction of disability in later chapters, in this chapter, first, we develop a critical understanding of the forces that are driving universal design in the online environment and we examine popular perceptions about the potential internet technology holds for greater participation in social life for the disability community. Second, we examine the W3C, the main organization responsible for setting internet standards. Following this, we turn to various legal challenges in relation to accessibility and the ways they have been influenced by conflicting and confusing government policy. In the next section of the chapter, we suggest that recent changes in community expectations have reconfigured the way accessibility is understood and approached, this is highlighted with case studies, including the Sydney Olympics website and that of Target.com in the United States. Finally, we assess a new term in web accessibility — "accessibility 2.0" — the capacity to access information in the format of choice when working within the largely unstructured environment of user-generated content.

Driving Universal Design in the Online Environment

Despite a more widespread awareness of accessibility amongst web developers, as web 2.0 becomes increasingly complex and reliant on graphics and diversity of content, accommodating for the needs of people with disability could potentially become a low priority due to perceived financial and time constraints. While it can be argued that the web is more accessible now than even just a few years ago, most new advances in technology are usually inaccessible at the inception stage. Rather than being an integral part of their roll-out, accessibility only comes later, usually as a reaction to demand and not by way of proactive intention. Joshua Miele, a research scientist at the Smith-Kettlewell Rehabilitation Engineering Research Center believes that people designing new technologies should change their approach and make a serious commitment to universal design and in-depth planning in the initial stages. Miele, as cited by Martinez-Cabrera (2010), claims this "really would be an amazing new world."

This "new world" discourse is invoked by both people with disability and the popular press. As Glenda Watson Hyatt (aka the left thumb blogger) articulates: "For someone who has always struggled to communicate verbally and who has often felt isolated and alone when in group gatherings, social networking has opened a world to me" (Watson Hyatt, 2008). While Watson Hyatt is an avid accessibility and disability advocate, the popular press, by comparison, does not usually consider the social responsibility nor civil rights requirement to make the web fully accessible — nor indeed recognize the flow-on benefits for able-bodied users (Ellcessor, 2010). By suggesting that the web enables access to the complete range of social activity for all — including work, sex, education, and recreation — these popular articles disregard the problems frequently faced by people with disability trying to access this new world. For example, online shopping is frequently celebrated in the popular press. Although we agree that the advent of online shopping has improved the lives of people with disability in life-affirming and radical ways, this says more about how difficult it was to access offline shopping than it does about how easy it is to access the online version. By accepting systemic inaccessibility, people with disability are manipulated into reaffirming the "normality" of their oppressor and, by extension, their own perceived difference. Low-profile accessibility issues — such as inaccessible blogs or missing alternative texts (alt text) for images and scans — must be addressed alongside more high-profile cases of inaccessible websites such as Target.com or the Sydney 2000 Olympic Games.

The increasing use of DRM software to protect online content from copyright infringement further complicates any attempt to access the information in alternative formats. Sklyarov's arrest for breaching the DMCA motivated disability activists to consider the exclusionary nature of DRM, despite copyright allowances for people with print impairments:

Mr Sklyarov's case broke new legal ground and has been controversial for several reasons. Among these reasons are its potentially profound implications for those writing access software for use by people with disability. EFF [Electronic Frontier Foundation] Intellectual Property Attorney Robin Gross states, "Dmitry programmed a format converter which has many legitimate uses, including enabling the blind to hear e-books ... The idea that he faced prison for this is outrageous." (Wilkinson, 2001)

The severe consequences of violating the DMCA foreshadowed a potential for further problems for people with disability attempting to access information via new technology. Digital rights management has consequences for those reconfiguring portals and platforms in different ways and it is time for web designers and programmers, as well as legislators and corporate leaders, to address this issue. The Advanced eBook Processor had been used by both people with vision impairments, seeking to access inaccessible documents and others who wanted to copy an eBook from one computer to another. The case represented an astonishing deployment of criminal law to enforce copyright, particularly since a national (US) law was used to charge someone from another country. Many countries seek to regulate and influence the development of new media by passing laws such as the DMCA and the Australian Broadcast Services Amendment (Online Services) Bill 1999. While these laws are technically limited to a single sovereign territory, they still have the capacity to affect those who reside in, or wish to do business with, that territory. Although not an American citizen, Sklyarov was charged with several offenses including conspiracy, trafficking, and copyright infringement (Wilkinson, 2001). This was despite the fact that these offenses were allegedly committed in Russia — outside the jurisdiction of United States' law.

The manipulation of data was central to the grand jury's decision to indict Sklyarov. As all accessibility software involves the manipulation of data, the fear is that unless permission is explicitly granted in each instance, any developer of accessibility software could face the same fate as Sklyarov (although in 2002, a jury found that ElcomSoft had not wilfully violated United States' law). The legal system chose to foreground compliance with copyright legislation, even though this negated anti-discrimination initiatives. This cavalier disregard for the impact on people with disability is not really new in society, but many expected better now that guidelines exist to address this issue.

Invoking disability law in the online arena has been problematic due to both its subjectivity and confusion concerning governance. Accessibility operates in two ways — legal and professional. Voluntary guidelines around web accessibility are recommended by the Web Accessibility Initiative (WAI) section of the W3C, while legal standards in the United States are governed by Section 508 of the Rehabilitation Act, which applies to Federal agencies and their contractors in the United States, and by the Americans with Disabilities Act (ADA). In 2006, more than 70 percent of commercial sites failed to meet either the recommendations of the WAI or the requirements of Section 508 (Ellcessor, 2010: 291). The various branches of the internet public service such as the W3C influence the discourse of accessibility. Yet while these bodies often argue that they make technical rather than political decisions, the two are intimately linked.

World Wide Web Consortium (W3C)

Tim Berners-Lee established the W3C in 1994 in order to maintain consistency and compatibility across the internet. It aims to enhance the web's functionality through universality and operates on a broad scale to develop guidelines and specifications by means of consensus and endorsement from the wider community. However, the W3C is a technical organization and its guidelines for accessibility, although encouraged, are not legally enforced. Without dispute, accessibility is regarded as an important factor. According to the 1999 WAI guidelines, web content developers should scrutinize and prioritize aspects of the online environment in terms of the degree of impact on prospective users. Three accessibility priorities were established:

[Priority 1]: A Web content developer *must* satisfy this checkpoint. Otherwise, one or more groups will find it impossible to access information in the document. Satisfying this checkpoint is a basic requirement for some groups to be able to use Web documents.

[Priority 2]: A Web content developer *should* satisfy this checkpoint. Otherwise, one or more groups will find it difficult to access information in the document. Satisfying this checkpoint will remove significant barriers to accessing Web documents.

[Priority 3]: A Web content developer *may* address this checkpoint. Otherwise, one or more groups will find it somewhat difficult to access information in the document. Satisfying this checkpoint will improve access to Web documents. (W3C, 1999)

Each priority group delineates a large number of checkpoints. For example, Priority 1 is divided into seven sections and has a total of 16 checkpoints, encompassing features such as providing a text equivalent for non-text elements. Using style sheets and logical tab orders come under Priorities 2 and 3 respectively. The sliding scale of these priorities has been embraced to a greater or lesser extent by the various companies and individuals developing content for the web. The categorization was endorsed by the White House in 1997 and following a recent update is now known as the Web Content Accessibility Guidelines (WCAG) 1.0.

While many Australian universities initially adopted Priority 1, in the last few years several have taken up adopting Priority 2 as well. Yet an accessibility audit of a number of Australian university websites in 2003 found that 98 percent failed to meet basic criteria. When this audit was repeated in 2007, inaccessibility had increased to 100 percent (Alexander and Rippon, 2007). This disappointing result reveals a problematic tendency of accessibility being most devalued in the environments where it is most required. The full inclusion of people with disability in the tertiary arena is vital for social change to occur on a broader level — both through the education of people with disability and through exposure to diversity for all people.

This lack of compliance is partially due to the fact that the WCAG 1.0 guidelines were developed in 1999 within the web environment at that time. In this decade of enormous web change, developers have found it difficult to apply these rather specific and prescriptive categorizations within the web 2.0 environment. Unfortunately, WCAG 1.0 did not account for rapidly changing technology, such as JavaScript, nor encourage web developers to build accessibility into the early design phases.

The perceived deficiencies of WCAG 1.0 led to the development and release of WCAG 2.0 in 2009. Unlike WCAG 1.0 priorities, which could be only effectively applied to html, WCAG 2.0 is designed with web 2.0 applications in mind (Kelly *et al.*, 2007). WCAG 2.0 is guided by the acronym, POUR — perceivable, operable, understandable, and robust:

> Perceivable: Content must be perceivable through sight, hearing or touch ... One of the main keys to accessibility is ensuring that content is transformable from one format into another, enabling your ... readers to perceive it in multiple ways.
>
> Operable: Content must be navigable or operable by various input methods. This means content must not be device dependent; for example, not mouse only.
>
> Understandable: Content and navigation must be understandable by your readers. This means writing the content in plain language and using consistent and intuitive navigation.
>
> Robust: Robust content works across operating systems, different browsers, and even on mobile devices. Your ... readers should be able to choose their own technologies to access read and interact on your [site]. This allows them to customize their technologies to meet their needs. Web content that requires a certain technology ... may exclude visitors who either don't want to use that technology or cannot use it because of their disability. (Watson Hyatt, 2009)

WCAG 2.0 aims to guide web designers both now and in the future and encourages the use of complementary "technology specific" documents. Thus, WCAG 2.0 encourages flexibility and considers the needs and capabilities of individual users. POUR seeks to put people at the center of the accessibility process. While WCAG 1.0 focused on technique, WCAG 2.0 emphasizes principles in a way that allows greater flexibility and puts users' needs first. Technical documents specific to certain devices and code are available as attachments.

Legal Challenges

Legal challenges in the area of web accessibility have been scant, in part due to the differences amongst jurisdictions and interpretations of the law. Here, we outline some of the significant laws and legal challenges regarding web accessibility and the ways companies, organizations for the disabled, and individuals have responded.

Effective communication and access to public spaces are central to the legal discourse of accessibility, both on the web and otherwise. Section 508 of the United States' Rehabilitation Act 1973 is the legal standard for web accessibility. The Act legislated against the exclusion of people, otherwise suitably qualified, on the basis of their disability (Ellcessor, 2010). Earlier in the Act, Section 504 evidences a rights-based approach to disability by legislating against discrimination and exclusion on the basis of disability (Ellcessor, 2010: 292).

Similarly, Section 255 of the Telecommunications Act came into effect in the United States in 1996. It applies to manufacturers of telecommunications equipment and requires that they consider ways to ensure accessibility and usability from the initial design process and that they outline ways the product can be used by people with disability when "readily achievable" (United States Access Board, 2010b). Section 255 posits that people with disability should be able to access the same information as easily as those without disability and, importantly, without having to use accommodating technology (Ellcessor, 2010: 300–301). If accessibility and usability are not readily achievable (defined as able to be accomplished without excessive cost), then the manufacturer must ensure the equipment can be accessed by peripheral devices commonly used by people with disability (Access Board, 1998).

In 2008, the United Nations expanded its definition of accessibility to position internet accessibility in line with the built environment (e.g. roads, buildings, etc). The W3C provided input and members of W3C were part of the ad hoc committee that established the UN Convention on the Rights of Persons with Disabilities. While it is acknowledged that there are a number of different organizations attempting to improve digital standards, the W3C study illustrates that these standards can be overlooked, if not actively ignored, in actual web design.

Australia is currently at the forefront of the international community in relation to promoting accessibility (Accessify, 2009). In Australia, the legal requirement in relation to web accessibility is clear. Section 24 of the Disability Discrimination Act (1992) [hereafter, DDA], like Section 508 of the Rehabilitation Act in the United States, proceeds from a social constructivist standpoint:

24 Goods, services and facilities
(1) It is unlawful for a person who, whether for payment or not, provides goods or services, or makes facilities available, to discriminate against another person on the ground of the other person's disability or a disability of any of that other person's associates:

(a) by refusing to provide the other person with those goods or services or to make those facilities available to the other person; or

(b) in the terms or conditions on which the first-mentioned person provides the other person with those goods or services or makes those facilities available to the other person; or

(c) in the manner in which the first-mentioned person provides the other person with those goods or services or makes those facilities available to the other person.

(2) This section does not render it unlawful to discriminate against a person on the ground of the person's disability if the provision of the goods or services, or making facilities available, would impose unjustifiable hardship on the person who provides the goods or services or makes the facilities available. (Australian Government, 1992b)

Like Sections 504 and 508 of the United States' Rehabilitation Act, Section 24 of the Australian DDA mandates that if goods and services are available to people without disability, then people with disability must be afforded the same access.

Changing Expectations

In the first successful legal challenge to an organization for discriminating on the basis of disability through an inaccessible website, Bruce Maguire was awarded AUD 20,000 in damages. Under Australia's Disability Discrimination Act, it was found that the inaccessibility of the Sydney Olympics website resulted in an unjustifiable hardship to Maguire (Worthington, 2000).

The Sydney 2000 website was an important public space for people to engage with the Olympics. It provided news, latest results, and ticketing information. Maguire requested the ticketing information be provided to him in Braille and the Sydney Organising Committee for the Olympic Games (SOCOG) refused, suggesting that he get his wife to read it aloud to him or that he call a helpline that they might establish for people with vision impairments (Lobez, 1999). Both options would involve Maguire listening to another person for several hours. For Maguire, who also has a hearing impairment, Braille provides a "greater sense of engagement with the text" (Hudson, 2009). The complaint requested that the SOCOG:

> include alt text on all images and image map links on the website;
> ensure access from the Schedule page to the Index of Sports; and
> ensure access to the Results Tables on the website during the Olympic Games.
> (Worthington, 2000)

The SOCOG refused mediation and argued that the initial AUD 2,000 set-up cost to produce the document in Braille was an unjustifiable hardship on their part. While Part 2 of Section 24 of the DDA does allow exemptions if the cost of allowing access for people with disability poses an unjustifiable hardship on the company, in this case the Human Rights and Equal Opportunity Commissioner (HREOC) found that this did not apply. Since the ticketing system for the Sydney Olympics cost several million dollars, it was unreasonable for them not to provide the alternative format at the stated cost of AUD 2,000. The Commissioner argued that the SOCOG should have thought about web accessibility when they began setting up their website, emphasizing that it would have been easy to do and beneficial for a number of people.

This kind of oversight is common and results in the internet being a disabling rather than enabling technology for many people with disability. Yet digital technologies are often presented as a way to eradicate disability as it is socially constructed, while issues regarding access are ignored or glossed over. This issue will be problematic as long as disability remains part of the private sphere rather than a civil rights or public sphere issue. Interestingly, Maguire was subjected to a backlash from both the general Australian community as well as those with disability. Maguire recalls the views expressed by both people with disability and those without following a talkback radio interview in which he argued that access to information was a right not a privilege:

> One woman said, "I don't know what it must be like to be blind, and my heart goes out to them — but he should get someone to read him the book". Shortly after this, a blind man rang in and said, "That Maguire's nothing but a b_____ troublemaker: doesn't he realize that we just have to accept things and not rock the boat". (HREOC, 2003)

When disability is individualized in these ways, the broader community is absolved of the responsibility of access — individuals and their families must find ways to cope largely unsupported. Maguire further explains that:

> In their different ways, these two callers were expressing the same underlying belief: while disability may be part of the reality of human experience, any suggestion that people with a disability can or have the right to participate with full equality is subversive. (HREOC, 2003)

Although he lodged the complaint for personal reasons, for Maguire this radio interview revealed that the broader impact was significant because everyone should have a right to public spaces, including the internet. The importance of laws such as the DDA should not be underestimated (HREOC, 2003).

The internet will only become accessible when the civil rights discourse of social models of disability is extended to the web as a public space:

> The web is not a *barrier* to people with disabilities, it is the *solution*. The web has the potential to revolutionize the day-to-day lives of millions of people with disabilities by increasing their ability to independently access information, communication, entertainment, commerce and other aspects of life that most people take for granted. However, for the web to reach its full potential for people with disabilities, *web developers must commit to always designing with accessibility in*

mind. Failure to do so risks turning a revolutionary solution into yet another barrier
in the lives of people with disabilities. (WebAIM, 2010a: italics in original)

Maguire's successful case against the SOCOG set an international precedent
which has assisted people with disability to pursue their right to access information online. More recently, in 2006 the Californian arm of the National Federation of the Blind (NFB) pursued civil action against Target.com in the United
States under the Americans with Disabilities Act (ADA), the California Unruh
Civil Rights Act, and the California Disabled Persons Act. They claimed that
Target's inaccessible website was denying people with vision impairment the
opportunity to access their goods and services online (Disability Rights Advocates, 2010). In 2008, Target reached an undisclosed settlement and pledged a
commitment to accessibility. This favorable outcome for the NFB has raised not
only community awareness but also the expectations of improved accessibility.

As part of the confidential settlement package, Target was required to make
changes to its website and internal guidelines under the direction of the NFB
(Arnold, 2008). Target.com is now recognized by the NFB as meeting the requirements of making the site equally usable by blind and sighted users. Indeed, the
NFB has awarded Target a Nonvisual Accessibility Web Certification. Although
Target.com is one of the first major retail websites to implement web accessibility, issues with keyboard navigation and color contrast remain a barrier for users
with low vision or people who are keyboard dependent (Dolson, 2010). It is also
significant to note that this renewed interest in accessibility is the result of legal
action rather than an implementation of universal design. Accessibility is, however, receiving greater attention recently with other online retailers, including
CVS and Staples, agreeing to adhere to accessibility standards as part of out-of-
court settlements (Martinez-Cabrera, 2010).

Some in the disability and accessibility community were disappointed with
the fact that the complaint was settled rather than proceeding to a legal resolution. This meant that there is still no precedent in the United States. Early
attempts to sue companies in the United States for inaccessible websites under
the ADA were thwarted when the advocacy group, Access Now attempted to
bring a suit against Southwest Airlines. The judge presiding over the 2002 case
refused to expand the definition of public accommodation beyond the physical
built environment: "To expand the ADA to cover 'virtual' spaces would be to
create new rights without well-defined standards. The plain and unambiguous
language of the statute and relevant regulations does not include internet websites" (McCullagh, 2002). However, as far back as 1999, this kind of view was
contested: "For the rights of the disabled to mean anything in today's world, they
must be extended to cyberspace no less than to parking spaces ... The Internet
is a new and critical kind of public space" (A More Accessible Internet, 1999
quoted in Ellcessor 2010). In 2010, the equivalence between the public space of
the built environment and the public space of the web is becoming more widely

accepted. The UN Convention on the Rights of People with Disabilities now describes cyberspace as equal to public space and encourages private entities and the media to make websites accessible to people with disability as a basic right (United Nations, 2006).

In the United States, the Section 508 Amendment to the Rehabilitation Act 1973 was first introduced in 1986 in recognition of technological advancements in communications technologies. In 1998, it was amended in such a way as to allow for both the elimination of barriers and the encouragement of new and accessible technologies. It requires that websites be made accessible to people with disability. There are six criteria that must be adhered to in order to achieve a minimum level of accessibility.

These criteria address a range of different impairments and disabling aspects of website design and they deal with both software applications and operating systems. One example is that a website should be easily navigable using a keyboard without a mouse as some people with physical dexterity impairment are unable to use a mouse. Similarly, people with vision impairments may exclusively use a keyboard and not a mouse. The importance of allowing for the use of screenreaders or Braille display through the inclusion of alt text is recognized via a focus on web-based information and applications. In the telecommunications sphere, there is an emphasis on the importance of compatibility with hearing supports, hearing aids, cochlear implants, assistive listening devices, and telephone typewriters (TTYs). The ability to adjust volume is noted to be important. Further, more than one media must be available via a variety of video and multimedia products. Self-contained, closed products — including information kiosks, calculators, and fax machines for example — address embedded software and allow for assistive technology.

These criteria are wide-ranging with respect to the types of disability they address. In addition, they give general users options as to how they access the web, for example, volume control and choice of media (video, text, slide show, etc). However, it is ineffective to rely solely on legislation to ensure accessibility, especially when it applies only to a certain group of websites. Despite relevant laws, accessibility protocols are still often set aside. Particularly in light of the trend toward user-generated content, the only way that accessibility will be guaranteed is if the principles of universal design become widely accepted as a fundamental part of web design.

It is difficult to apply much of the disability discrimination legislation to the web 2.0 environment because they were established prior to the wide uptake of the web in homes, government, and business. Although the first case of successful litigation against an inaccessible website occurred in Australia, there were no further attempts at corrective litigation in that country until 2009 when Les Karr initiated action against Virgin Blue, and also signaled his intention to similarly sue Yahoo Seven and the Australian Competition and Consumer Commission websites.

Motivated by his experiences as a person with vision impairment trying to navigate the online environment, in 2008 Karr began the onerous task of examining 30,000 websites to test their accessibility for people with vision impairments. He believed about 99 percent of websites to be inaccessible and initiated contact with several sites via their online contact information. After explaining the difficulties he, as a vision-impaired visitor, experienced with the particular site, he outlined the WCAG principles and encouraged the organization to bring the site up to standard. Only if the response was not favorable did he consider making a complaint to the Human Rights and Equal Opportunity Commission under the DDA.

Kerr did pursue action against Virgin Blue, citing difficulties in relation to color contrast and hard-coded text size. However, unlike Maguire's experiences with SOCOG, Virgin Blue agreed to mediation and made the necessary changes. This was applauded by the Australian Disability Discrimination Commissioner, Graeme Innes:

> Travel is something that we are all doing more and more of, and it is important that people with disability can participate equally in this activity ... Virgin Blue have been working productively with peak disability and advocacy organisations to improve access and their Independent Travel Criteria. The result is a policy which is far less restrictive.... Australians with disability make up 20 percent of the population, so I am pleased that this significant segment of the travelling market will now be able to share in use of Virgin's facilities more equitably ... I congratulate Virgin Blue on these changes, and the way that they have worked with people with disability to achieve a positive result. (Australian Human Rights Commission, 2009)

While it is good to see attitudes to accessibility on the web changing, this does raise some continuing questions. Why is it that these laws and regulations work, whether by design or practice, only in situations where a complaint is brought either by individuals with disability or by organizations outside of government acting on their behalf such as the NFB? In many cases, these laws and regulations seem to require that they are policed and enforced by the very people who are excluded from accessing the sites that require modification. While the FBI were active in seeking out and prosecuting Dmitry Sklyarov for breaching United States' laws relating to copyright, there seems to be no equivalent extra-jurisdictional enforcement of laws and regulations relating to accessibility.

The Australian Human Rights Commission takes W3C compliance into consideration when mediating disputes regarding web inaccessibility. WCAG 1.0 was the internationally-recognized standard for accessibility; this standard has now moved into its second generation with WCAG 2.0 and focuses on principles rather than technical specifications. By encouraging sites to follow the POUR principles, WCAG 2.0 is not invalidated by technological advancement. Like Berners-Lee's vision for the web, these guidelines highlight the importance of accessing the same information in different ways and using different adaptive technologies. They also fit into a core feature of web 2.0 whereby software is above the level of a single device (O'Reilly, 2005). This has become increasingly important as more people access the web, using a range of different portable devices. Robust sites which allow users to control and access information in a variety of ways are particularly important in the era of the mobile web.

At the time of writing, Section 508 is open for public discussion (for more, see Chapter 8). The move to update the Act is in response to the high level of non-compliance (including by the White House) and the emergence of social networking in e-government. Section 508 requires that all Federal online content is accessible to people with disability (Walker, 2010). As local governments look to moving their online content to Facebook and other social networking platforms (Towns, 2010), the accessibility of social networking sites is becoming increasingly important as a measure of Section 508 compliance. This update is long overdue.

Accessibility 2.0

Particularly in light of the expanding ethos of user-generated content, the spotlight on web accessibility must move beyond the domain of government regulation. This concept has been termed "accessibility 2.0." We use this term to refer to the capacity to access information in the format of choice when working within the largely unstructured environment of user-generated content. The philosophy of web 2.0 is to relinquish control by sharing ideas and building on what came before. In this way, web 2.0 invites collaboration and participation, with the only barrier to full democratic engagement being a problem of access. Allowing users to access information in the ways they want without restrictions is both robust and future-directed. It is also markedly different from the previous generation of broadcast communications where audiences were dictated to by broadcasters. Web 2.0 flourished where the early web failed because sites gave users control. The phenomenon will be discussed further in Chapter 4.

Unfortunately, compliance with the standards suggested by the W3C is voluntary and there is no fully effective way to enforce it. The differing interpretations of legislation amongst judges and jurisdictions make it doubly problematic, with some areas recognizing disability discrimination acts and others arguing that online spaces do not fall within the definition of public spaces and are therefore deemed to be exempt. Further, most disability discrimination acts were established prior to the advent of the World Wide Web era and their concepts do not easily translate.

Kelly *et al.* (2007) argue that accessibility options can sometimes get in the way of a satisfying user experience and that people should have choice about how information is accessed. An accessibility 2.0 approach describes "a renewed approach to accessibility, which builds on previous work but prioritizes the importance of the user." Accessibility 2.0 follows a social understanding of disability by focusing on the purpose of the resource. It assumes different people use the web in different ways and that accessibility is a process rather than a finite solution. Although accessibility 2.0 is lauded for moving beyond regulations and groups such as W3C and WCAG, this does not imply that there is no value in either their existence or the guidelines they have developed. Indeed WCAG 2.0, with its emphasis on principles rather than prescriptions, was actually a step toward the notions of accessibility 2.0 by allowing users to control the way information is accessed.

Accessibility 2.0 has been credited with moving beyond content in recognition of a web environment in which people both read and write. However, this presents an entirely new challenge to web designers who are trying to "do the right thing" by following web content checklists. Brian Kelly, who possibly first coined the term accessibility 2.0, anticipates a new set of resistance from the group that, historically, has supported the implementation of accessibility most forcefully:

> But how ... should we address the conservatism we're likely to face within the institutions which have adopted an approach to web accessibility which is based on simple conformance with checklists which simply cover the Web content? And what about the Web developers and content creators who, possibly for a period of almost 10 years, have prided themselves on implementing such guidelines? How should we change this culture? (Kelly, 2008)

Perhaps part of the answer is that everyone has a role to play in the future of accessibility, from government and policy makers, to hardware and software creators and finally, the web 2.0 community and the people actually accessing the sites.

Toolkits must be better developed in order to anticipate ways to allow for different impairments because there are many web developers and no one single way to ensure accessibility for everyone. For example, some websites, with the social networking site MySpace being the obvious example, automatically load audio. In this example the problem could be seen to be emanating from the creator of the MySpace page, or the browser (such as Internet Explorer or Firefox) or the operating system. As this interferes with the functioning of screenreading software, an accessibility 2.0 approach, in conjunction with WCAG 2.0, would see web standards implemented in a way to block the automatic loading of sound without impacting on the functioning of the screenreader (Popov, 2006), yet without having to turn off all audio.

As in the case of Dmitry Sklyarov and his Advanced eBook Processor, it seems that, sadly, the needs of the disability community are deemed to be of no consequence:

> But what about the fate of all those blind people who now won't be able to read e-books because Adobe will have disabled the read-aloud feature at some pub-

lisher's request? Typically, publishers ask Adobe to disable that feature when they fear it might violate their contracts relating to an existing audio version of the same book. But when you think about it, in those circumstances it might actually make more sense for a blind person to pay $15 to buy the audio book — a tape of a professional actor or the author of the work reading the book aloud — rather than pay $8 for an e-book and $99 for circumvention software, in order to hear voice-simulation software articulating the words in a robotic monotone. (McCullagh, 2001)

Even in 2010, when accessibility to print materials for people with disability is more widely understood by publishers, libraries, and universities, this argument does not actually reflect the real world situation. Publishers regularly lock pdfs (Portable Document Format) of their book prints without providing an audio book alternative and DRM is introduced to force device-specific access. If people with disability were to do as McCullagh (2001) suggests then they could be forced to purchase a new eBook reader for every book they read. That would be clearly unfair and disabling — text-to-voice software is an important accessibility and usability feature.

Usability is an important feature of accessibility 2.0 and borrows from recent developments in human computer interaction (HCI):

> The original and abiding technical focus of HCI is on the concept of *usability*. This concept was originally articulated naively in the slogan "easy to learn, easy to use". The blunt simplicity of this conceptualization gave HCI an edgy and prominent identity in computing. It served to hold the field together, and to help it influence computer science and technology development more broadly and effectively. However, inside HCI the concept of usability has been reconstructed continually, and has become increasingly rich and intriguingly problematic. Usability now often subsumes qualities like fun, well-being, collective efficacy, aesthetic tension, enhanced creativity, support for human development, and many others. (Carroll, 2009)

In the web 2.0 era, usability is not just about being able to use a site, it now embraces the concept of fun. But some have questioned whether this creativity is compatible with the prescriptions about accessibility. However, Lembree argues against the portrayal of accessibility as detrimental to fun:

> I think there's a misconception that a "Web 2.0" site or app [application] can't be cool or fun and be accessible at the same time. On the contrary, I find that it's quite possible. It's mostly a matter of planning it from the beginning, and implementing progressive enhancement. (quoted in Accessify, 2009)

Glenda Watson Hyatt (2009) acknowledges the balancing act between creativity/ aesthetics and usability/accessibility but affirms that site visitors' preferences should be paramount. People must be able to access information in any way they choose:

> [balance] your blog's aesthetics with usability and accessibility. Which do you value? Which is more beneficial to your readers? That is not to say a blog needs to

be butt ugly to be accessible. Find the balance. Perhaps ask your readers what works best for them. (Watson Hyatt, 2009)

Conclusion

Web 2.0 is governed by a user-centric approach that assumes technological innovation and that users will access the same information in different ways. Although the web as a platform is a web 2.0 concept, its origins are in Tim Berners-Lee's vision of the web as a platform to share information. Berners-Lee suggested that accessibility, regardless of disability, was a crucial aspect and established the W3C and WAI to ensure this vision was realized. WCAG 1.0 and 2.0, although released ten years apart, reveal much about the increasing value of universal design and differences amongst users and their access choices and requirements.

Legislation in both the United States and Australia embody civil rights terminology. Emerging alongside the W3C, their origins are in non-web telecommunications and accessible environments. This has been problematic to implement yet has resulted in some positive outcomes for accessibility. Despite initial reluctance, the public space of the web is now being conceptualized in the same way as the public space of the built environment.

Accessibility 2.0 embraces the underpinning philosophy of web 2.0 — the undeniable right of user choice — and could prove more effective than W3C in forcing large corporations to embrace accessibility. This is particularly important when we start to realize that new bottlenecks of resistance are emerging to thwart user choice of format. Although web 2.0 sites encourage community collaboration via user-generated content, surprisingly, many still attempt to force users to access information in a particular way. For example, Apple, whom we consider in-depth in the next chapter, has greatly improved their accessibility following user outrage. Yet they continue to operate outside of standards and dictate which technology users must adopt.

At the start of the century Skylarov was arrested, but was not convicted for circumventing DRM to grant a higher level of access, similarly at that time Maguire successfully pursued his action against SOCOG over the inaccessibility of their website. However by 2007, all Australian universities had websites that were no longer compliant with the WCAG guidelines. The legal action against Target.com was also successful in making the company's web presence more accessible and similar agreements have been reached with both CVS and Staples. However, all these outcomes required legal action to be taken. It seems that heading into the second decade of the twenty-first century that we do indeed stand at a crossroads in relation to web accessibility. The great potential that access to digital communications technologies provides, particularly for people with disability, remains in danger of being unrealized, yet there are many positive signs and developments.

2

iAccessibility from iTunes 1.0 to iPad

"Maybe I'm just being old-fashioned, but this iTunes, God bless 'em, it's going to kill music if they're not careful. It's a ... monster, this thing. It just worries me. And I'm sure they're just doing it all in the interest of making as much cash as possible. Let's put it this way, it's certainly not for the love, let's get that out of the way, right away."

(Brian Johnson, AC/DC lead singer, Daily, 2008)

"if we can find our tunes eyes-free, we are going to want to do many other things eyes-free. And that means a future where blind people like you and me no longer have to struggle for accessibility just moved a whole lot closer."

(Mike Calvo, 2008)

"Building a music library on your computer is cool, but a computer is a bit too bulky to replace your walkman. How do you take your music collection, or at least a portion of it, on the road? The easiest and lightest way is to purchase a portable MP3 player."

(Joe Kraynak, 2004)

MP3 is a form of compression; storage and playback that digitizes music. The format enabled people to build music libraries on their computers, while portable MP3 players allowed this library to go mobile. MPMan F10, the first device to utilize the MP3-encoding format, was launched in March 1998 (Smith, 2008). However, it was not until April 2003 when Apple launched the iPod that the market began the massive growth that has made the devices ubiquitous in everyday life. The "Pod" in iPod is inspired in part by the film *2001: A Space Odyssey*, and stands for "portable on demand". Apple's iPod is currently the most popular portable MP3 player and has been described as the single object which captures the zeitgeist of the first decade of the twenty-first century (Hesseldahl, 2009). In 2006, iPods were rated as more popular than beer amongst college students in the United States, according to *Student Monitor.* Beer had only been surpassed in popularity once before, in 1997, by the internet (Zeff, 2007)!

Then in 2007, Apple released a significant development in this line of products, the iPhone, which incorporated the popular MP3 player in an advanced mobile phone. The merging of mobile phone and music cultures through the Apple suite of products reveals both the active role Apple has played in influencing the convergence of online and mobile media and the active role consumers and external developers have played in developing the capability of these products. This confluence was further enhanced in 2010 with the introduction of the iPad mobile tablet. Like the iPhone, but on a larger scale, the iPad runs an operating system that resembles a small touchscreen-enabled laptop. Users add value to these products by personalizing their interaction and sharing content, and developing applications (or "apps") to enhance the experience for other members of the community.

The iPod touch, iPhone, and iPad all feature a touch-sensitive flat screen that serves as the interface for its operating system. While the design is striking, it also generates potential accessibility problems. As Crichton (2007) observes, there are obvious implications for those with vision impairments when there are no physical markers to point toward the phone's functions. This chapter looks at the specific case study of Apple's popular iPhone, iPod, and iPad hardware as well as the associated iTunes software.

Apple uses the iTunes platform to distribute music, movies, and television, and through iTunes U lectures and content for courses in higher education. While iTunes seems on the surface to provide enormous opportunity for people with vision impairments to access a broad selection of audio content, its design has previously worked to inhibit access to the platform for this group. Apple promotes the use of iTunes in educational settings through the iTunes U channel, and this potentially excludes those who have difficulty with access to the relevant devices. Critically, it is often these excluded people who, potentially, could benefit the most from the technology.

This chapter demonstrates the potential role for internet-based technology to be inclusive of people with disability, as well as the opposing danger that the social construction of disability in an online world will simply mirror pre-existing discrimination. We also examine the role of disability groups in informing the progress of this technology and the changes that have been made to improve access to this platform, especially within the new Apple operating system and its software development in the later model iPod and iPhone as well as the more recently-launched iPad.

In the first section of the chapter, we consider the difficulty experienced by people who use adaptive technologies in relation to iTunes and highlight the potential problems for universities who utilize iTunes U, particularly in light of the well-recognized right of students to universal access. The second section of the chapter recognizes the more recent accessibility features of later model iPods, iPhones, and iPads to foreground the innovations created by users with disability to improve access to this popular technology. Throughout the chapter, we reframe disability accessibility as a principle of universal access and design, and outline how changes made to assist users with disability can enhance the experience of all users.

The iDecade

With a mere six percent share of the American PC (personal computer) market, Apple, like a number of online businesses at the turn of the twenty-first century, was struggling (see Chapter 4 for a discussion of the dot-com bubble/burst period of web history). Rather than head for oblivion, however, Apple was able to tap into both mobile phone cultures and the cultures of the portable consumption of music to such an extent that the first decade of this century is now described as the "idecade" (Hesseldahl, 2010).

When introduced in 2001, Apple's iTunes was initially conceptualized as jukebox software to compile and organize personal music collections. By 2003 it had become a music store, introducing video two years later and in 2008 had become the world's biggest music retailer. iTunes is a free application that allows users to organize and play music and video, and can be used on both Macs and PCs. This media can then be synced to portable media players such as an iPhone, iPad, or iPod. The first iPod had a 5GB hard drive with the ability to hold 1,000 songs. More recent iPods are far more powerful — the iPod touch has up to a 64GB hard drive with enough room for 14,000 songs and up to 30 hours of audio playback, the current version of the iPod classic has storage for 160GB. The iPod was created in response to a perceived gap in the portable digital device market whereby cameras, personal organizers, and camcorders were small, sleek, and portable yet by contrast portable music players were not — they were large and chunky. In addition to this, there was the annoyance of carrying around phones, organizers, and MP3 players. Steve Jobs of Apple predicted that a single device that united these functions would be popular — and history shows he was absolutely right.

The first mobile phone to feature the iTunes application was developed in consultation with Motorola. The ROKR held 100 songs but could not directly download music (Goggin, 2009a: 234). In order to protect the iPod and their own mobile phone (iPhone) developments, Apple put in place tight restrictions on intellectual property and DRM. The phone would not play music from any other online store besides iTunes. This posed a problem for mobile phone carriers hoping to make money on data traffic through downloads or trying to introduce their own music download stores (Rose, 2005).

DRM, a control mechanism for Apple to protect its iPod, also prevents people with disability accessing content using adaptive technology (see Chapter 8 for further discussion). Yet both web 2.0 and the WCAG 2.0 prioritize software being written above the level of a single device. After some negotiation, Apple, Motorola, and the mobile carrier Cingular came to an agreement and the ROKR was launched. However, cracks quickly appeared in the relationship and the phone itself was unattractive. In order to protect the iPod's dominance, Apple chose to introduce its own mobile phone model. Apple focused on a sleek design with the iPhone which was in development as the ROKR was released. Apple's strength was apparent not only in its knowledge of operating systems but also in the company's understanding of the marketplace. The era has been characterized as one where style reigned supreme over substance and the practical features of the unattractive ROKR were no match for the sleek design of the new "must have" Apple iPhone. Indeed, *Wired* Magazine described the iPhone launch as bigger than the Apollo launch (Goggin, 2009a: 235) — a phenomenon again seen at the launch of the iPad.

Accessibility

The World Wide Web based its successful development on a set of common standards that worked across different software and operating systems. This interoperability held out great opportunity for the implementation of enabling software for those with disability. The increasing sophistication and diversification of online content has confounded this initial promise. Websites have become more complex, particularly with the rise of web 2.0 and the associated trends in coding and website design. This has aggravated attempts to mediate this content for a disabled audience through software (Zajicek, 2007).

As the content requiring translation — either from text into audio or onto a Braille tablet, or from audio-into-text captions — becomes less standardized and more complex, it becomes both harder for software to act as a translator and harder to navigate this media, once translated. This is particularly the case when links are generated on the fly for each view of a website and where images replace words as hyperlinks. As Wood (2008) notes, "these days many computers are used principally to access the Internet — and there is no telling what a blind person will encounter there".

Web 2.0 sites loaded with Ajax and Java scripting present a particular challenge for translation software (Zajicek, 2007). These sites overlay web content on the main webpage and confuse screenreaders (Krazit, 2009). iTunes, an iconic web 2.0 application, is a further step away from easily-translated content. Although iTunes as proprietary software operates though the internet, it does not conform to web standards. Many translation software packages are unable to read the iTunes software at all or are limited and only able to read part of the page, but not enough of it to use the program (Furendal, 2007). Apple's accessibility problems can trace their origin to before the development of the World Wide Web. Reihing, addressing another Apple product in 1987 observes: "The Apple Macintosh is particularly hard to use because it depends heavily on graphics. Some word processors 'paint' pictures of letters on the screen instead of using standard computer codes, and speech or Braille devices can't cope" (quoted in Goggin and Newell, 2003). As websites utilizing web 2.0 technology increase in complexity they become less attractive to users with vision impairments, particularly when dynamic elements cannot be accessed using screenreaders provided with the operating system (Bigham *et al.*, 2008). Technological innovation in screenreading technology appears to offer users with vision-impairment a choice. There are a number of screenreaders available and users should be able to customize their machines to allow use by their preferred reader. However, many sites, including iTunes, offer their own customized screenreader which implies that users with vision impairment must learn how to operate many different readers. This is a skill that must be learnt by the user with vision impairment above and beyond skills required by sighted users of the applications.

This denies a user with vision impairment the opportunity to engage with this popular software. To Apple's credit, they have taken some of these access concerns on board. The recent upgrade of both the Apple operating system and iTunes better enables Apple's own access software to translate the iTunes screen for blind users. However, this also illustrates the problems with this type of software operating outside of nominated standards as there are still serious problems with access to iTunes on Microsoft's dominant Windows operating system (Furendal, 2007).

Although Windows provides its own integrated screenreading software, the company acknowledges that this is not sufficiently powerful for regular use by disabled users. This group of users will need to use more specialized programs (Wood, 2008). When the Windows operating system upgraded from XP to Vista, the stipulation that there was a keyboard shortcut for each operation the system performed was abandoned. This has presented significant difficulties for those unable to use a visual interface on the screen to point and click with a mouse (Wood, 2008).

While accessibility should in theory move in line with technological innovation and advancement, historically this has not always been the case. Internet Explorer 4.0 had less accessibility features than Internet Explorer 3.0 despite Microsoft promising the National Council on Disability that they would increase accessibility in Windows across the board with a specific emphasis on screenreader compatibility (Goggin and Newell, 2003: 118). America Online (AOL) similarly decreased accessibility options between 2001 and 2002. In Chapter 4, we consider such disregard for accessibility as a symptom of the rush for market dominance during the browser wars and dot-com bubble. That moment of the web's history demonstrates the digital reflection of analog disability. Apple's insistence on their own standards and software largely written for a single mode of access is a problematic continuation of the rejection of common standards across different software and operating systems.

iTunes and iTunes U

iTunes is the enabling software supporting the iPod, iPad, and iPhone hardware. As well as commercial content, iTunes also acts as a distribution medium for other content that is free to use. It allows individuals or organizations to record and publish audio and video files — podcasts and vodcasts — that can be automatically downloaded from the internet as soon as they become available onto individual computers and iPods. Significantly, this technology has been embraced by the educational sector. iTunes U facilitates the delivery of lecture material in a very time-efficient and cost-effective manner.

While Apple has acknowledged that this is, in part, a deliberate effort to drive the uptake of iTunes (Udell, 2006), there are particular opportunities for the distribution of information through this channel. Duke University in the United States was an early adopter, distributing iPods to each of its first-year students for educational use as early as 2004. A study of students at The University of Western Australia (UWA) by Williams and Fardon (2007) found that those who listen to lectures through portable media players such as iPods have a higher attendance rate at lectures than those who do not. Despite this, academics often resist the recording of their lectures believing that students will stop attending in person.

Lecture recordings are used extensively in the provision of disability support at the tertiary level. Many students, with a range of impairments of varying degrees of effect benefit from the digital recording of lectures. For example, students with vision or mobility impairments can use lecture recordings when they are unable to attend classes due to fatigue or transport issues. Students with hearing impairments can connect the recordings to hearing aids and microphones at home or use note-taking services to access the lectures at times convenient to the note-taker. As lecture-recording software such as the Lectopia platform moves into providing transcripts of lectures, people without any impairment will benefit by being able to search for keywords while people with disability will be able to access the material independently.

In 1998, the same year that the first portable MP3 player was being launched, the Lectopia (or iLecture) lecture-recording and distribution system was introduced in Australia to enable students with disability better access to lecture materials. While there have been significant criticisms of this platform (Brabazon, 2006), the broad uptake and popularity of this technology, particularly in Australia, demonstrates how changes made to assist people with disability can potentially be mainstreamed to help the broader community. This underpins the concept of universal design where consideration given to people with disability also improves the lives of people without disability. Disability issues, such as access to digital content, improve usability for the community in general (HREOC, 2000).

The idea of universal access was integral to Berners-Lee's original conception of the web. However, the platform has developed into a more complex and less-ordered environment that can stray from agreed standards (Edwards, 2008). iTunes comes with its own accessibility issues. Furendal (2007) demonstrated that its design has added utility for some impairments, notably dyslexia and colour blindness. However, as noted previously, iTunes is highly problematic for those with other vision impairment particularly for people who are totally blind. As Regan observes:

> There exists a false perception among designers that accessibility represents a restriction on creativity. There are few examples that exist in the world that can dissuade designers of this notion. While there are no technical reasons for this division between accessibility and design, the notion exists just the same. (Regan, 2004)

The invisibility of this issue confirms that while an awareness of differing abilities can assist all users; a blinkered approach to diverse visual acuities is not only blocking social justice imperatives but also future marketing opportunities. The iPhone was initially notable for problems associated with use by people with disability, particularly people with hearing (Keizer, 2007) and vision impairments (Crichton, 2007). In colder climates the fact that the screen would not be activated by a gloved hand has also been a problem, its design reflects bias against not just the physically-impaired. Design decisions reflect the socially-constructed nature of disability where disability is related to how humans have chosen to construct the world (Finkelstein, 1975). The push toward iTunes U highlights the importance of digital accessibility for everyone, not just the disabled as this technology becomes ubiquitous. The wide adoption of platforms such as Lectopia in higher education demonstrates the value of flexibility of delivery to the whole student population, inclusive of the disabled.

Following the release of iTunes 8.1.1, the screenreader JAWS developed the J-Tunes skin for use with iTunes. J-Tunes is an interface which allows Job access with speech (JAWS) users to access iTunes using keystrokes rather than vision. J-Tunes boasts an impressive list of accessibility features and allows users to engage with the iTunes software on an equal level to people without disability.

In order to provide an authentic non-visual experience of iTunes, J-Tunes allows users to import whole CDs or individual tracks along with audio books or purchase these directly from the iTunes store. These tracks can be organized into playlists and transferred onto an iPod. J-Tunes can also automatically announce album names, the amount of space remaining, and the serial number.

Significantly, volume can be adjusted independently of the JAWS screenreader. Tracks can be played at random from the computer and playlists can be rearranged with an ability to skim forward and back through the tracks in a similar way to a CD player where the songs can be heard. J-Tunes also allows users to listen to internet radio stations, subscribe to podcasts, or individually download them. Keystrokes are designed to be easy to remember and a help-system groups together keystrokes around specific tasks. Finally, accompanying documentation aims to communicate clearly and succinctly. Reviews of the interface have been positive:

> I'll admit, when it comes to accessibility technology advances, I believe it when I experience it on my very own computer. So, while the news about iTunes 8 being fully accessible to screenreaders made me grin from ear-to-ear, I had to confirm it for myself. I'm thrilled to say that iTunes 8 and JAWS 10 are working like a charm. (Sims, 2008)

Yet the $75 price tag is prohibitive especially when JAWS itself costs around $1,000 already. Likewise, ten-minute free trials available prior to purchase were perhaps not long enough to fully master the features. However, just as iTunes had, J-Tunes locked users into a particular mode of access which led some to take issue with the fact that it wasn't compatible with other screenreaders such as Window Eyes. When Apple released iTunes 9, J-Tunes became incompatible with iTunes and for a time recommended that clients not upgrade to iTunes 9. J-Tunes is now at version 5 and includes an upgrade feature to enable a robust use of the technology. J-Tunes users need to upgrade their J-Tunes before upgrading their iTunes in order to work. The manufacturers, T&T consultancy do make allowances for people who use older screenreaders with suggestions regarding compatibility. This suggests developers of adaptive technologies may experience some difficulty in developing updates when updates for platforms provided by large corporations such as Apple are so rapid.

Accessibility and the iHardware

As people with disability become more aware of their rights, more people are turning to legal action in order to fight for accessibility and make the point that it matters. In 2007, the Hearing Loss Association of America filed a complaint against Apple claiming that the iPhone was not compatible with hearing aids in breach of Section 255 of the United States' Federal Communications Commission:

> The iPhone is not useable with a hearing aid, either on the microphone or telecoil setting. Clearly it was not designed to be hearing aid compatible. It should have been…. Apple set itself up for the dissatisfaction from the disability community.

> Expectations were huge, and they let us down. All the marketing hype just made it worse for them when they finally unveiled it, and it was lacking so much access needed for people with disabilities. (Keizer, 2007)

Apple responded positively by introducing a range of accessibility features for people with hearing impairments into the iPhone and iPods. These features include a captioning capability and password-protected volume limits as well as an audio out jack that allows the iPod to be connected to headphones or speakers. Hearing-aid compatible induction ear loops and remote wireless headsets are available as accessibility add-ons through external organizations, similar to the situation with J-tunes.

Other recently available accessibility features for the iPhone have been created by users, for example, a sign language app that users can download to their phone. These accessibility features have been incorporated into the iPad from its inception. If the launch of the iPhone was the equivalent of the Apollo mission to the moon, then it is hard to think of an appropriate metaphor for the iPad. The iPad sold one million units in the first 28 days, less than half the time it took to sell that number of iPhones when it was launched in 2007. The device's larger screen makes it potentially more useful than either of its two predecessors for people with a variety of impairments. These devices have been embraced as they enhance communications and accessibility for people with disability including those that affect manual dexterity and cognitive function who are able to gain better access through the larger touchscreen. As such, people who have had strokes, people with spinal cord injuries, cerebral palsy or ALS, a paralyzing nerve disease, and people with autism are afforded greater access (AAP, 2010).

For people with vision impairments, the new iPhone contained a built-in screenreader that incorporates the touch-sensitive screen to provide a tactile interface and turn the most obviously disabling feature of the original design — a featureless screen — into a tactile interface with the operating system. The new operating system also contains a range of voice-control features and the ability to provide an audio version of the auto-text feature for text messages. Other features for people with vision impairments include a zoom function and the ability to change the contrast of the screen as well as a range of alert functions utilizing sound, sight, and touch. People without disability are using these functions, especially the screenreader, to facilitate multitasking.

These moves suggest we are a step closer to Goggin and Newell's (2003) goal of seeing disability considered a social identity alongside race and gender, and Mary Reihing's fantasy of "… all you have to do is plug in your computer, and it'll be the answer to your access prayers" (Goggin and Newell, 2003: 117). As Calvo (2008) blogged at the head of the chapter, these moves could also mean less social distance between the disabled and able.

Apple Accessibility

These accessibility features also serve to illustrate that impairment is important and that a range of features and approaches to access needs to be implemented to enable access to the broader disability community. Yet, new technology is rarely accessible at in the initial stages and this was certainly the case with Apple's iPod and iPhone. Despite accessibility measures across other Apple operating systems, the iPod and iPhone were not similarly accessible as Kyle Buckley, a technology reviewer with vision impairment at online magazine, *Nillabyte* explains:

> When the iPhone and iPod touch were released, I was amazed at the technology, but had always passed it up as the initial models contained no accessibility tools for people like me. However, the new iPhone 3GS and the 3rd generation iPod touch now have accessibility features that grant access for blind and visually impaired users. (Buckley, 2009)

Accessibility and the iTunes Network

Later versions of the iTunes platform, such as iTunes 8 and iTunes 9, are far better for accessibility than earlier versions, allowing for better access for people with vision and hearing impairments, and acknowledge some of the difficulties potentially encountered by those users with difficulty with manual dexterity. iTunes U, Apple's higher education platform, has similarly focused more on accessibility issues, particularly for people with vision impairments (Buckley, 2009).

While we acknowledge the improvement Apple has made to accessibility for people with different impairments, we critically note that the iTunes platform still does not conform to W3C standards and that Apple must contend with its reputation of having inaccessible products. By operating outside of standards, much third-party software including several screenreaders will not be able to access this popular technology. Similarly, access to these accessibility features involves the purchasing of new hardware as earlier models remain inaccessible.

When Apple upgraded its OS X computer operating system from Leopard to Snow Leopard, the decision was made to overhaul accessibility. Apple now claims to sell the only computer that a person who is blind or vision-impaired can buy, turn on, and set up without any assistance from a sighted person. This is a fairly recent feature of the Apple suite of products and we, of course, applaud these accessibility features. Without a doubt, many members of the vision-impaired community have embraced Apple's commitment to accessibility. Yet for others, the inaccessible reputation remains as we discovered when asking a university student with a vision impairment studying arts at UWA what she thought about the recent iTunes and iPod accessibility measures:

> I actually haven't had any experience with the iTunes website, but I have also heard from another blind person that it is not accessible. I don't actually have an iPod (they aren't particularly accessible either). (Personal communication: name withheld)

This response suggests that the origins and history of inaccessibility should not be forgotten simply because of a recent overhaul. Bloggers and tweeters are also on the lookout for any accessibility issues with later model Apple products that promise accessibility. By working belatedly toward creating an accessible platform, rather than having it integral to the design, iTunes continues to represent the dangerous trend in digital design where socially-constructed disabling features from the analog world are migrated to the digital environment online. The issue of accessibility cuts across computing technologies in relation to hardware, software, and applications. In some ways, the accessibility features continue to represent a desire for control and market dominance on Apple's part as outside screenreaders do not work with Apple products and users must learn to use another product. Despite a reputation of putting users at the center, Apple wishes to maintain a stranglehold:

> Apple has its own well-defined interests in not opening things up too much; indeed the company consistently seeks to circumscribe use and circulation of digital materials, and to demarcate the arena of digital cultures in new ways, that serves its own interests. (Goggin, 2009a: 239)

Although Goggin is referring to Apple's battle with mobile phone carriers and the momentous change the iPhone initiated with regard to wireless access and mobile cultures, his comments hold relevance to an investigation of the ways Apple is attempting to dominate the hardware and software markets, now venturing into accessibility that does not work across operating systems, browsers, and mobile devices.

Apps and Accessibility

Accessibility 2.0, the next generation of accessibility introduced in the previous chapter, and the iPhone and iPad all purport to put the user at the center of the experience. Both emphasize context and usability. While accessibility 2.0 is a new way of understanding accessibility and allows users to choose the way they access information and values the role of the rest of the community in initiating accessibility features, the iPhone promises users that they can do just about anything using their iPhone. The iPhone created a new digital culture where users have more influence over what gets built:

> The iPhone cracked open the carrier-centric structure of the wireless industry and unlocked a host of benefits for consumers, developers, manufacturers — and potentially the carriers themselves. Consumers get an easy-to-use handheld computer.

> And, as with the advent of the PC, the iPhone is sparking a wave of development that will make it even more powerful. (Vogelstein, 2008)

Although initially Apple attempted to strictly control unauthorized use of the iPhone, through the well-established DRM regime developed over the years through the iTunes software, hackers almost immediately cracked and modified the iPhone. Applications, previously provided only by Apple are now open for public development, although still regulated by Apple who refuse to release certain apps.

Apps are being developed for people with disability by both Apple and other community members to enable a more accessible interaction with a world physically and culturally structured to exclude people with disability (Wilson, 2010). While Apple created the iPhone as a closed device, they now allow for open application development where consumers could develop their own applications to use with the iPhone. The potential to develop applications for the iPhone, and now the iPad, is exciting to both professional software developers and people outside the industry who have a good idea or want to see a change in the world. *Smashing Magazine* suggests there are four reasons to create an app:

> solve a unique problem
> serve a specific niche
> make people laugh
> build on someone else's idea to make it better. (Gordon, 2009)

Interactivity is a vital feature that must drive all four reasons. Attention spans are decreasing and people use iPhone apps for ease and convenience. Identifying an audience is vital to the development and marketing process. People with disability are emerging as an important audience as many apps have been created for and by this niche group to solve a number of social problems. A search for "disability" in the iTunes App store elicits a large number of apps that deal with a diverse range of impairments and issues for both iPhones, iPods, and more recently for iPads, from learning disability assistance, to disability rights lawyers, to understanding the Americans with Disabilities Act (ADA). Screenreaders and sign language apps are also available.

Just as people are creating and utilizing apps that rate the food in restaurants, people with disability are calling for apps to document the accessibility of the built environment before they decide on where to go. This in turn helps people with injuries, the elderly or parents pushing strollers. The success of these types of apps depends on the social network. A community of people interested in accessibility add "information about places that are wheelchair/cane friendly" (Sylvie, 2009) and the network gets stronger the more people add to it.

In 1983, Shworles predicted that people with disability were on the verge of a "culture gap" in relation to the imminent uptake of computing technology and recommended that "consumers and consumer representatives become a part of the problem solving process" (Goggin and Newell, 2003: 123). Although we are critical of Apple's discriminatory origins, we applaud their more recent accessibility moves as they have consulted people with disability. Further, open application developments that allow anyone to create an iPhone app have revealed a desire amongst the community to consider the access requirements of people with disability in both the digital and real world.

While the Apple website boasts a number of pages dedicated to their accessibility features, these read much like an advertising campaign and provide little information regarding how to make iPhone applications accessible beyond the comment: "iPhone 3GS offers accessibility features to assist users who are visually or hearing impaired. These features include the VoiceOver screenreader, a Zoom feature, White on Black display options, Mono Audio". Following the "learn more" links leads to an endless loop of PR that does not provide any practical information for software developers. The iPhone Development Centre, on the other hand, encourages developers to guarantee their application works with screenreader users by ensuring:

> Every user interface element with which users can interact is accessible. This includes elements that merely supply information, such as static text, as well as controls that perform actions.
>
> All accessible elements supply accurate and helpful information. (OS iPhone Reference Library, 2010)

Apple have built accessibility into the application development toolkit, so if developers use the standard UIKit controls their app should in theory be accessible. The site does provide more in-depth technical information for developers wishing to create apps outside the standard development toolkit and caution that it is up to them to ensure the app is accessible. Accessibility testing kits are likewise available. While in 2010 every professional web developer would have an understanding of accessible design, more novice users would not or indeed prioritize it at all. Thus in a very positive move, we hope that inaccessibility could now be a reason for having your app rejected by Apple. There is, however, still need for caution. The iPad is being marketed as a tool for accessing and reading traditional print media — the first totally accessible portable device. However, the first iPad edition of the technology magazine, *Wired* made all its content a picture of text, rather than text that would be accessible through the iPad's operating system. As Joe Clark observes:

> It also means there's no accessibility on the first computers that are accessible by default if you the developer do no extra work at all. (Follow the spec exactly and your app is accessible right away.) Think of how much effort it takes to blow an opportunity like that. (Clark, 2010)

While default settings may prove vital in creating greater accessibility awareness, further education is clearly required if the seminal technology magazine,

Wired actively sought to circumvent accessibility measures. This again reflects the false perception identified by Regan (2004) that accessibility restricts creativity. However, because Apple now has a larger number of customers with disability, *Wired* were unable to get away with this unscathed.

Conclusion

Gregg Vanderheiden noted the potential and problems of computing technologies for people with disability in 1983:

> We can use the computer to do all sorts of wonderful things which can assist individuals who have various disability. At this point the computer still looks like a "good guy". But that's only half the story. Let's look at the other half — where computers have the great potential of creating new barriers and widening the gap between disabled and able-bodied people rather than helping the disabled individual overcome these gaps. (quoted in Goggin and Newell, 2003: 109)

This chasm can certainly be seen in the example of Apple computers, iPod, iTunes, and iPhone technologies but possibly in the reverse order. Initially, Apple was seen as a "bad guy" in terms of accessibility but following the legal and political mobilization of people with disability, Apple have subsequently embraced accessibility features with value obvious for the non-disabled as well. For example, using accessibility features in later model iPhones, users can verbally command their phone to play all their David Bowie songs — and it will.

Goggin and Newell (2003) observe that new technology is a prominent component of social, cultural, and political changes with the potential to include people with disability in more aspects of social life. However as is demonstrated by the changing implementation and operation of iTunes, this mitigation is far from an inevitable consequence of technological development. Despite this, James Edwards, author of the Brothercake blog, is optimistic that technology does have an important role in decreasing social disablement in the wider society:

> Technology is the last, best hope for accessibility. It's not like the physical world, where there are good, tangible reasons why some things can never be accessible. A person who's blind will never be able to drive a car manually; someone in a wheelchair will never be able to climb the steps of an ancient stone cathedral. Technology is not like the physical world — technology can take any shape. Technology is our slave, and we can make it do what we want. With technology there are no good reasons, only excuses. (Edwards, 2007)

Internet-based technologies have the potential to be inclusive of people with disability, and are often presented as a way to eradicate disability as it is socially-constructed. As we will discuss in Chapter 5, new technologies characteristic of the Information Age have been heralded as initiating an offset to many of the prejudicial attitudes established during the Industrial Revolution, where technology was established around able-bodied norms. The example of the Apple suite of hardware and software illustrates that digital technology is constructed in the same social world that people with disability are routinely disabled by. The Lectopia system, on the other hand, enables students with disability to access lecture materials and highlights the concept of universal access, the original ideology underpinning the design of the web. Lectopia has been widely utilized by many different types of students, not just the disabled, who are seeking flexibility. While we should be optimistic, we must also be aware as noted by Goggin and Newell (2003), the internet cannot be fully accessible until disability is considered a cultural identity with unnecessary social restrictions placed on a devalued biological fact. Accessibility is a universal design issue that potentially benefits both those with a disability and the wider community.

In the next chapter, we expand the discussion of how people with disability are driving change on the internet and consider the possibility that people are beginning to recognize that disability is a socially-created form of discrimination.

3

Building Digital Stairways
Nice View, But What About My Wheelchair?

"[I] worried about the fact that [computers] were going to someday be ubiquitous and people with disabilities need to not be able to do just special things on them, but regular things."

(Gregg Vanderheiden, quoted in Ellcessor 2010: 293)

"An accessible Web site is but the gateway ... There is no reason why disabled people, including blind and partially sighted people, should be excluded. ... [However] for some this may still sound like science fiction."

(Weisen et al., 2005)

Science fiction is experienced and defined intertextually across literature and films which adopt certain thematic tendencies, such as a fear of technology or disbelief with the non-existent and unfamiliar. The rapidly advancing and changing internet environment has inspired several cautionary titles within the science fiction cinematic genre since the 1970s including *Logan's Run*, *The Net*, *The Matrix*, *Minority Report*, *Tron*, and the *Terminator* movies to name a few. While these are cautionary tales, they are also a celebration of digital technologies and their potential. Problems seem to arise only when opportunities for participation are limited to a certain type of person or institution. Any attempt to decrease or eradicate diversity results in untold mayhem within the science fiction genre. By focusing on disability throughout this book, we are attempting to identify a similar problem in relation to narrowly-defined notions of citizenship. In the process, we do not wish to condemn the web. Rather, we seek to expose the assumptions made about humans, bodies, and who has access to this technology.

This chapter is a celebration of the web and an examination of how it is becoming a more ubiquitous part of life. Through a critical examination of trends toward greater inclusion and exclusion of people with disability from the internet, as it is set against a backdrop of increasing democratization, this chapter considers the current digital environment to chart the rise of web 2.0 — focusing especially on user-generated content. These sites present particular challenges for universal design and disability. As we consider the ways people with disability are excluded from participation, we also look to how people with disability are affecting and participating in opportunities for collaboration allowed via web 2.0 platforms such as YouTube, blogs, and Twitter.

As the web becomes a more ever-present part of everyday life, the potential costs of being excluded from that environment grow. Currently, people with disability are excluded from many aspects of the web experience. Yet, disability and accessibility will impact on the next generation of the web as user-generated output potentially enables an "accessibility 2.0" of user-generated content. By putting users at the center, they can determine the way material they view is delivered and their individual accessibility requirements. With the digital world at a crossroads, user-generated output and accessibility 2.0 as it focuses on universal design and access, represents a possible future for the web. Alternately, the web can continue to move away from universal design principles, while at the same time increasing the social and economic costs to those who are then excluded.

The Early Web

The internet was initially established as a network to connect researchers across different locations and incompatible operating systems. As such, it was difficult to master and required an advanced understanding of computing technologies. When Tim Berners-Lee developed the World Wide Web in 1989, access to the internet was greatly enhanced. He believed that a more simple and intuitive interface connected via hyperlinks would allow a common information space and facilitate easier connections among people. Enabling access for people with disability was central to his vision. The text-based early web worked well with adaptive technologies that were widely adopted by personal computer users with disability during the 1980s.

Chieko Asakawa (2005), an IBM research fellow who specializes in the non-visual web, describes an enormous accessibility chasm between the early web and web 2.0:

> Lynx, a text based web browser, which was developed in 1992, was very accessible for screen reader users, since it could be controlled with just a keyboard. By pressing the cursor right or left keys, for example, users could move to the next or previous link texts. I was able to access the Web for the first time using Lynx in 1994, with a DOS screen reader through telnet by accessing a UNIX server. (Asakawa, 2005)

The internet environment Asakawa describes in this quote was paradoxically a much-less-accessible experience for the average person. Specialist software was required to connect to the network as well as the (at the time) specialist hardware of a modem. Lynx is an early text-based web browser which, at the time, did not process pictures and images. As a result, a screenreader could easily read the text-based web and a mouse was unnecessary as a computer user could navigate to different links using the tab button on the keyboard. However, other factors contribute to ease of access because computing technology is more than hardware and software (Kent 2008).

The hardware of the computer hosts the software of its operating system and other programs. The fusion of these two elements enables the digital environment to be represented on the user's computer. This then interfaces with wetware — the person using the device and their knowledge and experience. This atomized convergence creates a matrix of these elements which determine if access is possible and the quality of that access. As an employee at IBM Tokyo research, Asakawa likely had more advanced hardware, software, and wetware than the general population. While Asakawa's experience is important, equally we need to recognize that her case is an unusual one. What she was doing in 1994 is not representative of what the average person was doing.

Of course, the ability of most people to access the World Wide Web in 1994, regardless of any level of disability, was quite limited. Asakawa's experience reflects considerable skills and the literacy in, what was at the time, a very new technological medium. This ironically also meant that a lack of access was less of a disabling factor at that time, since it was still a long way from becoming a mainstream part of everyday life.

The first widely-distributed web browser, Mosaic, was launched in 1993. A year later there were less than 50 million internet users, mostly concentrated in North America. In contrast, by 2010 there were more than 1.8 billion internet users, with North America-based users making up less than 15 percent of the online population. The internet has gone from a relatively marginal medium in the early- to mid-1990s to one that is much more mainstream in the early 2010s. Unfortunately, this growth in the use of the medium has also seen it become less accessible for people with disability.

The move into web 2.0 with its associated plug-ins and multimedia was, and continues to be, particularly disabling to users with vision impairment. Asakawa argues that a blind web-user could not authentically experience the web in 2005 and recommends further research so that both IT-savvy and novice, blind internet users could benefit from the web as an information resource (2005). Asakawa may be vision-impaired, but she clearly has an in-depth knowledge in this area and significant wetware in relation to the operation of the internet and the World Wide Web. She is reflecting on her use of the 1994 web environment. This was just three years after the first website went online.

A collaborative space where people could share ideas was a motivating factor for Berners-Lee's proposal for a hyperlinked network to allow a common information space. His boss, Mike Sendall, felt the proposal was "vague but promising" and allowed Berners-Lee to continue development. Throughout 1989 and 1990 Berners-Lee, together with Robert Cailliau, developed a way to share information over the internet using hypertext. This platform eventually came to be known as the World Wide Web. The first websites were administered through their place of employment, the organization Conseil Européenne pour la Recherche Nucléaire or CERN. The first website to go online, on 6 August 1991, was info.cern.ch and it contained information about hypertext and how others could create their own page. There were not a large number of hits at this time, and in order to be effective as a collaborative space, more sites needed to emerge.

Throughout 1991 the web remained research-based, and a number of other institutions began developing servers and websites. The network was governed by an "acceptable use" policy established by the National Science Foundation (NSF), the United States government research arm to support the backbone of the internet. A ban on commerce was an integral aspect of this policy. However, in 1992 this ban was lifted as the US government, unable to continue funding the increasing costs of the growing technology, turned to corporate America to fund the medium's progression. The internet and web then emerged as an everyday communications tool. In 1994, people were able to shop on the internet for the first time. In that same year, Pizza Hut launched an online ordering system. Asakawa describes ordering a cake from an online store using her Lynx browser and a screenreader.

After the commercial ban was lifted, browser development began in earnest and Netscape Communications and Microsoft, in particular, began competing with each other for market dominance through the rapid release of browser software. As a result, there was greater emphasis on producing new features at the expense of both fixing bugs and ensuring accessibility. That Internet Explorer 3.0 was more accessible than its successor Internet Explorer 4.0 is a famous example of the problems experienced during this period. Common standards established during the research phase of the web were lost. At its most obvious level, this meant that different sites would announce that they had been optimized for, or best-viewed, using a particular browser. A serious consequence of this was that developers of adaptive technology were unable to keep pace with these changes.

During the 1990s, there was rapid growth in the online population and a rapid growth in the value of companies that were developing online applications. This growth, however, was unsustainable as the dot-com stock price bubble burst at the turn of the century. We will consider both of these issues in greater depth in the next chapter with particular reference to the consequences of this for people with disability. Following the 2001 collapse in stock prices, we have witnessed the rise of a new type of web culture around the loosely-defined concept of web

2.0. The overriding principle of web 2.0 is that the web is a platform and can be used in dynamic ways. There are endless possibilities for participation and innovation. The user-generated content that characterizes this next generation of the web allows or enables just about anyone to access and contribute to it.

Web 2.0 allows people to contribute to information and act as co-developers through wikis, blogs, social networking, and file-sharing. It is popularly considered to be "easy" when compared to the early web. Difficulties navigating sites are usually blamed on the user rather than the site itself. The idea that anyone can become a blogger in less than three minutes characterizes this phenomenon. However, for people with disability, there are accessibility issues that do, in fact, relate to the structure of the site. For example the "Captcha" (completely automated public Turing test to tell computers and humans apart) technology designed to differentiate between a person signing up for an account and an automated computer process is a disabling technology that can prevent people accessing sites. This system, often used for verification purposes on web 2.0 sites, presents an image of a word deliberately blurred and disfigured so that it cannot be readily identified by a computer, which can only be translated by a human user. However, this presents an obstacle to people relying on transcription software which is unable to read the image, and to those who may have trouble translating the image on the screen.

Although accessibility 2.0 is of most benefit to people with disability — and especially those with vision impairment — older people and people in the developing world, the recent trend toward mobile internet use suggests the majority of internet users will benefit from accessibility options (Zajicek, 2007: 1). The move from "reading the web" to "writing the web" is an important point in the evolution of the internet, in cementing its place in people's lives. While a plethora of avenues exist in terms of generating content, opportunities for how this information is accessed and viewed are limited to the restrictions established by the creators of sites.

Digital technology allows the manipulation of information in terms of appearance, text size, color, and mode of output including, for example, text-to-sound or Braille. In theory, digital information can be accessed by many users with different needs in different ways, as Asakawa's early experiences demonstrate. However, in practice this is not always the case, particularly as the web becomes more complex and a more ubiquitous part of life. Donna Smillie of the Royal National Institute for the Blind (RNIB) fears that as web 2.0 becomes more complex, accessibility will be considered too hard, expensive, and time-consuming, despite a more widespread awareness:

> We will see a reduction in the accessibility of sites as Web 2.0 technologies and
> functionality are implemented. Because it can involve more complex programming
> and interactions between browser and server, there is a risk that functionality will
> initially be implemented in ways which cause problems for those using assistive

technologies such as screen readers. Some Web developers still struggle with issues as simple as providing meaningful ALT text for images! (Zajicek, 2007: 2)

As the web becomes more complex and dependent on visual imagery, alternative (alt) text is paramount. Alt text is a tag attached to the image which describes what the image is attempting to communicate in the context of the site. This text enables a non-visual, authentic experience of the web.

As a way to participate in social networks and advocate for a more equitable and extensible world, the web is a crucial medium for people with disability. Web 2.0 allows a number of different ways to communicate using, for example, text, still and moving images, and sounds. The opportunities to participate in the creation of user-generated content in ways that suit the user have proved invaluable to people with disability. However, restrictions on the ways this content can be viewed is potentially blocking out people with disability. We suggest a focus on user-generated output as a way to remedy this. Accessibility 2.0 describes a continual focus on accessibility to prioritize the user (Kelly *et al.*, 2007). Web 2.0 could be and, in some cases, is fantastic for people with disability. Problems arise when people are forced into a certain way of doing things. As we move into the future of the web beyond web 2.0, the opportunity for grass-roots collaboration to replace user-generated social networking could be compromised if bottlenecks that restrict ways of viewing content continue to develop.

The internet and particularly the web and web 2.0 applications have become increasingly more important within our day-to-day lives. Most people in the developed world manage their finances using internet banking and pay their bills online. Likewise, entertainment is gravitating more toward online formats with companion websites for popular movies and television shows. People organize and recommend books on the LibraryThing web service and share movie reviews on the Internet Movie Database (IMDB) or Everyone's a Critic.

The collaborative focus of web 2.0 platforms is also acting as a Fourth Estate — as was envisioned for the media during the eighteenth century when the press claimed "a central role in the management and maintenance of a representative democracy" (Schultz, 2002: 102). As conventional media is increasingly being questioned for its inability to speak for the public interest, user-generated content is taking over the role of maintaining this representative democracy. Social networking and mobile connection also allow people on-the-ground, experiencing newsworthy events and natural disasters — such as the London bombings, protests in Iran, and the earthquake in Haiti — to upload images and accounts which can then be passed on to the conventional news distribution channels.

User-generated social networking also acts as a Fourth Estate to monitor the government and big business. For example, in 2009 Twitter users responded to Amazon's (Amazon.com) decision to remove sales rankings for books which contained, or had vague references to, homosexual themes by reclassifying them as "adult content". This decision meant these books became difficult to search for and they were unable to be recognized in the bestseller list. People considered this an incidence of censorship and initiated a public-sphere debate. As far more people picked up on this through Twitter and its trending topic #Amazonfail, Amazon claimed a software glitch and returned the sales ranking to the affected books.

Increasing Democratization

The public sphere is vital to the formation of public opinion which, in turn, legitimates democracy (Habermas, 1962: 176). The public sphere, simply put, is a space, real or virtual, where citizens can come together to explore ideas and form a public view. In order to work effectively in the maintenance of democracy, it must be free from both government and economic influences (Price, 1995: 24). For Habermas, accessibility is a core tenant of the public sphere — it must be free of restrictions.

Habermas' conception of the public sphere is often applied to the internet as a democratic and politically powerful medium. However, just as the Habermasian public sphere has been derided for being a bourgeois fantasy replete with race and class inequalities, the internet too has limitations — described as the digital divide. While questions of equality of access, in relation to race, sex, age, income, and geographical location, are well-asserted, the challenges faced by people with disability are less well-considered (Ellcessor, 2010: 290).

Examples of an increasing democratization available via the web can be seen in the political use of the early web, particularly through email, personal websites, and chat. Sen and Hill (2000) credit the internet with facilitating the fall of Suharto's rule in Indonesia over a two-year period. The medium allowed the disaffected middle-class to get around mainstream media regulation and, likewise, enabled students to plan their protests while gaining international support (Sen and Hill, 2000: 194). The radical social and political change was made possible because Indonesia's government was unable to regulate local shopfront telecommunication stores who were more interested in paying by-the-hour customers than vague government policy. Lunat (2008) suggests the cyber cafes created "public spheres of discussion and dissemination".

More recently, web 2.0 platforms such as Facebook, YouTube and most significantly, Twitter, kept the rest of the world abreast of developments in Iran following the 2009 presidential elections. Similar to the reach of email and personal websites during the overthrow of Suharto in the 1990s, Twitter was able to circumvent media regulation. Users influenced the administrators of Twitter to postpone a scheduled maintenance shutdown at the time of this unrest so that it would remain online during the period. Likewise, YouTube softened its "non-violence" policy to disseminate footage of the protests that took place in Iran.

Twitter

Created in 2006, Twitter is a social networking and micro-blogging site. While currently at third-most-popular social networking site, Twitter's popularity is growing the fastest. The 140-character limit on tweets or text-based posts was conceived to be compatible with SMS messaging and slang. This simple interface has spawned an exciting era of innovation with users directing its evolution and use (Johnson, 2009). The simple design invites collaboration with users, the Twitter interface, and third-party platforms. Most Twitter users access the software using third-party applications designed for use with mobile devices such as iPhones and BlackBerrys. These applications and other tools, including photo links and maps to connect Twitter's community members to others "tweeting" nearby, have been created by users. Twitter claims a mix of public and private technologies that allow an easier, global connection. It is predominately a social networking system and is heavily dependent on the mobile web (Twitter, 2010).

Personal moments can be transformed into wider social and political issues, as Giroux (2009) suggests of the broadcast of the green movement's protests in Iran in June 2009. For Giroux, new communication technologies, and especially social networking sites, are far more than depoliticized "personal tools" or "entertainment devices."

The combination of social networking and mobile technology awakened a "reservoir of political activity" allowing people within and outside Iran access to information that would have otherwise been stifled (Giroux, 2009). Tweets of 140 characters and photo links were effective methods to disseminate information following the limitations placed on mainstream media during the conflicts.

Political activists in China have similarly embraced the micro-blogging site and access to it was blocked by the country's government to prevent discussion of the twentieth anniversary of the Tiananmen Square massacre. While our position regarding Twitter's role in political mobilization is celebratory, others are more cautious suggesting that the only reason Twitter was not blocked in Iran was because the government used it for surveillance (Lake, 2009). While Twitter may not be inherently political, its format has invited political mobilization in many areas, including disability and accessibility.

Twitter has attracted a number of people and organizations interested in promoting the importance of web accessibility, including the World Wide Web Consortium's web accessibility initiative, which has a Twitter account (@w3c_wai). The strong accessibility community on Twitter is giving public exposure to issues relating to disability that have historically been considered personal problems that an individual must overcome. While there are number of people who use Twitter to tweet about accessibility issues, Twitter itself is inaccessible and does not have an accessibility policy. Dennis Lembree outlines several inaccessible features of Twitter that he addressed in his third-party platform, Accessible Twitter:

no keyboard access to favorite/reply/delete
lack of headings
favoriting requires JavaScript
custom colors may not be readable
code doesn't validate
code could use better semantics
password field is missing a label: select lang missing label
field sets used without legends
layout width is static not flexible; doesn't "stretch" with browser width
Javascript required for details on latest tweet (time, in reply to) (quoted in Accessify, 2009)

He argues that people with vision impairment are being excluded from Twitter and the web in general because of time and money constraints, as well as a general lack of imagination. Although he believes this group is "not intentionally neglected online", we argue that the assumption that every web user has the same ability to access the web is an example of what Goggin and Newell (2003) call "doing production". Doing production, while not intentional in a malicious sense, is a reflection of the underpinning moral order, as it intersects with technology and culture and digitally disables people with certain bodies. We explore this concept further in Chapter 6, with particular reference to the social networking site, Facebook.

Lembree has addressed many of the inaccessible features of Twitter to ensure it adheres to web standards. Accessible Twitter adopts a simple and consistent layout, and navigation can work with or without JavaScript. JavaScript is a functional programming language which is used to make webpages more dynamic and interactive. As an add-on to HTML, it has traditionally posed a problem for users with disability. Although screenreaders that were developed more recently are better equipped to handle JavaScript, a certain percentage of people choose to browse without JavaScript while others use older versions of screenreading software. Therefore, it is still an important business and accessibility issue to ensure a page works with or without JavaScript.

Lembree has also ensured "forms are marked up for optimal accessibility" This is a relatively easy-to-achieve feature which includes clear identification and labelling, while also allowing exclusive use by either the keyboard or mouse. This is an important feature for users with a mobility impairment who cannot use a mouse, and people without disability who prefer to use keyboard shortcuts as a timesaver. Accessible Twitter has a large default text size that adopts a high color-contrast in line with the stipulation that a site must be "perceivable" under WCAG 2.0. The site allows users to access it in either high or low resolution in line with Berners-Lee's vision that the web be accessible regardless of disability. Finally, Lembree has made a commitment to expanding the accessibility features of Accessible Twitter "every day". For example, when Twitter introduced the list function, Accessible Twitter began developing a functionality to allow a similar experience. Lembree was not surprised at the inaccessibility of the original Twitter, even given its reputation for being simple and easy-to-use, because of the misconception that web 2.0 cannot be fun and accessible at the same time. He recommends a focus on accessibility from the planning stages to ensure all users can navigate and benefit from a "cool" site. Progressive improvement with changes in technology is also vital.

The inaccessibility of Twitter is a reflection of the poor quality of accessibility on the web in general and Lembree's Accessible Twitter has been enthusiastically received by those with and without vision impairment in the Twitterverse. The project has raised the visibility of the importance of accessibility in the rapidly-evolving online world. Appreciative users have called on Lembree to turn his attentions to an accessible Facebook:

> Twitter.com is extremely off-course as far as web accessibility goes. Basic things such as proper use of headings and keyboard access are not implemented. I received an email from a blind user who really enjoys Accessible Twitter. He even asked, I think jokingly, if I could make an accessible Facebook, which is also terribly inaccessible. (quoted in Accessify, 2009)

Although Twitter did not even rate a mention in the AbilityNet (2008) report on social networking, the charity found a number of social networking sites were inaccessible to users with a number of different impairments. Since that time, the importance of accessibility has been demonstrated after Facebook and You-Tube, two sites criticized by AbilityNet, revamped their accessibility features with far-reaching success with audience satisfaction while MySpace, which was also criticized, has done nothing, losing a significant proportion of its worldwide market share (Cahill, 2009). Twitter should take notice of the intersecting relationship between accessibility and market share. However, the existence of Accessible Twitter does not let them off the hook:

> Accessible Twitter is designed to be easier to use and is optimised for disabled users, but it is yet to be seen whether such a move will prompt Twitter into action or have the reverse effect, letting them feel that they can more easily shed all responsibility. In such a competitive market and with other social media players innovating and leading on accessible design, accessible design is becoming central to the development and continued growth of online businesses. This fact should be food for thought for a savvy startup like Twitter. Leaving it too long might just signal the beginning of the end. (Cahill, 2009)

Despite its reputation for being simple and easy-to-use, and its perceived importance as a tool for democracy and political mobilization, Twitter invokes digital disability by failing to consider accessibility. However, by encouraging a community of members to create Twitter applications, its accessibility was achieved through a network of community. Lembree's Accessible Twitter shows that accessibility in social networking is possible. Although this adoption of community accessibility gives cause for great optimism, it is equally important for corporate leaders such as Twitter and Facebook to lead the way by building accessibility features into their toolkit.

Work, Education, Web 2.0, Accessibility and Disability

While the early web centered on research and was mainly used by scientists and physicists, the web has now become a part of our everyday lives. Likewise too, the web is something used by people with disability to do "regular things" as predicted by Vanderheiden in the quote at the beginning of this chapter. The benefits of the internet and web 2.0, in particular, for people with disability have been recognized in relation to community-building through social networking sites and virtual worlds. These sites have been much celebrated for the opportunities they provide for the independence and self-empowerment of people with disability. With reference to chat, popular during the early web, Seymour and Lupton (2004) argue that communication is central to social life and find the internet allows people with disability to develop and maintain friendships. They also observe that internet technologies allow many people with disability to work from home and use adaptive technology and ergonomic furniture to tailor their work environment to suit their bodies.

People with disability are often cited as a group that would particularly benefit from the telecommuting possibilities available through the internet. The opportunity to work from home marks a move from the industrial era to the Information Age (Holloway, 2007: 3). As we will discuss in Chapter 5, the industrial revolution, as outlined by Finkelstien (1980), was particularly disabling because machines were constructed to suit a certain type of body — the "norm". The development of digital communications technologies is especially important to people with mobility and sensory impairments because the remote access it allows saves physical energy without compromising contact with employers (Roulstone, 1998: 20).

Technologies such as email that enable workers to telecommute are also beneficial to workers with disability in the physical work environment. Email as a communications tool addresses several disabling aspects of the physical environment, including way-finding and inaccessible paper, notes and also allows ready access to information. Web 2.0 — style platforms such as wikis and cloud computing are providing similar opportunities for employees with disability. A recent Pew Research Center survey found that the majority of technology experts predict that cloud computing will be more dominant than desktop computing by 2020 (Watters, 2010). Cloud computing which saves documents to a server rather than a desktop computer will allow a greater number of people to engage in telecommuting, including people with disability. Students can likewise make use of online platforms to complete their degrees.

Online social networking is an important part of the university experience for many young people and, increasingly, educators are introducing web 2.0 technologies into teaching and administration as a way to reach this group (McGee and Diaz, 2007). The experience of students with disability demonstrates the issues of bringing web 2.0 platforms into the academy, in terms of disclosure, diversity, and network disablement:

> A student who is in a wheelchair can control the disclosure of their disability online, deciding when, where, and if their disability is relevant to a social network discussion. For some disabled students controlling disclosure in this way can facilitate social presence with potentially positive learning outcomes. However, it should be noted that for other students print impairments, such as dyslexia, may represent uncontrollable disclosure, with a negative impact on confidence and contributions. In these circumstances a student is disabled by the network, and both the student and network can suffer as a result. (Liccardi *et al.*, 2007)

Online spaces have been credited with allowing more students with disability the possibility of participating in an educational experience. More flexible study options, such as the delivery of lectures online, addresses some of the problems students with disability need to overcome in a traditional face-to-face learning format (Alltree and Quadri, 2007: 164). Techniques and technologies that include people with disability act as a useful reminder to meet the varied needs of a diverse population, which includes students negotiating paid-employment or combining family commitments with study.

While theories of good pedagogy have shown this has long been the case, the widespread uptake of web 2.0, digital technologies, and broadband internet access has provided new opportunities for inclusion. Multimedia, in particular, has been heralded as a way for students with learning disability to both improve their writing skills and provide an alternative to writing (Li and Hamel, 2003: 35). The point of effective disability — internet policy is that it not only improves the lives of those with mobility, visual, or auditory challenges, but also increases the usefulness of the internet for everyone. As we discussed in Chapter 2, Lectopia, as it provides recordings and more recently transcripts of lectures, benefits people with disability by increasing their independent access. Likewise, it benefits people without disability who are engaging in revision or catch-up on lecture content. Adaptive, customizable, and flexible technologies are better technologies.

A number of tertiary institutions are embracing the pedagogical benefits of the virtual world Second Life, particularly in terms of fieldwork, the demonstration of social constructions, and the possibility to bridge the crossing between education and the everyday. Participation in Second Life potentially allows students to question what appears to be fixed biological categories such as "disabled" (Mullen *et al.*, 2007: 23). For some, non-disclosure is liberating:

> For the different, the hybrid, the disabled, and others, it is experienced as tremendously liberating not to allow an embodied physical "fact" to be so determining; and the Internet is proving a fascinating site of experimentation in how people move beyond these embodied physical facts, not for the sake of "escaping" them or denying them, but for *changing what they mean to us and to others.* (Burbles quoted in Mullens *et al.*, 2007: 24 [italics in original])

Writing about text-based multi-user dungeons (MUDs), the virtual worlds of the 1990s, Turkle also sees potential for the fluid formation of identity as people choose how they manifest in text-based descriptions, "the obese can be slender, the beautiful plain, the 'nerdy' sophisticated" (Barr, 2002: 250). As we will discuss in Chapter 7, virtual worlds engender both opportunities and challenges for people with disability. While virtual worlds and social networking do not require disclosure of disability, they do not eliminate the body, as accessibility issues can and do remain. Rather than make disability invisible — in order to change what it means to us and others — perhaps confronting an ableist world with the reality of social disablement would be more effective. With reference to media and film production, David Hevey (1997) recommends disabled producers adopt imagery that does not conform to an able-bodied worldview.

YouTube

In the 1990s, activists, academics, and media producers of the disability cultural movement argued that people with disability should be in charge of their image and, further, those images must make the able-bodied audience feel uncomfortable in order for social change to occur (Hevey, 1997). Web 2.0 participatory media, such as Google's YouTube, realizes this vision, and allows people with disability a new voice — a way to tell their stories and force the non-disabled world to take responsibility for the disableism that devalues the perspectives of people with disability in film and media. Systemic ableism is perpetuated by traditional media which promotes individualized representations of disability to absolve society of responsibility for creating inaccessible environments (Ellis, 2010). Mainstream media frequently represent disability in a way that reassures able-bodied people of their normality (Ellis, 2008). Digital video has long been used to subvert this and offer more complex realities of disability. Web 2.0 now provides an effective platform for the dissemination of these grass-roots videos.

Disability film festivals that feature different representations of disability, and strive to make each film accessible to any type of disability by including audio descriptions as well as subtitles, are an important way to increase the visibility of disability in the media and culture. However, the video-sharing website YouTube may prove more effective, as film-makers do not have to get past a judging panel bound by time, programming, and philosophical restrictions to have their films seen.

YouTube has a growing community of people with disability, with subgroups emerging around different impairments. Grass-roots videos question social constructions of disability and the motivations of mainstream media as it seeks the "expert opinion" of people with no direct personal experience of living with disability to perpetuate cure — care stereotypes. Many lively discussions have taken place in the comment space below videos, as users question each other's perceptions and experiences. For example, a radically different representation of autism is presented in silentmiaow's YouTube film, *In My Language* (Ellis, 2010). The short film has been reviewed by *Wired* Magazine (Wolman, 2008) and other medical and technology publications and has received significant attention across the blogosphere. By offering an interpretation, the film constructs people with autism as a linguistic minority who communicate differently and puts the onus on people without autism for failing to understand. YouTube is a popular platform with a large audience. People with mental illness are also using YouTube to revise the negative stereotypes more commonly seen in the mainstream media. While a space for community has emerged via this avenue, YouTube has recognized the need to work on accessibility to allow more people with disability an opportunity to participate at their site.

In 2009 Ken Harrenstien, a deaf Google software engineer for YouTube announced on the Google blog that YouTube was now automatically captioning videos:

> Since the original launch of captions in our products, we've been happy to see growth in the number of captioned videos on our services, which now number in the hundreds of thousands. This suggests that more people are becoming aware of how useful captions can be. ... Captions not only help the deaf and hearing impaired, but with machine translation, they also enable people around the world to access video content in any of 51 languages. Captions also improve search and even enable users to jump to the exact parts of the videos they're looking for. (Harrenstien, 2009)

Captioning had been available from 2006, but had not been universally adopted because it was not considered important by the users generating content for YouTube. Harrenstien (2009) has set a long-term goal to make videos accessible. While this first generation of automatic captioning has some flaws, and applies only to videos produced in English, it is an important step in making YouTube more accessible and we expect future technological advancements will lead to further improvements. As YouTube becomes a more accessible social and political space for people with disability, blogs similarly hold great potential for people with disability as a space to generate content, socialize, and educate the non-disabled.

Blogs and Social Networks

People with different impairments have embraced various forms of blogging, depending on their preferred method of access. For example, people with vision impairment have embraced audio and adopted podcasts while people with hearing impairments opt for video blogging as it allows communication via sign language. The social and personal commentary enabled by this medium, blogging, potentially advances a social understanding of disability that moves between the medical and social divide (Goggin and Noonan, 2006: 165). The BBC's Ouch! website represents a particular disability-blogging experience — one that recognizes the perspectives of people with disability while also striving to educate a non-disabled audience (Goggin and Noonan, 2006: 168).

Ouch! is a BBC-affiliated disability lifestyle website which utilizes web 2.0 platforms to bring a disabled voice to the majority. Aimed at anyone interested in disability — including those without it — the site consists of articles, blogs, a message forum, and a downloadable radio show. Intended to reflect the "lives and experiences of disabled people", Ouch! claims the site is meaningless without people with disability (Ouch!, 2010). While Ouch! has been criticized for relegating the expert opinion of people with disability to the fringes of media rather than mainstream BBC output (Zajicek, 2007: 3), it encourages grassroots participation of people with and without disability via mainstream web 2.0 media, including blogs, cartoons, and audio or video blogging. The site has been integral in redefining the way disability could be imagined in the community, through an irreverent tone that reclaims the way disability has previously been reported. Charity discourses which see the disabled as poor unfortunates in need of charity are debunked:

> But disability is really dull ... I'm off!
>
> Dull? Are you JOKING me? Maybe some of the reporting has been a bit odd in the past, but disabled lives are far from dull. There's so much complexity and variety, and so many things to think about. Dull? Sheesh!
>
> Some of this stuff is quite funny — can I laugh?
>
> You complete sicko. Why would you want to laugh at the plight of the disabled? Seriously though, Ouch! Is really into using humour positively. Disabled people are uniquely placed to see some of the stupidest things around. So there's plenty to chuckle at. Ouch! Never laughs AT disabled people; we laugh WITH them. (Ouch!, 2010)

This approach is evident in Disability Bitch's blogs on Ouch! She brings disability into the mainstream popular culture and has received an international cult following by showing that women with disability experience the same social pressures as other women:

> In principle, I've always been a supporter of high heels. Think about it. As types of footwear go, they at least put disabled and nondisabled women on a level, and

they render even the most Amazonian and able female slightly mobility impaired. (Disability Bitch, 2008)

Disability Bitch takes news articles that don't appear to have anything to do with disability, such as the claim that high heels improve your sex life, and then draws out the disability relevance in a playful and irreverent way. Her pop-culture icon status was achievable because web 2.0 platforms put Ouch! on an equal level with mainstream BBC media productions. By bringing together all of the BBC's representations of disability at this one site, the relevance of disability in the mainstream is emphasized not diminished.

Conclusion

We celebrate the increased opportunity the web provides to people with disability. Increasingly, people with disability rely on the medium to provide more independence, work opportunities, and social interactions. However, user-generated content is providing challenges for universal design and disability. Unknown and unused accessibility features in web 2.0 platforms complicate attempts to access information in alternative formats. Digital media and online technology hold the promise that people with disability will be included in social life, diminishing the impact their impairment has on their social life. However, when the technology disables different bodies, the result is what Goggin and Newell (2003) describe as digital disability. While Mary Zajicek (2007) argues that web 2.0 accessibility is of most benefit to people with disability — and especially those with vision impairments, older people and people in the developing world — the recent trend toward mobile applications and internet usage suggest the majority of internet users would benefit from accessibility options.

The digital world is at a crossroads and user-generated output and accessibility 2.0 represents a possible future for the web. This future could see a move back toward universal design and access that was integral to Berners-Lee's prediction for a common information space. His grand vision became the World Wide Web and greatly enhanced access to the internet for everyone. Significantly, the early web as a text-based environment worked well with adaptive technologies. Early users of the web such as Chieko Asakawa (2005) now describe an enormous accessibility chasm between the early web and web 2.0.

Web 2.0 is a platform that enables the web to be used dynamically by means of user-generated content — blogs, social networking, and file-sharing. Web 2.0 is popularly considered to be "easy" when compared to the early web. The opportunities to participate in the creation of user-generated content, in ways that suit the user, have proved invaluable to people with disability. However, restrictions on the ways this content can be viewed is potentially blocking out people with disability. Accessibility 2.0 is a mode of accessibility and user-generated output which prioritizes the accessibility choices of individual users. However, many web 2.0 platforms restrict people to a certain way of viewing information. As we move into the future of the web, beyond web 2.0, the opportunity for grass-roots collaboration to replace user-generated social networking could be compromised if accessibility 2.0 is prevented.

The move from "reading the web" to "writing the web" was integral to the establishment of the web as an everyday communications tool. Although a plethora of avenues exist in terms of generating content, opportunities for how this information is accessed and viewed is limited to the restrictions established by the creators of sites. In theory, digital information can be accessed by users with different needs in various ways. The user can determine the way the information is displayed visually, altering the size of the text and its background or, alternatively, have images relayed as sounds through a screenreader or as refreshable Braille using a Braille-output device. In practice, this is not always possible, with the options available to a user to select their own output being limited by the platform they are using, particularly as the web becomes more complex and a more ubiquitous part of life.

Despite its reputation for being simple and easy-to-use, and its perceived importance as a tool for democracy and political mobilization, Twitter builds in disability at the point-of-production by failing to consider accessibility. However, by encouraging a community of members to create Twitter applications, accessibility was achieved via a network of community. Dennis Lembree's Accessible Twitter shows that accessibility in social networking is achievable. While Lembree's adoption of community accessibility gives cause for great optimism, it is equally important for the corporations to lead the way by building accessibility features into their toolkits.

Google's YouTube has recently begun building accessibility into its user-generated content toolkits with varying degrees of success. YouTube has performed an important function in the grassroots' political mobilization of several groups associated with different impairments — by allowing a medium for representations that would not normally be granted mainstream media exposure. While a space for community has emerged via this avenue, YouTube has recognized it needs to work on accessibility to allow more people with disability an opportunity to participate at their site.

Similarly, blogs, which can be posted in many different formats depending on the effects of impairments, have enabled a social and personal commentary which speaks to overtly political paradigms of disability and more personal narratives. The BBC-affiliated Ouch! draws together mainstream media output and the experiences of ordinary people with disability to reveal the stupidity and hilarity of social disablement. We celebrate the increased opportunity provided to people with disability by the web, but caution against glossing over issues of accessibility.

There is a need to focus on the ways in which technologies can be redesigned to eliminate ableist oppression that keeps people with disability from being able to participate fully in all aspects of the material and social world. As the example of YouTube's automatic captioning demonstrates, new technologies which address accessibility must be put into practice because the technical skill required to create a blog, wiki, or webpage is minimal. Accessibility features built into the initial toolkit will flow on to end-users (Gibson, 2007: 4).

The central thesis of this work is information that is held as convergent digital media should be accessible — both to generate and consume — through a wide variety of different platforms. These platforms have the potential to be inclusive of many different types of impairments. Just as disability is generated by society in an analog world, the failure to make information accessible through alternative digital platforms is a socially-constructed cause of disability in the online environment. Through the user-generated content associated with web 2.0, the disabling process takes on a dynamic form of production.

While assistive technologies worked well in the early web environment, as bandwidth and processing power have grown, the environment has become much more complex. Digital design is triggering disability when it was initially established to be inclusive. The next chapter expands on this history to track the development of the World Wide Web from its not-for-profit origins through its commercialization and the dot -com bubble at the turn of the century, to elaborate further on the rise of web 2.0. Each of these developments had implications for universal design and access by people with disability to the online environment, as disability is dynamically reproduced.

Part II
How Did We Get Here?

4

We Want You in Our Network
Universal Design v Retrofitting the Web

"The boundaries of the internet are essentially only dependent upon barriers to access."

(Trevor Barr, 2002: 251)

"Another important area of professionalism is accessibility awareness. Everyone should be accommodated, especially when around 20 per cent of the population have special requirements. In fact, Microsoft said recently that nearly 50 per cent of people need to make some sort of adjustment to their system to interact with it. Having turned 50, I'm very aware of receiving email with very small fonts — people don't want to use their spectacles to look at a Web page!"

(Tim Berners-Lee, 1998)

When Vannevar Bush, Franklin D. Roosevelt's chief scientific adviser, published the essay *As We May Think* (1945), calling for understanding rather than destruction in scientific research, he laid the groundwork for the web as it now exists. He envisioned a "collective memory machine" that would transform the information revolution into a knowledge revolution. His essay predicted the emergence of hypertext, personal computers, the World Wide Web, scanners, speech-recognition, print-on-demand, digital photography, mashups, and Wikipedia. For Bush, collaboration and ease of access were essential features of the "memex" or "mechanized private file and library" (ibid: 9) on which people would store and access both personal and public materials:

> Most of the memex contents are purchased on microfilm ready for insertion. Books of all sorts, pictures, current periodicals, newspapers, are thus obtained and dropped into place. Business correspondence takes the same path. And there is provision for direct entry. On the top of the memex is a transparent platen. On this are placed longhand notes, photographs, memoranda, all sorts of things. (Bush, 1945)

While Bush did not mention people with disability, the emphasis on speech-recognition and the ability to insert personal comments following "pertinent items" signals toward features of assistive technologies developed for people with disability such as screenreading, dictation, and research and collation tools that everyone can benefit from.

This chapter tracks the development of the World Wide Web from its origins as a technology developed at the CERN particle physics laboratory by Tim Berners-Lee and then given away for free to anyone to use as they liked, through its commercialization and the rise of the dot-com bubble at the turn of the century, to the more recent rise of what has come to be known as web 2.0. Each of these developments has had implications for universal design and the ways people with disability access the online environment.

A robust engagement with hardware is a core feature of WCAG 2.0 yet in the current web 2.0 environment, a number of bottlenecks have emerged to dictate the way their site's content can be used and accessed. This has consequences for people with disability, in particular those who wish to access content using assistive technologies. As we outlined in Chapter 2, Apple's iTunes software potentially block out people with disability if they do not have the Apple-branded software and hardware.

To be completely understood, the problems with accessibility and the rise of gatekeepers or bottlenecks needs to be viewed as emerging from the historical context. Throughout this chapter, we consider these issues in relation to the internet and the World Wide Web. The first part of the chapter delves further back to the history of the internet itself and considers early internet networks as revolutionary but more significantly, exclusionary. A consideration of Advanced Research Projects Agency Network (ARPANET) will demonstrate the ways universal design was not valued in the environment that led to the development of the internet in the 1960s. We then look at the origins of the World Wide Web and the ways accessibility was prioritized in this vision. We will also consider the evolution of the World Wide Web as the browser wars split the universal nature of the web. Finally, we identify a return to standards following the dot-com bubble and burst. Integral to this analysis is the intersection between software, hardware, wetware, and cultware (or "culture-ware") (Kent 2008) as it facilitates or impedes access.

Each person ultimately accesses the internet on their own; each individual computer screen is designed for a solitary user. This point of access involves the synthesis of a number of separate elements. The hardware of the computer hosts the software of its operating system and other programs. The fusion of these two elements enables the digital environment represented at the analog edge of the computer screen, this then interfaces with wetware, or the person using the device and their knowledge and experience. This atomized convergence creates a matrix of these three elements which determine both if access is possible and the quality of that access. The fourth element — cultware — describes the digital and analog environment in which the user is embedded, and the value and characteristics of that environment. While the first three elements describe one point in the digital landscape, cultware provides a broader view of the surroundings both through the screen in the digital space it creates, and also in an individual's analog setting. It measures the social networks that might enrich online experience as well as those networks, both digital and analog, that might determine an individual's ability to enhance their own knowledge and experience through their social network. Disability and impairment have a significant impact on each of these four elements and the interface between them.

Not-for-Profit Origins

The internet began life in 1969 as a text-based network connecting computers to one another in universities and research institutions. It did not become an everyday communications technology until the 1990s, with the advent of the World Wide Web. The internet is a communication system, a network of networks that allows computers to connect to each other whereas the web is the platform that facilitates connections. In his seminal 1945 essay, Vannevar Bush urged scientists to embark on the development of a connected machine as soon as the war commitments were over. In 1960, Joseph Licklider recognized that computers were then powerful enough to realize Bush's vision and extended the idea with the prediction of a "thinking center." According to Licklider, this communication network would connect modern libraries with future advancements in information technologies within 15 years:

> The picture readily enlarges itself into a network of ... centers, connected to one another by wide-band communication lines and to individual users by leased-wire services. In such a system, the speed of the computers would be balanced, and the cost of the gigantic memories and the sophisticated programs would be divided by the number of users. (Licklider, 1960)

This "universal network" prediction inspired his successors to develop ARPANET, the network from which the internet evolved. Subsequent to the United Soviet Socialist Republic (USSR's) 1957 launch of the Sputnik, the Defense Department's Advanced Projects Research Agency (DARPA) was established in 1958 by the US government. In 1969, DARPA began to develop a nuclear-war contingency plan to decentralize information away from a potentially vulnerable central location. The result was ARPANET — the internet in 1969. Although a highly classified project, civilian academic researchers were invited to participate in its development. This led to an open source environment where researchers could participate in a "feedback loop" to engage in peer review to make the technology better through collaboration and contribution (Hartley, 2002: 122). The military and United States' research universities and institutions were the first to connect to this network but by 1973 the University of London had joined — thus, establishing an international collaboration. During the 1970s, government funding of the infrastructure grew and a number of non-commercial networks appeared. The only people using the internet at this stage were computer professionals and there was no consideration given to universal design. Personal computing had not yet emerged, nor had the widespread use of computers in work environments. The internet was only being used by experts who had the training and expertise to enable them to learn a very complex system.

As researchers came to realize the benefits of sharing information in such an effective and economical way, the network continued to expand. Subsequently, when Cold War fears decreased the military's involvement in the development of the internet's "backbone", other federal agencies began to find uses of the technology. ARPANET split to become two agencies ARPANET, which would service the academic community and MILNET, which was interested in military networks. MILNET was eventually subsumed by the National Science Foundation (NSF) which had been working on its own network. The NSF took responsibility for the backbone and laid down terms for "acceptable use" including the standardization of email, ftp (file transfer protocol), and telnet as well as a strict ban on commerce. With these standards, the internet started to become easier for non-experts to use. As the internet grew during the 1980s, the United States' government which had been the primary funding source for the development of the network, began to look to private funding to bear the increasing cost. In 1992, the internet, previously a commerce-free zone abandoned the prohibition on profit and the NSF network was switched off.

While the rapid development of hardware technology is a driving force behind the internet's level of network utility, the software applications partnering with this hardware also play a major role in determining the nature and accessibility of the online environment. ARPANET, the precursor to the modern internet, was designed to facilitate communication between computers at different research institutions, despite otherwise having incompatible operating systems.

In 1971, Ray Tomlinson played a crucial role in standardizing email communication on the ARPANET network via the introduction of the @ symbol into email addresses. By 1973, three-quarters of all traffic on that network consisted of emails. Communication between people, rather than computers, became the driving application, colloquially known as a "killer application" (Jordan, 1999). As late as 2003, email continued to be the most popular online activity (Madden and Raine, 2003). Another so-called "killer application" to become the driving force in the progression of this technology was the World Wide Web developed by Tim Berners-Lee in 1991. He emphasized the importance of universality, particularly in relation to access regardless of disability. The World Wide Web was envisioned to be an open, accessible space.

In both email applications and the web, the potential enabled by the software drove growth in the network and increased the network utility. The web, in particular, made the internet more accessible to those individuals without training in computer science — that is the majority of the population. As Berners-Lee noted prior to the World Wide Web, the internet was "too much of a hassle for a non computer expert" (1999). Software helped reduce the level of technical knowledge (or wetware) that was required to utilize a greater proportion of the network, and through that increased its utility value for an individual user.

An individual highly trained in the use of internet-mediated technology has an aligned and highly complementary level of wetware. For example, Chieko Asakawa (2005) who we cited in the previous chapter had a highly advanced wetware during the 1990s as she was a computer programmer at the time. However, as Gregg Vanderheiden (quoted in Ellcessor, 2010: 293) explains, during the 1980s he began to worry that people with disability would need computers for everyday life some time in the future. His prediction was correct, computers are now ubiquitous as is the use of the web in everyday life. In addition to appropriate hardware and software, people need a corresponding level of knowledge about how to use them — wetware.

With more developed wetware, people are better able to make use of a given set of hardware and software. They are also able to expand the point at which access is available by making better use of any marginal levels of software and hardware that are available. The types of wetware required to facilitate these two functions are not the same. Wetware, like hardware and software, is not homogeneous and varies in suitability to different tasks. Web 2.0, the second generation of the World Wide Web is designed to be easier to use than the first generation of the web — the required wetware is not as complex. However, a consideration of cultware indicates that this is not always the case for people with disability, particularly when corporations or developers act to restrict the use of external adaptive technologies.

Cultware determines the circumstances of the interface between the onscreen access and the offscreen analog world that the individual user inhabits. Cultware will influence the impact and availability of the other three elements of access: hardware, software, and wetware. The growth in processing power and communications bandwidth together with the development of the World Wide Web have served to improve the levels of network accessibility from hardware and software. This is evidenced in the rapid growth of the internet, particularly since 1993 as the World Wide Web has become ubiquitous throughout society.

All four elements of internet access impact on people with impairments. It is well-recognized that if either hardware or software is designed without adherence to universal design, this will result in inaccessibility. This, in turn, will require subsequent modification or third-party development of add-ons such as eye-tracking hardware, or screenreading software. Additional wetware will be required to both interface with these systems and utilize any modifications. It is the interface between the digital and analog that universal design can provide greatest benefits to access. While "the screen" is an inherently visual metaphor, screenreading software reconfigures it as a place where the person and computer interface, the place between hardware/software and wetware. Adaptive hardware and software can provide an alternate interface for people who are unable to access the traditional mouse and keyboard, subtitles and sign language can provide a translation for audio for those who have difficulty accessing that medium. Critically all these additions will help access for everyone, not just those with specific impairments, to the network.

Similarly, many people with disability face potential challenges in the realm of their cultware. Mobility and communications impairment can negatively impact on a person's ability to create and maintain social networks and contacts, particularly "off line" in the analog world. Both biology and society impact on cultware because difficulty in forming social relationships can sometimes be the direct result of the effects of a particular impairment as well as related to the establishment of social structures and protocols, it can't be solved purely through social manipulation. As Roulstone (1998) notes, the disability community has one of the highest rates of unemployment and lowest rate of education, further exacerbating these problems with developing and maintaining cultware and digital social capital.

The development of the World Wide Web software by Tim Berners-Lee in the early 1990s led to the enormous growth in the population of people using the internet. At its most basic level, the World Wide Web enabled a greater potential for access by eliminating one mode of literacy a user needed to access content on the internet. Berners-Lee prioritized people with disability as a population of people that would benefit from ease of access. Not only was the content organized in a way that facilitated easier access, but the level of wetware, or training required to use a web browser, was much lower than the preceding internet-enabling software. Software could be used to stretch the space for access, limited until that point by the requirements of wetware.

Prior to the late 1970s, the only people using computers were information technology experts. Access required advanced wetware, to use the equipment and cultware, to be entitled to use the equipment. As easier-to-use software and hardware systems evolved, everyone became a potential computer user. Usability needed to be redefined. It needed to become more user-friendly for the average person — more useable for someone without a high-level wetware and cultware. Accessibility will be possible when the individual and social needs of the broadest potential user are prioritized, as Berners-Lee recommends in the quote at the beginning of the chapter, via a consideration of the access requirements of people with disability, the elderly and essentially, all people (Carroll, 2009).

Browser Wars

Vannevar Bush, Joseph Licklider, and Tim Berners-Lee all imagined a communication system that allowed people to freely share and access information to revolutionize the Information Age. Universality was central to each of their visions. Browsers were integral to the realization of the "memex", the "thinking center", and the web as a shared communication space. Browsers gave people without technical knowledge the means to engage with the web — to "point and click." Mosaic was developed at the National Centre for Supercomputing Applications (NCSA) and was distributed freely on the internet (Thomas, 1997: 187). People could download it and commence browsing on the web. Mosaic allowed people an unprecedented ease of access and transformed the way people communicated with both computers and each other (Wood and Smith, 2005: 37) However, with the wide uptake of the World Wide Web, ecommerce became a very attractive proposition. By 1995, a browser war was in full swing and Mosaic had been overthrown by Netscape.

In 1994, Netscape began to implement measures that would strengthen its commercial and competitive advantages by adding extensions to html that could only be decoded by Netscape browsers. If the site was accessed using another browser, what could be seen as images, color, and other stylistic features on Netscape would result in error messages or nothing at all (Castro, 2003: 16). In order to corner the market, Netscape rejected the universality that Berners-Lee argued was central to the web and people with disability using assistive technologies suffered.

When Netscape became the most popular browser, Microsoft began developing Explorer in earnest, loading it by default onto every computer with the Windows operating system. As a result, Netscape and Microsoft both started displaying sites in slightly different ways. Computers were no longer able to freely communicate across different platforms and the web lost its power of universality. During the Netscape and Explorer browser war, new versions of their products were released in quick succession for competitive edge. New features were introduced at a faster rate and with greater priority than repairing existing bugs. Proprietary features were added instead of adhering to standards.

A common language is vital to any communications system and essentially, Microsoft and Netscape were communicating in different languages. The lack of standards during the browser wars had a profound impact on the disability community who were frequently ignored in the rush for a new version:

> As websites were being built with ... non compliant code, people would have a very different experience when accessing the site depending on what browser or device they used, their language, if they used assistive technologies (screen readers, screen magnification, voice input) or even if they just tried to change font sizes and colours in their browser. If sites are built using non-standard code you run the risk of the

site breaking for the user. If you build a site with standards code you can be more confident that all users can access the site. It also makes the site easier to manage and maintain. (Iheni, 2008)

Microsoft was eventually able to edge out Netscape because the majority of home computer-users used Windows operating systems; however, market dominance was the aim and accessibility was not necessarily prioritized as Internet Explorer 4.0 was released with fewer accessibility features than previous versions. Following customer backlash, Microsoft did rectify the error and released version 4.01 a month later (Microsoft, 1998). However, the damage was lasting as many started to question whether accessibility was taken seriously by Microsoft or if it was all lip-service. At the same time, that browsers were foregoing research in the rush to release new products without fixing problems with prior versions, new businesses were rushing online to take advantage of what appeared to be a new economy that could make investors a lot of money.

Dot-Com Bubble and Burst

The web reduced the level of technical knowledge required to access the technology and enhanced the utility of the internet. This was a driver for the massive growth the medium experienced from the mid-1990s (Burnett and Marshall, 2003). The ideology of the early adaptors ensured that the software required to enable the web should be free and easily available. This, in turn, led to the uptake of the medium by the wider population.

With the wide take-up of the internet, the ideology of the internet as a free shared-space was abandoned for the ideology of capitalism and the market. When the ban on commerce was lifted, commercial interests infiltrated a number of areas including email, pornography, website-hosting, internet access, domain-name registration, and e-commerce (Goggin, 2005: 260). This led to a boom in the commercial use of the internet — sometimes referred to as a digital gold rush. During the internet boom years at the end of the twentieth century as the "dot-com bubble" of tech stocks expanded, the internet was seen to have enormous potential for profit. There was less focus on access, except in terms of potential online consumers yet to be active participants in the new economy.

The popular uptake of internet sites and the technology industry during the 1990s resulted in a massive rise in the value of stocks for businesses that went online. These businesses came to be known as "dot -coms" for the ubiquitous conclusion to their web addresses and business names. With claims of a new economy that "suspended the rules of business and economics" (Goggin, 2005: 262), the internet became a zone for commerce, and success was popularly believed to be a given. Between 1995 and 2000, a number of new start-ups entered the arena attracted by the prospect of tapping into the growing number of people using the internet who could potentially form a substantial customer base. The stock market value of these businesses rocketed as they continued to attract large numbers of investors. By March 2000, dot-coms were trading at an average of $55.92 per share.

The companies were seeking to "get big fast" by expanding their customer base as quickly as possible without necessarily making any profits. The "get large or get lost" rhetoric led to a number of publicity stunts. At times, product was given away for free in the hope of securing a brand-following to make profits later. The dot-coms relied on raising money through initial public offerings that they burned through without earning any revenue.

In January 2001, 17 dot-com companies spent over $2 million each for a 30-second ad at the Superbowl. However, by the time of the next Superbowl, only three dot-coms could afford to buy ads. Half way through 2001, 345 dot-coms had gone out of business or become bankrupt. The NASDAQ (National Association of Securities Dealers Automated Quotations) exchanges value peaked on 9 March 2000 at 5048.26, a value that had more than doubled in the preceding 14 months. It declined just as quickly. By October 2002, the market had lost 78 percent of this value to close at 1,114.11. The dot-com bubble had burst (Munro, 2001). In the rush for profits, people with disability were left behind. The dot-com bubble had seen a rush to market by many companies trying to cash in on the boom, this often left accessibility features overlooked or ignored. As the investment bubble burst, it left in its wake many collapsed enterprises and an understandable reluctance to invest in online enterprises, once again limiting the opportunities for online participation by people with disability.

There are different measures of internet growth that have been used over time. This is indicative of the changing nature of the way that the internet is thought of and understood. While some commentators have measured the actual flow of data, most of these measures of growth have focused on the interface between the internet and the people who use it. One of the original measures of the growth and size of the internet focused on the number of host computers connected. As the internet moved out of the exclusive realm of academia and government and into more general use, measures of the internet moved to focus on the number of people who had used, or had connection to, the internet. Then, with an increased focus on commercialization of the internet, much attention was focused on the growing amount of economic activity online, both between businesses and between businesses and their consumers. Concerns of a digital divide emerged along with the initial growth of the dot-com stock values with the United States Commerce department releasing a report defining the term in 1999 (McConnaughey *et al.*, 1999). All these measures are valid within their relevant context. They highlight the changing emphasis from wanting to know "how many computers?" to "how many people?" to "how much money?" to "who has access?". Questions of "why" and modes of exclusion that are masked by languages of progress, development, and growth are increasingly more difficult to reveal.

This growth in the size of the network tracks growth in both the total value of the network and the amount of that value which can be easily accessed by an individual. The development of the World Wide Web, by reducing the level of wetware required to access the internet made it accessible to a greater number of users. This in turn increased the value of the total network, attracting still more users. While this was occurring, the continued rapid development of hardware and the capacity to support more complex software further increased both the total network value and the ability of users to access that value. This correspondingly attracted even more people online. However, the rapid growth in the proportion of the population online is starting to taper off in "developed markets" for internet penetration. Up until this point, the network has been able to attract users who have the prerequisite wetware and cultware to enable them to access sufficient network utility, a population that grew as a result of the lower computer-literacy requirement allowed for by the development of the World Wide Web. This drop in the growth of internet penetration indicates the end of expansion throughout this population. This raises questions about the consequences for those left without access. New measures are needed as people with disability are being left behind and technology continues to build in disabling features.

Accessibility Case Study: AOL

At the height of the dot-com boom AOL (America Online), established in 1983, merged with Time Warner to create the largest "walled garden" online gateway to access the World Wide Web. A walled garden refers to a web service provider that controls and restricts access to non-approved content and people. In 2000, 19 million subscribers accessed the web through AOL, however, people who were blind or vision-impaired were unable to access the web through AOL because it had an inaccessible interface (Goggin and Newell, 2003: 130). Instead of providing accessibility features such as alternative text and keyboard access, AOL used proprietary software, graphics did not have alternative text, and certain sections of the interface could only be accessed with a mouse. The impact was felt by screenreader users, in particular, who were blocked from using AOL due to such a high level of inaccessibility (Pierce, 1999).

When the last of the public-funding was removed from the internet and it began to rely on commercial networks, AOL came online and was the gateway through which many people accessed the web. In 1993, this growth in numbers of new users came into conflict with what until that point had been seen as more traditional internet culture in the form of Usenet newsgroups. As worldwide discussion forums, the Usenet groups are an important precursor to modern social networking.

In September 1993, AOL gave its subscribers access to these newsgroups. Usenet regulars were familiar with new people joining as each new class of students joined university networks at the start of the academic year in September. These new users were unaccustomed to the established protocols of participation. The AOL customer base, however, represented a far higher number of users. This connection became know as the start of the Eternal September for Usenet as the influx of new users overwhelmed the existing users' established protocols. AOL was criticized at the time for making little attempt to educate their users about the nature of Usenet and its nature as a forum that was outside AOL's provided content and the established rules for participation. Through this Eternal September, AOL claimed to be opening up the web to everyone yet certain aspects of their websites remained inaccessible and automatically excluded people with disability.

Many complained to the National Federation for the Blind, who then attempted to communicate with AOL for a number of years before initiating legal action under the ADA in November 1999. The lawsuit was eventually dropped in July 2000 when AOL began working with the NFB to bring its pages in line with accessibility requirements. Accessibility officers were appointed and a disability policy was established, yet AOL's 2002 software 7.0 release was incompatible with JAWS screenreader (Goggin and Newell, 2003: 121).

However, by 2007 the NFB reported that AOL had steadily improved accessibility in the years since 2000 and AOL 9.0 could be used effectively with screenreaders such as JAWS and Window Eyes — although JAWS worked better. Unfortunately, AOL suspended accessibility testing on their new software platform, Open Ride, citing difficulties finding appropriate testers. The NFB admitted that this could be seen as a step backwards but applauded AOL for continually improving its accessibility between AOL 6.0 and 9.0. The NFB-endorsed solution was to recommend that clients not upgrade to Open Ride (Chong, 2007). AOL now has a section on disability and accessibility on its website and also claims that accessibility and adhering to standards is a core feature of their move to web 2.0 (Mason, 2008).

Web 2.0

Without doubt, the burst of the dot-com bubble in 2001 had very significant ramifications. As a response to the bursting of the dot-com bubble in 2001, a so-called web 2.0 conference was held in 2004 to try to restore faith in the industry and to examine why some companies survived where others failed (O'Reilly and Battelle, 2009). The term web 2.0, borrowing from naming protocols of software versions, signified a post-PC software era. Where previously software was seen as an artefact, the new era saw software as a service that must be maintained and updated on a daily basis (O'Reilly, 2005). Web 2.0 principally refers to the web as a platform where users control their own data and are treated as "co-developers" by the software companies. The web 2.0 philosophy that "the service automatically gets better the more people use it" can be seen in the way both Amazon and Google (survivors of the dot-com bubble burst) utilize users' searches as rankings to improve their service. It creates more integrated links between software and cultware. Web 2.0 is a revolutionary new way to collaborate:

> Web 2.0 is the business revolution in the computer industry caused by the move to the internet as platform, and an attempt to understand the rules for success on that new platform. Chief among those rules is this: Build applications that harness network effects to get better the more people use them. (O'Reilly, 2006)

Tim O'Reilly (2005) offers a list of web 2.0 features and suggests users rank sites that claim the title against these points, cautioning that "excellence in one area may be more telling than some small steps in all seven":

> Services, not packaged software, with cost-effective scalability
> Control over unique, hard-to-recreate data sources that get richer as more people use them
> Trusting users as co-developers
> Harnessing collective intelligence
> Leveraging the long tail through customer self-service
> Software above the level of a single device
> Lightweight user interfaces, development models, AND business models. (O'Reilly, 2005)

Although accessibility is not explicitly mentioned in any of these seven points, its significance can be seen across all of them, particularly in relation to how information is accessed and the goal of encouraging more members. A commitment to accessibility would result in excellence in each of the seven areas. We are particularly interested in web 2.0 as a strategy for harnessing collective intelligence in the ways O'Reilly described five years after the term was initially coined:

> Chief among our insights was that "the network as platform" means far more than just offering old applications via the network ("software as a service"); it means building applications that literally get better the more people use them, harnessing network effects not only to acquire users, but also to learn from them and build on their contributions. From Google and Amazon to Wikipedia, eBay, and Craigslist, we saw that the value was facilitated by the software, but was co-created by and for the community of connected users. Since then, powerful new platforms like YouTube, Facebook, and Twitter have demonstrated that same insight in new ways. (O'Reilly and Battelle, 2009)

The term web 2.0 has entered the popular zeitgeist, and the phenomenon has caused a cultural shift in the way the web is used such that the passive former audience now drives the media agenda (O'Reilly, 2005). The important message to take away from the web 2.0 philosophy is that networks are stronger the more people are in and contributing to them. It makes little sense to exclude an entire group of people — those with disability — from a network that gets stronger the more people use it. People with disability who use adaptive technology likewise mirror the importance of software being non-device specific. The obstacles faced by people with disability shed light on the potential problems each of us could encounter if excluded from the web and should lead us to question whether the web is the democratic medium it is held up to be (Liccardi, 2007). An exclusion of people with disability is at odds with what the World Wide Web was intended to be, in either its first incarnation or web 2.0.

The web provides people with disability important opportunities for education, employment, entertainment, and social interaction. The possibilities for people with disability to participate in broader society via digital avenues are an important outcome and focus of the move to web 2.0. Yet, the increasingly complex online environment that produces a richer experience for internet users creates accessibility problems that the World Wide Web sought to alleviate. In articulating his vision for a platform to share information, Berners-Lee believed that access for everyone regardless of disability was a crucial factor. Although arguably integral, disability is rarely recognized for its central role in Berners-Lee's vision for the web. Even in cultural and media studies of the digital divide, disability is rarely foregrounded as a case study. The internet and World Wide Web will remain inaccessible to people with disability as long as disability continues to be culturally-framed as an individual's problem, or damaged body. It is important to now look at disability as a cultural identity. Digital technologies associated with the internet and World Wide Web hold great potential for the increased participation of people with disability in social life, yet these technologies are often designed in such a way as to perpetuate ableist oppression.

Web 2.0 is a generation of web design that has changed the way the web is used and developed:

> With more users and sensors feeding more applications and platforms, developers are able to tackle serious real-world problems. As a result, the Web opportunity is no longer growing arithmetically; it's growing exponentially. ... 1990–2004 was the match being struck; 2005–2009 was the fuse; and 2010 will be the explosion. (O'Reilly and Battelle, 2009)

Web 2.0 is also characterized by a rhetoric that suggests more people will be included in the network, which in turn will get stronger via collaboration. While accessibility issues are more widely understood, decisions not to address them remain in large part due to a continuation of social prejudice. The migration to web 2.0. demonstrates that disability and accessibility are integral to the web as a democratic medium for all. As we move toward 3D, mobile devices, and augmented and virtual reality, accessibility will be of great significance to the next generation of the web. The return to standards is a feature of web 2.0 that is intended to allow users to take control of the ways information is displayed and accessed, using both browsers and assistive technologies.

Return to Standards?

The first browser war of the late 1990s was characterized by rapid innovation and the rapid release of updates to software by both Microsoft and Netscape. In the rush to get the latest version to the market, this was often done at the expense of fixing existing bugs in the software and security problems. As noted previously, this was in disregard to a commitment to universal design and accessibility. Following the conflict and with the dominance of Internet Explorer well-established, there has been a return to standards. This has been facilitated by greater clarity in the W3C guidelines/recommendations. To some extent, the seeds of a new browser war between Internet Explorer, Safari, Firefox, and more recently, Chrome can be seen at the end of the previous one. Netscape placed the source code for its Navigator program in the public domain with the Mozilla Corporation, leading to the development of Firefox. Similarly, the development by Apple of the Safari browser can be seen as a response to Microsoft's decision to discontinue Internet Explorer for the Mac operating system in 2003.

This return to a competitive market for browsers has not followed the same path away from accepted standards, partly because of consumers' greater concern with their security. Firefox, one of the organizations driving competition, as an open-source project, is ideologically committed to common standards. However, while at the browser level, there seems to be a commitment to common standards and accessibility, there is a trend to return to the "walled garden" approach in many online platforms, alongside the embrace of cross platform web 2.0 principles. As we will discuss in Chapter 6 many of the new social networking sites that are home to much of today's web traffic, while accessible through any browser maintain their own rigid design. In many cases, this impedes access to people with disability. Similarly, as discussed in Chapter 2, Apple's software and products for its successful iTunes/iPod platforms have their own standards and consequent challenges to accessibility. While one area seems to have developed a commitment to common standards that enable universal design, there are other areas of the internet that are still in disregard of these core principles.

Accessibility and browser issues have recently re-emerged. The latest release of Google's Chrome browser for the Mac OS is not able to access any of the accessibility features of that platform. The newly released html5 code is designed to be "forward-compatible" and should be able to be viewed in any web browser as future technological advancement occurs. However, instead of ignoring unrecognizable tags while still rendering the content normally, Microsoft's Internet Explorer does not recognize html5 and will not "apply styles to the new tags or allow them to be used as part of CSS [Cascading Style Sheets] selectors" (Andersen, 2010). To overcome this accessibility barrier, an accessibility hack has been developed in the spirit of community accessibility (Ellis and Kent, 2010) to force Internet Explorer to correctly render html5. This user-led revolution is expected to have a positive effect on accessibility (Andersen, 2010). It also shows that people will no longer allow browsers to dictate different ways of rendering communication. Perhaps, universality can be regained.

Conclusion

The internet and World Wide Web are relatively recent communications inventions, however, their existence was predicted long before their realization. Initially used only by computing professionals, the internet was complicated and did not embrace universal design or usability. In frustration with the "hassle" of using the internet, Tim Berners-Lee developed the World Wide Web with a focus on universality to enable an ease of access. He prioritized use by people with disability. Shortly after this, government support for the internet's backbone was removed and the ban on commercial interests was lifted. As a result, the online environment was commercialized and popularized through online businesses, introducing services such as email, pornography, website-hosting, internet access, and domain-name registration.

The internet came to be seen as a place where profits could be made quickly and in order to gain competitive edge, browsers in particular rejected the notion of universality by refusing to adhere to common standards. Sites built with standards code enable access to all users. This is particularly important to people with disability using adaptive software and hardware. However, the triumph of universal design and access was rejected in the rush to make money off the new environment and online economy. Now, we must retrofit the web.

While the hardware/software/wetware matrix is a useful intellectual tool for understanding access to communications technology, the new fourth element, culture-ware or cultware enables a more complete understanding of access. Cultware seeks to provide insight that reaches beyond the atomized individual and allow for this individual access to be understood in the wider context in which it occurs. The historical development of the World Wide Web from its not-for-profit origins through to its commercialization and the dot-com bubble at the turn of the century, to the more recent rise of what has come to be known as web 2.0 has had implications for universal design and access for people with disability in the online environment.

We continue the discussion of the ways disability is manifested digitally in the next chapter, when we offer a critique of the social model of disability as it both under- and over-emphasizes impairments. We argue that the biological and the social overlap and intersect in the creation of disability and suggest that in order to develop appropriate adaptive technologies, the effects of impairment, and the everyday experiences of people with disability must be acknowledged.

5

(Physical) Disability is a Form of Social Oppression?

"It is not individual limitations of whatever kind, which are the cause of the problem, but society's failure to provide appropriate services."

(Michael Oliver, 1996)

"The 'correct' thinking holds that disability is never the problem; it's barriers in the outside world, including barriers of attitude, that are the problem. This is a bit de trop, in my experience. Here in the real world, the general issue of accommodating people with disabilities does relate to the specific disability and to what the person is trying to do. One cannot separate the two."

(Joe Clark, 2002)

"Given that modern life paradoxically means that independence is achieved through greater dependence on others, the question, then is how does this differ from the requirements of disabled people?"

(Vic Finkelstein, 1980)

Technology is a feature of modern existence designed to make our lives and daily tasks easier. Why then do we devalue the adjustments people with disability make or the technologies they use as weak or special? Assistive technologies are stigmatized in ways that technologies used by people without disability are not. While people with disability may regard the accommodations or the assistive and adaptive technologies they use as an ordinary part of life, as non-disabled people would a kettle, washing machine or even computer, the technologies used by people with disability are stigmatized. Further, people with disability are often treated as helpless or dependent for using them (Wendell, 1996: 30).

There is no doubt that technology can revolutionize the lives of people with disability. Alan Roulstone (1998) argues that technology intersects with the wider sociocultural environment and can be understood in three ways with regard to its use by people with disability. The first framework he explores is technicism which ignores the social relevance of technological change. Technicism concentrates on technological change rather than the corresponding social change. Roulstone's second framework considers a rehabilitative discourse of disability deliverance through technology. Adopting a right-wing political perspective, this framework rests on technological determinism and adopts a discourse of deficit. This is the model adopted by medical or deficit discourses of disability. As Stienstra and Troschuk (2005) suggest:

> [A] deficit model is widely used, by medical and technical "experts," to create new and specialized technologies to address the gaps between the person and their limited abilities as a result of their impairments. The technological solutions are viewed as requiring a case-by-case approach rather than as something to be developed in the mainstream. The deficit model identifies the relationships between disabled people and technology primarily as those taking place at the individual level — between a single person or a cluster of individuals with similar impairments, whose life or lives can be made better by the development and application of technology. (Stienstra and Troschuk, 2005)

This is the model society is collectively most familiar with — it locates the problem of disability within the individual and suggests disability can be cured through medicine or technologies. While these technologies can compensate for impairment in a "non-disabled" world, their cultural interpretation and relevance remains contested. At times, people with disability are used as motivation within a rehabilitative discourse for the creation of technologies such as the bionic ear and recent hopes for a bionic eye and ignore society's role in creating disability (Goggin, 2008). Throughout this chapter, we will attempt to outline a way to rethink this discourse in combination with a social understanding of disability to develop better technologies and modes of inclusion.

In Roulstone's third framework, disability can be recognized as a social construction. Although theorists interested in this politicization have accused technological development of contributing to the further disablement of people with impairments (see Oliver, 1978; Davis, 1995), technology, in a broad sense, is integral to the politicization of disability, particularly as we move further into an Information Age of both employment and leisure. This perspective invites links between personal perspectives, technological support, and the potential for wider social change that we wish to develop further.

This chapter will critically examine the importance of technology to the formation of a social understanding of disability. In response to recent criticisms and the increasing importance of the internet — and especially web 2.0 — to all members of society, not just the disabled, throughout this chapter we suggest a framework for bringing the social model into the twenty-first century. A consideration of impairment will allow a future in which people with disability will benefit from a networked digital society. The Information Age is vital to the development of a new phase of disability. This chapter starts with a specific examination of the social model of disability before turning to technology and its role within the social model. We conclude by exploring digital impairment and disability.

While some argue that digital technologies have created an environment that supersedes the work of Oliver (1996) and Finkelstein (1980), we do not believe that the social model has outlived its usefulness. Rather, we suggest that the implicit focus on impairment that has always been present in the politicization of disability, be recognized in order to move forward into the Information Age and toward notions of universal design that would see a realization of both Finkelstein's (1980) third phase of disability development and Tim Berners-Lee's (1997) equalizing vision that the web should provide a platform for all, regardless of disability.

The Social Model of Disability

Disability, as a form of social oppression, is a concept that emerged following civil rights movements in other areas such as race, gender, and sexuality. The social model of disability as it considers social and cultural interpretations and origins is an attempt to demedicalize disability by placing the emphasis on the social factors that influence disability. The difference between disabling social attitudes and actions and the impairment of the body has traditionally been an important distinction in this model. Michael Oliver (1996) describes disability as a form of social oppression distinct from any physical abnormality. Significantly, Oliver also concentrates exclusively on "physical disability" suggesting that there are some gaps in this model.

When the social creation of disability is emphasized, the social responsibility of finding solutions to these issues become relevant. This allows disability to be reconceptualized within the discourse of civil rights. Disability is created according to how humans have chosen to construct the world (Finkelstein, 1975). Finkelstein (1980) illustrates the social model of disability by reversing the disempowerment experienced by people with disability through a hypothetical place physically and culturally structured for wheelchair users only. It is the "able-bodied" visitors to the world, who become socially disabled as they experience difficulty navigating an environment built exclusively for wheelchair users:

> Door and ceiling heights [would be] be lowered substantially. If now, able-bodied people were to live in this community they would soon find that they were prevented from "normal" social intercourse — they would be constantly knocking their heads against the door lintels! Apart from bruises the able-bodied would inevitably find themselves prevented from using the wheelchairuser-designed [sic] environment and aids. They would lack jobs and become impoverished — they would become disabled! (Finkelstein, 1980)

Similarities exist between Finkelstein's hypothetical place and the island community of Martha's Vineyard from the seventeenth to early twentieth century (Groce, 1985: 13). Due to an unusually high incidence of hereditary deafness on the Massachusetts island, the entire community learnt how to use sign language so that they could all communicate with each other. For deaf people, the barrier to full participation is not their inability to hear but rather the lack of common mode of communication with the hearing community.

Nora Groce (1985: 4) conducted an anthropological study of deafness on Martha's Vineyard and maintains that deafness is socially isolating because of ignorance and misinformation — the bilingual community of Martha's Vineyard show us that adaptation on the part of the non-disabled population results in the full integration of people with disability. Martha's Vineyard suggests Finkelstein's fantasy could work in the real world and that disability is related to social norms rather than individual's bodies. Because everyone spoke sign language regardless of their hearing capabilities as a standard mode of communication, deafness did not become a disability in relation to communication. Society, on the island, was constructed to be inclusive without regard to a person's hearing ability.

Similarly, the web was created as a shared information and communication space that could be accessed by anyone regardless of disability. As a result of the widespread uptake of personal computing during the 1980s, the use of adaptive technologies likewise became widespread. In the early predominantly text-based web environment, adaptive technology similarly flourished (Ellcessor, 2010). Adaptive technology allows the user to determine the way information is communicated and displayed according to techniques that may bypass the effects of impairments. Digital information allows the adaptation of size, color, and output, unless restrictions are put in place to prevent these. When the web was mainly text, adaptive technologies integrated well. While this freedom of access allowed the web to develop, eventually commercial interests, described in the previous chapter, led to a situation whereby disability was disregarded for profits, and standards were no longer prioritized or even adhered to. Similarly, the more complex graphical web 2.0 environment has problematized access using adaptive devices.

The deficit model of disability sees adaptive technologies as part of a rehabilitative discourse that assumes the relationship between the individual and user is one of dependence whereby experts without personal experience of disability dictate technological forms of cure and care. While Vasey (quoted in Dewsbury, 2004) argues that the social model does not aim to promote ways to compensate for every bodily dysfunction through technology, Marks (1999) suggests the tendency to exclude personal experience from the social model has allowed a theoretical vacuum to be filled by deficit and individualistic perspectives. Adaptive technologies acknowledge ambiguities and everyday experiences of people with disability whereas the social model perhaps does not.

The intersection between digital technology and the changing social position of people with disability was highlighted in 2006 when the theme at that year's International Day of Disabled Persons was E-Accessibility. ICTs (Information and Communication Technologies) were heralded as having most of the answers to the exclusion of people with disability:

> no longer do the societal barriers of prejudice, infrastructure, and inaccessible formats stand in the way of participation. When available to everyone, information technologies foster individuals to reach their full potential, and for persons with disabilities it allows them to play their part in society's development. (United Nations, 2006)

Although the web does provide excellent potential, information and computer technologies are not an automatic source of liberation. Digital documents on the internet enable people with disability greater access than physical spaces, such as libraries, especially for the more than 38 million blind and vision-impaired people who utilize screenreading technology (Bigham *et al.*, 2008). However, digital does not always mean accessible since infrastructure issues can remain. Online documents are often presented in an image format that cannot be read by the user's screenreader. Before they can be considered accessible, they must be converted and corrected by a sighted person. Despite the E-Accessibility rhetoric of the International Day of Disabled Persons, a massive gap still exists between the spin and the reality. Barriers continue to exist just as utopian discussions around the web and the benefits for people with disability abound. These celebrations do much to reassure the non-disabled of their normality and privileged position by disregarding the importance of disability as a public sphere issue.

In *Everybody Here Spoke Sign Language*, Groce (1985) recounts an interview with a 90-year-old woman who had lived on Martha's Vineyard 50 years earlier. After Groce asked her about two residents who were deaf, the woman recalls that they were excellent fishermen and only remembers their hearing impairments when Groce prompts her. People with disability wish to be recognized for the contribution they make and/or their personality rather than exclusively for their impairment, which is often the first thing people notice. However, before this can happen, the world must be accessible or adapted to ensure people with disability can contribute. This happened on Martha's Vineyard because non-verbal communication was normalized. Many herald the web as affording people with disability the opportunity to showcase their talents without their impairment being a factor at all. However, these discussions often sidestep the issue of accessibility and center on social interaction without consideration of the built-in "digital disability" (Goggin and Newell, 2003).

In a similar fashion to arguments that the web is both gender and race neutral, people with disability need not identify as disabled in online spaces and can instead be judged on their personality first. Communicating using information technologies allows a person to totally hide their physical appearance:

> Unlike [face-to-face] interactions where one's physical appearance is obvious, it is assumed that one could potentially be completely free of these physical cues in [computer mediated communication]. It is a well-established finding that physical appearance is an important cue in social interaction. People treat others differently based on gender, race, age, ethnicity, physical disability, and attractiveness. Without these cues, individuals are unable to project stereotypes on others and thus, expectations for behaviour based on these stereotypes should diminish. (Christopherson, 2007: 3045)

It is assumed that disability is not always a factor in the social encounter when people with disability are freed from their social roles. The web allows people with disability to interact with others in a way that is not usually possible in general society. This has been especially celebrated in relation to social networking sites and virtual worlds where people can choose their physical appearance (or avatar identity) and how much information they disclose about themselves. Many see this as an opportunity for a heightened understanding of social roles.

These discussions highlight the importance of fluid identity formation in terms of independence and self-empowerment for people with disability, and like the social model usually center on the experience of people with mobility impairments. While certainly an important discussion, there is potential that it ignores the disabling infrastructure of the internet and web — accessibility is still an issue. However, the frequent focus on disability in terms of mobility impairment reveals a wider tendency to focus on ability in discussions around the internet and disability. Despite its importance, such a focus potentially crowds out discussions of the ways impairments impact on initial and continued access. This focus has resulted in a lack of understanding around accessibility for those with vision and hearing impairments or cognitive impairments such as dyslexia, and those with a mobility impairment who can't use a mouse and/or keyboard, particularly as web 2.0 sites become more complex and harder to translate using assistive technologies.

The idea that issues around race and gender are no longer relevant on the internet is a contested one. Similarly, if these differences were to vanish when online it might serve merely to mask inequalities in people's analog lives. Disability can be a crucial factor in the way people engage with the web and denying its existence is rarely empowering, especially if it means exclusion from the web in the first place. As web design has moved away from the promise of access by anyone regardless of disability, the medium itself has come to play a more prominent role as part of participation in broader society. Technologies can be redesigned to eliminate the ableist oppression that keeps people with disability from being able to participate fully in all aspects of the material/social world. Continued inaccessibility suggests certain bodies are valued over others. Further redevelopment is required to include people with disability.

Difference and normality are framed through an interaction between technology, people, work, and society. Finkelstein (1980) identified three phases of disability "creation" — the feudal era where there was no separate disabled group, the industrial revolution when the concept of able-bodied normality was established and a third stage yet to occur when the gaze would be taken off the body and put onto society. He paid particular attention to the second stage where the construction of disability as dependency was consolidated. This stage occurred during the Industrial Revolution, when production lines were geared toward able-bodied norms and institutions caring for the disabled and insane were established. Boundaries of "normality" and disability were created during this era of rapid technological development.

For Finkelstein (1980), the second stage of disability, as it emerged out of the Industrial Revolution focused too heavily on impairment, which in turn stressed a "medical" model. The clear extension of this argument is that in order to highlight a social model of disability, the focus must be taken away from the impairment. Although articulating a powerful political strategy, this does not adequately fit into his third stage of disability. It likewise ignores and alienates some people who have impairments. As Paul Abberly (1999) argues, regardless of a barrier-free utopia, some people will just not be able to work due to their impairments. It is time for the social model of disability to refocus its philosophy to incorporate a consideration of impairment as an integral part of the experience of disability.

Finkelstein's phases relate directly to important periods of social change as they are tied to economic history. Economic social history can be divided into four revolutions, including the Agricultural, Industrial, Electrical, and the Information Revolutions. The Agricultural Revolution corresponds to Phase One while the Industrial Revolution and the Electrical Revolution together mark Phase Two. Finally, Phase Three is characterized by technologies integral to the Information Revolution. Bob Sapey (2000) suggests the social model of disability (particularly the work of Oliver and Finkelstein) may be superseded as a result of the grand scale of the Information Revolution. In response to the ability of the internet to shape space — time relations and produce and distribute products, he contends:

> It would make sense then to suggest that if the demands of clock-time were instrumental in the construction of disability during industrialization, then a new social meaning of time which involves greater speeds may be more demanding. However, this may not be the case as much of the work being undertaken at such speeds is being carried out electronically and as Finkelstein (1980) predicted of phase three, such developments may assist in the ending of disablement. (Sapey, 2000)

However, Sapey (2000: 6) also finds evidence that people with disability are excluded from informational occupations (computer programmers are least likely to employ people with disability) to a greater extent than industrial and agricultural sectors. This corresponds to Goggin and Newell's (2003: 153) contention that "technology will never deliver society from the reality of disability, [and that] disability continues to be constructed through that technology." They suggest that as a society we have choices to make about whether to enable or disable through new technologies and questions must be asked regarding whose bodies are included and excluded. The future is bleak if we continue to reproduce disability digitally, yet there is optimism also that digital technologies will allow disability to unfold in unexpected ways to benefit everyone (Goggin and Newell, 2003: 153–54). In order for this to happen, recognition of the impact of impairment on the ways we interact with this technology is vital.

Finkelstein's (1980) faith in technology rests in notions of technological determinism where structural changes to society and hence, discriminatory attitudinal barriers will be the direct result of innovations such as Braille keyboards that allow people a non-visual way to engage with computer keyboards. He believes technological change will directly result in a change to institutions, practices, and ideas. However, patterns of technology are influenced by the cultural traditions of the society that produces them. The social model recognizes that disability is created in and by society — it is the negative social reaction to impairment.

However, at times the social model does not go far enough, as Sally French argues "some of the most profound problems experienced by people with certain impairments are difficult, if not impossible, to solve by social manipulation" (1993: 17). There have been calls for a social theory of impairment to note the existence and relevance of impairment. Likewise, Wendell finds that "the biological and the social are interactive in creating disability" (1996: 35). Working from these expressions of dissatisfaction with the model and parallels drawn with feminist theory, Carol Thomas (1999) defined "impairment effects" as ways to articulate the experience of impairment within the social model. Thinking about impairment effects is particularly relevant to designing assistive technology and enabling people with disability digital access.

While the social model was integral in raising the self-esteem and political awareness of the disabled community, this model requires urgent revision. Biology does affect the lives of people who have impairments and to deny this is to deny a huge part of the lived experience of people who have impairments. Accessibility 2.0 puts the needs of the user at the center — adaptive technology which recognizes impairment effects is central to this. We seek to consider the interaction between society, impairment, and technology as a way to move forward into the Information Age. Finkelstein and Oliver argue that disability is the result of a capitalist mode of production, whereby bodies were judged on their ability to operate heavy machinery and submit to regimes of productivity. Deliverance from this disabling environment rests on a new mode of production. The digital era has initiated a new mode of production which values adaptation and ergonomics for maximum productivity.

Technology and the Social Model of Disability

Technology is often broadly presented within the social model of disability (see Finkelstein, 1980; Oliver, 1996) as a single entity that can be seen to alleviate impairments and enable people to enter the workforce. A consideration of impairment as well as socially created disability offers a more nuanced approach to the social construction of disability. Universal design is a principle that can be uniquely applied to a digital environment in a way that works for different users without working against each other's interests. A consideration of impairment is vital to the full inclusion of people with disability in the digital arena, as features that enhance accessibility for groups with a certain type of impairment can diminish accessibility for another. As suggested in Chapter 3, there is enough variety in digital adaptation to allow different modes of access depending on impairment, for example people with hearing impairment blog in sign language using webcams, while people with vision impairments adopt podcasts and so on. In Chapter 7, we will examine the way this manifests in the virtual world Second Life and the importance of keeping access options open. As an aspect of universal design, accessibility 2.0 prioritizes the needs of users who access the web in different ways and for different reasons (Kelly *et al.*, 2007).

Technological change and participation in the workforce features prominently throughout Finkelstein's three stages of disability. For Finkelstein (1980), the second stage has had the greatest influence on the world as we know it now. Machines were created to be used by a number of different people and therefore could not be modified to suit individual needs or impairments because mass (and quick) production was the aim. This phase followed a period (the first phase of disability) where people with disability existed in the margins of society and worked as part of the family unit. Small machinery was adapted to suit "individual physiques" and people with disability worked as part of the family unit (Finkelstein, 1981). Disability moved into the second phase, when production lines were geared toward able-bodied norms and people competed for work (Finkelstein, 1980). The notion of able-bodied normality was created and the construction of disability as dependency was consolidated. In theory, the third phase of disability or the Information Revolution should be similar to the first phase because workstations can be adapted to suit individual physiques and ergonomics are valued amongst people working in the information economy. Web 2.0 empowers the individual who was previously subsumed in the industrial revolution when able-bodied normality was established. However, the stigma initiated during the second phase remains in the third as adaptive technologies are devalued and accessibility is ignored or foregone for the sake of speed and profit. However, if the web 2.0 philosophy that everyone controls and personalizes their web experience is extended to include people with disability, attitudinal barriers will decrease.

Finkelstein (1980) sees disability as a social construction based on lack of access. He is confident that the third phase, characterized by technological change, will offset many of the prejudicial attitudes established during the second phase. While he specifically refers to Braille keyboards to illustrate this paradigm shift, a more recent example would be the popularity of SMS or text messaging on mobile phones amongst the deaf community. SMS has been described as having the potential to unite hearing and deaf communities by allowing a common language similar to the widespread use of sign language on Martha's Vineyard (Power and Power, 2004: 333).

While the absence of hearing technologies was a crucial factor in deafness not being considered a communication disability on Martha's Vineyard, stigmas attached to some technologies but not others demonstrate the way disability is socially constructed. Intolerance is integral to the disempowered position of people with disability in society. When power imbalances are related to institutions rather than individuals, institutions maintain their power through the creation of deviant groups who are then "treated." Institutional medical care has established people with disability as the "problem":

> disabled people have been viewed as passive, unable to cope with normal social relations and dependent upon others. The professions came into being with this assumption as the key to the relationship that developed over the centuries between the active able-bodied helper and passive disabled object of attention. (Finkelstein, 1981)

People with disability are socially created as a deviant group and stigmas attached to the alternative or assistive technologies used by this group to navigate daily life perpetuate their deviant status and the need to be treated. The on/off switch at the front of the computer was developed for the benefit of people with disability using personal computers, yet it is of great convenience to the rest of the community so it is not stigmatized in the same way that a screenreader is. However, it is possible that in the future, the ability to use computers without hands or eyes will become increasingly important. Perhaps then, screenreading technology will be considered differently.

It is important to consider the ways technology is used and the social environment through which it emerged. The impact of the uneven distribution of power on people with disability can be demonstrated through changing technology. When accessibility is added onto media and communications technologies, rather than built into the design from the beginning, solutions are considered "special" and are stigmatized (Goggin and Newell, 2003: 148). These technologies become attributed to "spoiled identities" (Goffman, 1963, republished 1997) while other technologies that enrich everyone's lives are interpreted differently.

Take for example communication technologies, such as TTYs (Telephone typewriters), voice/TTY rely services, fax, email, and SMS, that are used by people who are deaf and hard of hearing. While TTY is a cultural artefact of the deaf community, the others are used by the wider community and are not stigmatized in the same way:

being able to mainstream technology without any adaptation or intermediary appeals to Deaf people both because it lessens the stigma attached to needing equipment to be modified and it is less expensive than "special" equipment. SMS and fax machines ... although not designed with Deaf people in mind ... suits their purposes and solves what were previously difficulties in communication from afar. (Power, Power and Horstmanshof, 2006: 81)

Of particular interest is the example of SMS because it has been widely adopted by the entire community. It also allows deaf people to benefit from the telephone in a mainstream way for the first time. This group has been integral in driving developments in SMS, including both abbreviated vocabulary and the expansion of interconnectivity amongst different providers. Condensed messages lacking in syntax, tense, and other key markers of written expression were used in TTY conversations, long before SMS (Power and Power, 2004: 335). Anecdotal evidence suggests deaf people introduced this new genre of English expression characteristic of SMS communication.

As mobile telephony has become increasingly important, the convenience of SMS cannot be ignored. Mobiles provide people another way to communicate and participate in society. A common form of communication is integral to building communities. SMS, an unexpected feature of mobile phones, gives the hearing and deaf a common language (Power and Power, 2004: 333). Deaf people who SMS ten times more than people without hearing impairments (Harper, 2003: 159) are able to achieve greater autonomy through this technology.

Digitizing Impairment and Disability

Digital technology has potential to move the markers of what disability is. HCI (Human Computer Interaction) is a discipline of study which seeks to understand the relationship between computers and the people who use them. It combines computer science with many other fields of enquiry such as design and psychology to develop technologies in ergonomic and culturally appropriate ways. However, HCI has been criticized for assuming a particular type of body. A more in-depth consideration about the ways different bodies interact with computers would facilitate a move beyond the assumption that the body is universal.

A lack of awareness has resulted in a failure to consider the needs of people with disability during the design and evaluation of software and hardware. However, we are now seeing an increase of awareness as a result of greater contact between disability organizations and software developers as well as the increased possibility of legal action. A more developed form of HCI investigation accounts for the impacts of specific contexts, cultures, and bodies. Including accessibility within the already interdisciplinary arenas of HCI is becoming more important as computing technology is spreading across every aspect of our lives. Soon, designers will need to consider the user who cannot see, hear or touch as a matter of course.

The embodied experience of disability, that is recognition of impairment, therefore advances HCI and software and hardware design in such a way that benefits our increasingly digitized world. This merging of disability, ability, and the needs of the "general population" goes some way in instigating the much-needed "interrogation of the unmarked category of 'able' and 'ability'"(Goggin, 2008). This interrogation looks to the ways ability is constructed rather than disability. An interrogation of ableism is important precisely because without it, we could not have a "concept of difference" (Campbell, 2009: 6). In the information economy, technology should be adapted to suit individuals and the rhetoric of compulsory correction is peripheral to a recognition that we all depend on different technologies to participate in work and social life.

In Britain in the 1970s, the Union of Physically Impaired against Segregation (UPIAS) developed a document entitled *Fundamental Principles of Disability* in which they problematized the notion that disability is an individual's problem that can be located within a damaged body (Oliver, 1996). The participation of people with disability in the workforce was one of the key motivating factors for the UPIAS when they developed this document. The document was a response to the way that the organization of work since the industrial revolution has been structured around a set of values which disable people who have impairments (Barnes, 1999). Web 2.0 technologies are changing the workforce and the role people with disability play in it. When impairment and accessibility 2.0 is considered, the values that disable people who have impairments could potentially change.

Although influenced by the social model of disability, as it separates disability from impairment, we recognize disability as an embodied experience of physical difference *and* social stigma in line with Sharon Snyder's argument that disability: "no longer means a condition, an incapacity, or lack that belongs to the body, but rather a product of interactions between self, society, body, and the variety of interactions (from political economies to personal commitments) that they engender" (Snyder, 2006). Snyder's definition recognizes the body as an aspect of disability and does not compromise on society's part in creating disability. Integral to the social model of disability is the separation of disability (socially created) and impairment (biological). As a way of maintaining political significance, this model has been dedicated in its adherence to this separation, refusing to consider the impact of impairment on the lives of people with disability for fear it would weaken the model. While social disablement is a major contributing factor, the effects of impairment are likewise central to the experience of people with disability. A model of empowerment needs to recognize this, not push it further into the private sphere. For Joe Clark (2002), cited at the beginning of this chapter, a consideration of impairment in the digital arena is integral to addressing the question of disability discrimination.

Roulstone's (1998) second framework of disability deliverance through technology, and Finkelstein's (1980) characteristics of the second phase of disability (the Industrial Revolution) both relate to an oppressive rehabilitative regime being imposed onto people with disability. Yet people with disability can and do benefit from technology appropriately adapted, so as to enable participation in the workforce and social life. The social model has suffered from a theoretical vacuum which unfortunately has perpetuated the deficit model of disability. When personal experience is left out of the discussion, the space is subsumed by the more dominant deficit voices which perpetuate a rehabilitative regime. When we come to recognize the significance of impairment in the ways technologies can be designed around different bodies, the cultural difference between the able and disabled could in fact become as simple as a "variation in the way things are carried out" (Dewsbury *et al.*, 2004: 154).

In 2006, Shakespeare previously highly critical of these critiques, introduced his own powerful critique of the social model of disability which for the first time foregrounded the experience of impairment. While acknowledging that the social approach as it has separated disability and impairment is successful in shifting attention away from individuals and onto society, he also finds that "the strength and simplicity of the social model of disability has created as many problems as it has solved" (Shakespeare, 2006: 31). These problems relate to impairment and the refusal of the social model to acknowledge the effects of impairment on the lives of people with disability. Impairment can create difficulties that cannot be attributed only to a disabling society (Shakespeare 2006: 38–39). Recognition of impairment is necessary in creating an accessible environment because different adaptations may be required. Acknowledging the intersection between self, society, and the body without stigmatizing impairment is accessibility 2.0.

Curb cuts are an example of the way features that enhance accessibility for groups with a certain type of impairment can diminish accessibility for another (Shakespeare, 2006: 46). This is mirrored in the digital environment. Innovations that may aid one group of users, such as people with vision impairments, may exclude another, such as those who are deaf or hard of hearing. Different impairments mean a different navigational experience. Individual choice is important and usability and user-generated output must be prioritized. Therefore despite claims to the contrary, a social understanding of disability must take into consideration impairment because universal design cannot be aggregated. This also holds significance to the creation of online accessible spaces where assistive and adaptive computer technologies have been described as "electronic curb cuts" (Westin, 2005).

The rapidly changing digital realm is not slowing down and is becoming increasingly important to everyone, not just the disabled. Significant changes that have taken place since 2006 when E-Accessibility was recognized as holding enormous potential for people with disability. Arguably, the "E" prefix is already out of date as internet users gravitate more toward "I". A move into "U" to embrace universal design and usability is the next logical step. Technology, in a broad sense, often features in discussions that both problematize and perpetuate individualized notions of disability. The workforce is undergoing huge changes as a result of informationalization (Castells, 1996 quoted in Barnes, 1999). This "web-orientated information-based economy" (Westin, 2005) will impact on and enable the participation of people with disability.

In the absence of appropriate adaptive technologies, informationalization acts as a form of marginalization that further excludes people with disability who as a minority group are already socially, culturally, and economically excluded. People with disability are often considered unable to contribute to the economy and therefore left out of policy debate and discussion. However, E-governance could bring people with disability into the democratic policy process (Stienstra and Troschuk, 2005). The manipulation of time, space, and communication also holds significance in the creation of a disability community and other social activities amongst this group (Seymour and Lupton, 2004). The growing importance of digital technologies and web access in fully participating in society provides the social model of disability the opportunity for revision.

Conclusion

The social model of disability (re)defines disability as society's unwillingness to meet the needs of people who have impairments. Three clear stages of disability creation have been identified by Vic Finkelstein (1980): The feudal era (no separation); the industrial revolution (formation of able-bodied normality); and a future third stage in which technological innovations will directly result in a change to institutions, practices, and ideas. In order to develop appropriate non-stigmatized technologies and change institutions, practices, and ideas, it is time to bring forward the implicit focus on impairment that has always been present in the politicization of disability (Oliver, 1996; Finkelstein, 1980)and embrace the Information Age and notions of universal design. This would see a realization of both Finkelstein's third phase of disability development (1980) and Tim Berners-Lee's grand vision for the web. From the social construction of disability, informationalization, and the importance of impairment to a discussion of disability studies and accessibility, in the next chapter we turn our attentions to social networking, at the cutting edge of debates regarding disability and platforms for participation.

6

Does That Face-"Book" Come in Braille?

Social Networking Sites and Disability

"i'm using jaws 10.0 and when i start to use facebook, it was verry verry hard for me. now, i know some details and it works but it's not fine. would be better, to get more navigatin points and more headings and such things."

(Post to The Official Petition for a more Accessible Facebook
(McKay, 2007: spelling as in the original)

"I am a totally blind user and switched to facebook because it was the most access-able compared to myspace."

(Post to STOP Facebook discriminating against disabled users
(Hawkins, 2007: spelling as in the original)

Online social networking is defined by the concept of community; while at the same time social networking is redefining what community means. The social networking sites, Facebook and MySpace have been credited with changing the way social connections are made. However, the inaccessibility of these sites prevents access by many people who want to participate. The post by the JAWS user at the beginning of this chapter continues by saying that Facebook is the world's leading social networking site and he wants to participate. Facebook has evolved from a way for Harvard University students to socialize amongst themselves, to a popular cultural phenomenon, to a human rights issue.

At the More than Gadgets conference held in Australia in 2009, Australian Human Rights Commissioner Graeme Innes stressed the importance of social networking sites to people with disability. He suggested that social networking could open a new world to people with disability and commented that in the future people not using these online tools (including people without disability) would effectively be disabled as they would not have access to vital information and ways to communicate.

As we noted in Chapter 1, social networking is now being used as platform for E-government. These sites have emerged in an era where the concept of a local community in which everyone knows everyone has gone. Instead, we find an atmosphere of individualism and a sense of being alone in the global world. Online social networking sites reproduce and mediate community by reinventing aspects of the local village in this global environment. They facilitate an extension of existing social relationships through the medium of the internet and provide a convenient way for people to maintain an awareness of the activities of a potentially large number of people.

The origins of using the internet as a place for social activity can be traced back to the bulletin board systems of the 1970s. Social networking sites as we understand them today, trace their origins back to the mid- to late-1990s. An early example was the Six Degrees.com site, launched in 1997. However, it was not until the advent of MySpace in 2003, and subsequently Facebook in 2006, that these sites became a major feature of people's internet use. MySpace was the most visited website online in the United States in 2007, but then lost its place to the Google search page. Significantly in early 2010, Google was itself supplanted by Facebook as the most visited site (Sinclair, 2010). The Chinese language interface QQ.com, operating since 2006, is also a significant player with more than 200 million users (Waunters, 2009). The relatively brief history of social networking sites is one of ongoing evolution with each success, and subsequent failure, providing a launching pad for the next success. Since their inception in 1997, the total number of people involved in the use of these sites has grown dramatically. At its peak, the Six Degrees.com site had one million users whereas by mid-2010 Facebook had more than 400 million users.

Throughout this chapter, we use the examples of the current industry leader in social networking sites as well as their immediate predecessors in Facebook, MySpace, and Friendster to argue that inaccessibility is a reflection of a disabling social worldview. The first part of the chapter uses the "doing production" framework established by Goggin and Newell (2003) to explore the way third-party applications such as screenreaders are incompatible with some design and layout. This framework places digital disability in the context of the wider social disablement of people with disability. The second part of this chapter then recognizes and celebrates the potential that social networking sites hold for people with disability regarding opportunity for political mobilization and social interaction. Finally, we consider the inaccessibility of Facebook and detail what the site has done, if anything, to address these problems. While Facebook is the main focus of the chapter, we also briefly consider the inaccessibility of other social networking sites such as MySpace. These examples demonstrate the importance of choice and the minimal impact that addressing these accessibility concerns has on users without disability. Such features might even enhance the user experience for non-disabled people.

The possibilities that information communication technologies, and social networking in particular, hold for people with disability are well-documented (see, for example, Seymour and Lupton 2004; AbilityNet 2008; Ellis and Kent 2010). For example, Raskind *et al.* (2007) consider the potential that social networking sites hold for young people with learning impairments. They argue that because people are more willing to share personal information over the internet than in face-to-face conversations, youth with learning disability, and other "special needs" are able to express their feelings more easily because the fear of social rejection is removed.

Doing Production

Throughout history, people with disability have been viewed as a deviant group in need of treatment. According to Michael Oliver (1996), disability is a category or "good" that is produced to give value to an underlying discourse. He separated disability and impairment to argue that ableist social values attribute negative meanings to impairment and so people who have impairments are disabled by an unadaptive world rather than their bodies. Prejudicial attitudes are integral to the perpetuation of the disempowered position of people with disability in society. Deviant groups are created according to power imbalances within society and people branded deviant are "treated". In the context of people with disability, this invokes a charitable discourse that sees the person with disability being "helped" and non-disabled as the charitable "helpers" (Finkelstein, 1981). Supports or alternative ways of doing things, using adaptive technology for example, become stigmatized. The example of TTY as a cultural artefact of the deaf community versus the more mainstream SMS considered in the previous chapter demonstrates this tendency. The production of disability is a dynamic process that is shaped by technology, culture, and the underpinning moral order (Goggin and Newell, 2003: 21). Disability exists in society and is a negative social interpretation of impairment that empowers dominant groups and institutions.

Doing production applies to web 2.0 when an aspect of a site or its sign-up process, such as Captcha, prevents interaction, collaboration or social networking. In the digital arena, it should be possible to accommodate for many different impairments through universal design. Exclusionary mechanisms that create disability are brought in from the existing disabling social context. Internet-based technologies have the potential to offer greater inclusion to people with disability, and are often presented as a way to eradicate socially constructed disability. Finkelstein (1980) believes new technologies characteristic of the Information Age will offset many of the prejudicial attitudes established during the Industrial Revolution, where technology was established around able-bodied norms. However, digital technology is constructed in the same disabling social world and should be understood in that context. While we should be optimistic that web 2.0 represents the next stage of the Information Age and could see a realization of Finkelstein's (1980) predictions, we must also be aware that as long as the cultural project of ableism is sustained, the internet will not be fully accessible. Accessibility is a universal design issue that potentially benefits both those with a disability and the wider community. Online social networking may provide a novel solution to inaccessible built environments and impairment effects which prevent networking and socializing in the analog world. They may also allow for a global connection of political advocacy. However, inaccessibility built in at the point of production is a disappointing trend that must be addressed as all people, not just disabled people, become more reliant on these networks.

Facebook

Facebook is currently the most popular social networking site with more than 400 million accounts (Facebook, 2010). It was created in 2004 by Harvard University student Mark Zuckerberg and two of his dormitory mates. Zuckerberg's vision was for a more open world where people, things, and events were better connected. Like Berners-Lee his grand vision was the open sharing of, and access to, information to allow people to become better connected:

> openness fundamentally affects a lot of the core institutions in society — the media, the economy, how people relate to the government and just their leadership. We thought that stuff was really interesting to pursue. ... We talk about this concept of openness and transparency as the high level ideal that we're moving towards at Facebook. The way that we get there is by empowering people to share and connect. The combination of those two things leads the world to become more open. And so as time has gone on, we've actually shifted a bit more of a focus not just on directly making it so people can use Facebook and share and be open on Facebook, but instead on making it so that the systems themselves have open properties. (Vogelstein, 2009)

Zuckerberg considers this openness and transparency "a better world". He has spoken extensively about how this concept will translate to more efficient modes of communication (Raynes-Goldie, 2010). Within a few weeks of its creation in 2004, over half of the student population at Harvard had created an account and the site then expanded to allow students from other colleges to join (Solove, 2007: 27). Since then Facebook has experienced phenomenal growth to become the most used social networking site amongst college students, then people aged 40 and above, with new demographics rapidly embracing this brand of social networking. The importance of Facebook, in allowing the disability community to mobilize politically and share disability-related news and information as well as break social isolation, has been highlighted by Haller (2010).

Facebook operates around the concept of a profile that an individual user creates and a list of people the user knows who agree to be associated as "friends". Once a registered Facebook member, you construct a profile by uploading a profile picture, filling in information about your age, where you went to school, your political views and relationship status, etc. You then search for people you know and add them as friends. The main feature of Facebook is the "wall" where friends post comments and users can update their current status by answering the ever-present question "what's on your mind?" This relatively simple interface has evolved to include a news feed, a live feed, and real-time chat. Facebook also allows users to create their own applications and a variety of quizzes add a dimension to the version of self that the community of Facebook friends come to know. Of these features, the most innovative and important is the news feed that automatically broadcasts updates made about any individual to all their friends. This includes the user's own status updates, and also any comment made about them, either in relation to those updates, or in relation to photos of them posted by other users. Rather than having to explore the site to find out what your friend and contacts are doing, you are provided a news feed of these events each time you log in.

Unlike in the generation of social networking prior to Facebook, including MySpace and LiveJournal, or the generation before, that encompassed chat interfaces such as Internet Relay Chat for Microsoft Windows (MIRC) or Internet Relay Chat (IRC), in Facebook members use their real name. Facebook does not constitute any particularly radical technological advancement over the social networking sites that have come before, although it does seem to scale very well. Rather Facebook's success has been based on the way it has developed the social side of its application. The social rather than the network has led the way. However, Facebook has been widely criticized by both disabled members of the Facebook community and outside organizations for the level of inaccessibility built into its interface. The fascinating thing about these accessibility problems is that the strength of Facebook as a platform stems from the social bit of its social network, rather than any set of technical specifications. Facebook often changes the interface it uses, rarely without complaints from its users, but it is the social function and the atmosphere of relative openness that allows people to link their Facebook identity to their real life that is its true value. Given this, its initial reluctance to address accessibility issues is highly surprising.

Four months after the launch of Facebook to the wider community, the first petition appeared on the site criticizing Facebook's level of accessibility for people with disability along with a call for changes. As the platform was developed in a university dorm room over a short period of time, it could be argued that an expectation that it would launch with all the accessibility options in place is unreasonable. However, rather than seeing the fact that it was designed by students as an excuse, this should be seen as a failure of the education system in prioritizing the inclusion of people with disability. Newly minted digital developers should be made aware of the benefits and requirements of accessible universal design in developing internet applications as part of their education.

Facebook has been accused of perpetuating race and class inequalities with boyd (2007a) labelling it a continuation of hegemonic society. However, the significance of the exclusion of some people with disability was left unremarked in her investigation. If Facebook's evolution can be seen as a continuation of class inequality, as boyd (2007a) contends, then the exclusion of people with disability from Facebook fits into a wider social structure. As Roulstone (1998: 7) suggests "the way that new technology is experienced cannot be understood in a social and theoretical vacuum." Due to longstanding social inequality, the disability community has one of the lowest rates of education and highest rates of unemployment. Facebook and all social networking sites are valued as businesses based on their participants.

Social networking sites have commodified people's friendship networks and opened them up as a marketing opportunity. The higher the number of people involved, the greater the value of the network and the greater the potential for commodification of socialization and communication within the network. Viewed from boyd's (2007a) perspective, Facebook's skewed socio-economic membership profile should be criticized. However, viewed from a commercial perspective, this skewing toward the top end of the socio-economic scale makes perfect sense as an active business strategy. Similarly, it follows that Facebook should try to grow the size of its network in order to increase value in the market. Facebook's activities in this area have often come under criticism for issues, such as making it hard for people to leave the network by deleting their account. Likewise, people who are not part of the network are identified through the network as a way of leveraging them into joining, just to see what information about them is already being shared on the network. If someone tags you in a photo on Facebook and you are not a member, the site identifies you, and sends you an email to let you know you have been tagged. However, if you want to see the content you have to start an account. As Innes (2009) suggests, when attitudinal barriers are the greatest barriers experienced by people with disability, access to social networks such as the increasingly important Facebook are vital for full participation in our connected world.

Viewed from Facebook's perspective, growth in membership translates to growth in monetary value. Viewed from the member's perspective, growth in membership translates to a wider network of "friends". This value both for Facebook, through advertising potential, and for people using the site, to keep in contact, is enhanced through the direct linkage of online and analog identity. How this linkage of identity then works with Raskind *et al.*'s (2007) findings may be less positive. A fear of social rejection could continue to exist on Facebook where people manifest as their "real" selves. As Raynes-Goldie (2010) observes "users are supposed to be their 'true' selves [and] interact with 'real' friends" on Facebook. This value of the network — both corporate and personal — comes with a significant counter. As the value for those who are already part of the network grows, so too does the cost of exclusion for those who are prevented from joining.

Facebook for Everyone?

When Facebook celebrated the milestone of 2.5 million members, they created a group called Facebook for Everyone. Facebook users were encouraged to join the group to tell stories about how they were able to reconnect with people from their past. Around the same time, other groups began emerging to claim that Facebook is not for everyone. The fact that people with vision impairments were unable to access the site's content without assistance from a sighted person is an important example of the way people with disability are excluded from Facebook. This has been an ongoing problem highlighted by the Facebook group, The Official Petition for a more Accessible Facebook. Launched on the anniversary of Louis Braille's birthday in 2007, the group has had some success in achieving their aim of a more accessible Facebook. However, it is significant to note that Facebook's first response was to create an accessible version of the gift shop — a service members pay to use.

The Official Petition for a more Accessible Facebook claims that Facebook "repeatedly ignored accessibility", making it virtually impossible to interact with the interface using any type of adaptive technology. With a focus on potential Facebook members with vision impairments or learning disability that use screenreading or magnification software, the group outlines seven key areas of concern:

Captcha
Gifts
Newsfeed preferences
Drop down menus
Drop down boxes
Adjusting text size
Webpage layout (McKay, 2007)

The issues they highlight address features of Facebook that are essential to the Facebook experience. In order to sign up on Facebook, a user must initially decode a Captcha. This technology is designed to differentiate between interaction with a real person who is signing up for an account and an interaction with an automated computer process. This filtering tool involves presenting blurred and disfigured characters that must be retyped accurately. As transcription software is not able to read images, people using adaptive technologies are unable to decode and reproduce this string of characters.

Theoretically, Captchas present a problem that humans can solve but machines cannot because according to University of California at Berkeley computer vision professor, Dr Jitendra Malik:

> Abilities like vision are the result of billions of years of evolution and difficult for
> us to understand by introspection, whereas abilities like multiplying two numbers
> are things we were explicitly taught and can readily express in a computer program.
> (Robinson, 2002)

This basis for telling humans and computers apart therefore rests on a very narrow definition of humanness. According to the rationale behind Captcha, a human can be distinguished from a machine on the basis that humans can see and read, or in the context of audio Captchas, hear. Now that both visual and audio Captchas can be cracked by computers, their continued use is confounding. Malik's assumption also suggests that reading inherently involves vision when this is not the case for all people. AbilityNet's (2008) research into the accessibility of social networking sites found a number of sites including, Facebook, were inaccessible to users with a variety of different impairments. This study noted the use of Captcha and several other issues awarding the site only a one star rating.

The use of this process means that potential Facebook users who rely on adaptive technology must enlist the assistance of another person in order to register for a membership account. This is a significant hurdle that could exclude some people from ever becoming members of Facebook. This casts some doubt on the idea that anyone can join Facebook and is contrary to Zuckerberg's vision. In addition to signing up, Facebook also uses Captcha to verify other activities including sending messages to other users, particularly when the computer being used is located in public locations such as an internet café or university computer lab. For Foley and Voithofer (2008), the use of Captcha is a determining point in the way we interact with the technology of Facebook and reflects the disabling values of the people who design and maintain these limiting applications. As the previous quote from Malik clearly demonstrates, the values operating behind the creation and continued use of Captcha is that a definition of a human rests on physical and sensory ability that is tied to evolution.

While asking a sighted person to assist in the sign-up stage may not seem like a very significant issue in the grand scheme of things, this needs to be considered within the history of the individualization and pathologization of disability. Historically, people with disability have had a helper/helped relationship with the able world — people with disability are attributed the helped position and identity (Finkelstein, 1981). Captcha unnecessarily disables people with vision and cognitive impairments and puts them in the helped position, inviting charitable interpretations. Access needs to focus on independence rather than benevolent assistance.

Three months after The Official Petition for a more Accessible Facebook was launched, Leah Pearlman, a product manager at Facebook, responded to the stated concerns with a blog announcing that the Facebook gift shop was now open to everyone. She contended that as Facebook grows, it becomes more diverse and explained to users how some Facebook members use adaptive technology to access the internet. She did offer a word of caution that screenreaders aren't "people smart":

> In order to work properly, they require the program or website they're reading to adhere to certain guidelines. For example, a screen reader can't figure out who is in a picture, but if a picture has a clear descriptive caption, a blind user can better understand what's on the screen. (Pearlman, 2007)

Pearlman attempted to assure the Facebook community that most of Facebook adheres to accessibility and that their commitment to accessibility can be demonstrated via the launch of an accessible version of the gift shop off the help page. In the spirit of social networking and collaboration, Pearlman invited feedback from the Facebook community:

> We know there are areas on the site that still require accessibility enhancements. While balancing those enhancements with the rest of the work we have to do, we plan to make those changes soon. If you notice anything else we can do to improve access to Facebook, as always, feel free to submit your suggestions. (Pearlman, 2007)

While the group was encouraged by Pearlman's invitation to submit accessibility suggestions and applauded Facebook for crossing one item off their list of seven, it appeared to have ended there because almost exactly two years later Official Petition discussion threads continued to focus on Captcha in Facebook's sign-up process as the major barrier to participation. Captcha is notoriously difficult even for people without any type of sensory impairment. Trying to ascertain whether a distorted character is a 1, I, l or | for example is virtually impossible. Lynx users also find Captcha limiting and discriminatory.

Like The Official Petition for a more Accessible Facebook (McKay, 2007), AbilityNet (2008) highlighted Facebook's use of drop down boxes as problematic. Drop down boxes rely on JavaScript to be read. Screenreader users will often turn off JavaScript when using the web because it can change the content of the page without refreshing the page itself, thus taking control away from the user with vision impairment (Foley and Voithofer, 2008). While JavaScript provides much potential for web designs, some accessibility issues beyond the obvious lack of control arise when assistive technology is prevented from access. Hidden and unexpected content often cannot be accessed with assistive technology, making navigation difficult and can disorient the user (WebAIM, 2010b). Drop down boxes are not only disabling but, in fact, have little to add to the general population irrespective of impairment when lists or check boxes are equally as effective. As Facebook has rapidly and repeatedly changed its layout, the navigation of drop down menus in particular has become increasingly complex. In this case, an accessibility 2.0 where users can decide on the way information is received would be especially useful.

While Facebook uses sans serif font, a recommended style for users with vision impairments and dyslexia, the text size is "hard-coded" so that it can not be resized. Being able to change text size benefits a large portion of population. The use of social networking sites such as Facebook and Twitter is on the rise amongst all sectors of the population. Facebook statistics reveal that one of the fastest-growing demographics of Facebook users are people over the age of 55 (Smith, 2009). As the population, along with the Facebook demographic, ages, accessibility options become more important to a greater number of people.

Facebook also serves as a platform for a number of applications run by outside companies. Farmville, the most popular application on Facebook, run by a firm called Zynga, has more than 80 million users (Walker, 2010). However, this game, along with Vampire Wars, Pirates, and Café World is inaccessible. There is no need for the applications developed to be inaccessible, another popular game Mafia Wars can be accessed through a screenreader.

How much responsibility can Facebook be expected to take for these projects run by external developers? There are more than one million developers operating from more than 180 countries (Facebook, 2010). However, Facebook has in the past placed requirements on external developers. They suspended the popular Scrabulous game under legal threat from Hasbro, the owners of Scrabble. There are also regulations regarding which data on users can be accessed by different applications. Imposing an accessibility policy would be within their power. Given it would increase the potential audience for many of these different games and applications, it would also be within their interest.

These points provide an opportunity to reflect on the internet as a disabling technology for people with disability despite the promise of the opportunity to fully participate. Addressing these concerns will enable a better internet experience for all users regardless of disability or impairment, particularly as we move into greater use of mobile devices. Website accessibility features are of great benefit to mobile internet users. Like many disabled users, mobile users have lower bandwidth, smaller screens, no mouse, and limited functionality. It is predicted that within five years, more people will be accessing the internet through mobile wireless devices than desktop PCs (Morgan Stanley & Co., 2009). Recent studies have also shown that much of the recent growth in mobile internet use is closely tied to the use of social networking sites (Caverly, 2009). More than 100 million people access Facebook through mobile devices (Facebook, 2010).

Web 2.0 is characterized by "interaction, collaboration and social networking" (Gibson, 2007: 1). Facebook embodies Berners-Lee's vision where people can share information by reading and contributing. Berners-Lee envisioned the web as a network and recognized that networks become more powerful when more people become members. He saw universal access as a critical component to the success of the web as a network. Facebook is likewise based on the notion of networks as people connect to read and contribute information. It makes little sense to exclude an entire group from independent participation in the network. The Facebook network gains value for each additional member. Given that Facebook has a policy for keeping accounts active for people who have died (Fletcher, 2009), setting in place universal design practice and policies to ensure access for disabled users is in their interest. However, people with disability are often excluded from social life and Facebook exists within an already disabling social environment.

Disableism is perpetuated in society via stereotypes and negative attitudes. Facebook's (2010) mission statement claims to "give people the power to share and make the world more open and connected" and emphasizes equity and respect in their rights and responsibilities including, "you will not post content or take any action on Facebook that infringes or violates someone else's rights or otherwise violates the law." However, while people are better able to recognize racist content and use the Facebook reporting mechanism to mark it offensive, disableism is less widely understood. When Tom Shakespeare (2009) investigated the occurrence of prejudice against people with disability on Facebook, he found over 500 groups that mock or otherwise humiliate people with restricted growth. He suggests these groups incite hatred and harassment of people with disability and probably violate anti-disability discrimination laws. They almost certainly infringe Facebook's rights and responsibilities. This investigation, while limited to a particular impairment, is reflective of the broader treatment of disability on Facebook.

The Facebook group STOP Facebook discriminating against disabled users attracts discussion relating to the inaccessibility of Facebook. The recent suggestion that if the applications created by outside developers were inaccessible then Facebook can't be held to blame raises some important points regarding the future of an accessible internet. Again, accessibility features must be built into content creation toolkits in order to have an impact on users, with limited skills and insight, creating content.

Potential for Political Mobilization

The Facebook group The Official Petition for a more Accessible Facebook revealed the inaccessible features of Facebook that were integral to the site's construction and operation. With over 2,500 members, this group also demonstrates the fantastic potential Facebook holds for people with disability interested in political mobilization. While the similar group STOP Facebook discriminating against disabled users only has 275 members, more specialized groups are much larger. For example, Blind Students on Facebook has 762 members, Deaf and Hard of Hearing has 1,742 members and Dyslexia has 1,149 members. The relatively newer fan page function is also attracting large numbers of fans for deafness and dyslexia, in particular. These groups show that Facebook is also used by people with disability including those for whom inaccessibility has the greatest impact.

Despite the inaccessible origins and attitudes amongst some members, Facebook and social networking hold significant potential for people with disability. Social networking is an important career resource for people whose impairment may prevent them from physically networking at events such as conferences (AbilityNet, 2008). The emergence of disability specific social networking sites such as Disaboom.com in the vein of Facebook has resulted in increased employment opportunities for people with disability and marketing opportunities for large corporations (Haller, 2010).

Seymour and Lupton (2004) found a similar suggestion when they analyzed the use of internet chat amongst people with disability. While many commented that online communication with like-minded people provided emotional support, the significance to employment opportunities also emerged as paid-employment could be accessed from home in an ergonomically appropriate environment with assistive technologies already in place. Online social networking addresses many issues people with disability experience when attempting to mobilize politically or socially including transportation, insurance, and communication barriers.

Cultural Pressure: Facebook's Response

In 2007 when Facebook founder Mark Zuckerberg declared "once every 100 years, the way that media works fundamentally changes" many agreed Facebook had "jumped the shark" or descended into the ridiculous. Zuckerberg was promoting the now defunct Beacon system. Beacon was an advertising system that directly targeted the user's circle of friends. Following privacy concerns raised by members, Zuckerberg and Facebook were forced to backtrack (Morrissey, 2007). In addition to the Beacon back down, unpopular decisions regarding the structure of the news feed and ownership of copyright of photos have been reversed. If they think it's important enough, Facebook will bow to cultural pressure when its members complain about changes or new initiatives. As part of Facebook's stated commitment to transparency, inclusion, and communication, Zuckerberg (2009) invites consultation amongst Facebook members regarding changes and initiatives:

> History tells us that systems are most fairly governed when there is an open and transparent dialogue between the people who make decisions and those who are affected by them. We believe history will one day show that this principle holds true for companies as well, and we're looking to moving in this direction with you. (Zuckerberg, 2009)

Despite being targeted by dissatisfied users as early as 2006, Facebook did not adequately respond to the issue of accessibility until 2008. Facebook was signalled out in both 2006, by the American Foundation of the Blind (AFB) and in 2008, by AbilityNet for being inaccessible to people with vision impairment. Yet, by 2009 it was ranked as the most accessible social networking site by Media Access Australia (Cahill and Hollier, 2009: 3). When compared to Skype, You-Tube, Flickr, Twitter, and MySpace, Facebook was commended for its response to previous criticisms in relation to its inaccessibility. Facebook overhauled its site in consultation with the AFB in 2008:

> The menus, in particular, are very clear and positioned where you would expect them to be — along the top of the page and the left-pane. Forms are simple and well laid out. The registration process is still reliant on CAPTCHA with an audio alternative, but this can cause problems in some cases. Graphical icons can also disappear when users adopt contrasting colour schemes, however Facebook has done a good job of providing text alternatives. (Cahill and Hollier, 2009)

With the newly available audio Captcha, html-only version and keyboard short-cuts, Cahill and Hollier (2009) describe Facebook as a "good choice for people with disabilities." MySpace, Facebook's main competition, on the other hand, is ranked least accessible. While it is heartening to see that the company has made changes to better accommodate people with disability, if Facebook, despite the documented accessibility problems, now rates number one as the best network for people with disability, what does this say more generally about the status of people with disability in relation to the developers of these increasingly important virtual environments?

MySpace and Friendster

Between June 2006 and April 2008, MySpace was the most popular social networking site in the United States. In mid-2007, MySpace attracted three times more traffic than Facebook, making it not only the most popular social networking site in the US but also the most popular website. In April 2008, MySpace lost its crown to Facebook which became and remains the most popular social networking site (Ostrow, 2009). Like Facebook, MySpace is a social networking site that connects people via a friendship list, or a friends space. Similarly, users update their statuses and write on each other's pages — MySpace calls this comments rather than writing on the wall.

MySpace started as a networking site inspired by the potential of its predecessor Friendster, danah boyd (2007a) described Friendster as the first social networking site to popularize the features that are seen in contemporary networks of this type. It was conceived as a social component to the Ryze professional network and designed to compete with the popular Match.com dating site (boyd and Ellison, 2007). By imposing limitations on the numbers of contacts a person could have, Friendster deviated from the Facebook/MySpace model in quite significant ways. Yet, like Facebook, it wanted people to present as their "real" selves using their actual name. The ability to link to others in the network was linked to a relationship between people being friends of friends. Initially each person was limited to 150 people, as a reflection of the Dunbar number limit to the size of an individual's social network.

However, early adaptors to the network did not embrace this rigid top-down structure and sought to increase their access to the network beyond Friendster's proscribed limitations. This was done, in particular, through the use of individual collector accounts who would allow people to access a greater number of friends. These "Fakester" accounts would often be in the name of a popular fictional character, as well as bands and musicians seeking to extend their fan base. The use of the network in this fashion caused technical strains on the Friendster network and the company sought to impose its will on its users, leading to what became known as the Fakester genocide (boyd, 2006) and the subsequent exodus from the network. The relevance of accessibility 2.0 can again be seen in the mass exodus from Friendster. Accessibility 2.0 prioritizes the preferences of the user and within the domain of social networking could allow both increased customer satisfaction and better access for people with disability. A rigid structure that did not value the user's interests resulted in Friendster's failure and allowed MySpace developers to capitalize with a new, more open platform. However, accessibility issues were intensified in a different way.

MySpace was developed rapidly by the company eUniverse to take advantage of the potential that they could see in sites like Friendster. While Facebook was initially limited to Harvard University students, MySpace's original members were eUniverse employees. In 2003, MySpace benefited from the exodus from Friendster and actively modified its operation to facilitate this transition, particularly encouraging bands and musicians to make use of their network. In 2004, when the site began to become popular amongst teenagers in the United States, the network dropped its age requirements to facilitate this. In 2005, MySpace was purchased by News Corporation for $US 580 million.

While little has been written about accessibility in relation to Friendster, MySpace has been notorious for its unwillingness to facilitate a greater level of accessibility to the site for people with disability. The documented accessibility problems with MySpace impact on people with vision impairments and cognitive disorders as well as people who have migraine headaches and epilepsy (WebAIM, 2010b). MySpace's failure to live up to its obligations to the disability community needs to be read in the development of the history of a network that essentially based its success by being accommodating to users, leaving a more rigidly controlled structure. In this context, their reluctance to enforce changes to accommodate access could be part of their broader strategy of not dictating to their user base.

However, there is no requirement that accessibility should impede the use of the network by others. Universal design would help make the site more accessible to everyone. More importantly, if universal design principles had been applied when the site was first designed both in the overall interface and in the tools provided to users to modify their individual pages, then the network would have been accessible from the outset. Just as there was no excuse for undergraduate students failing to consider accessibility in the context of Facebook, the professional developers at eUniverse and the subsequent multinational owners in News Corporation should doubly be expected to have knowledge in this area.

In contrast to Facebook, where every user's page has essentially the same layout, users of MySpace are encouraged to "pimp their page" by adding features unique to their identity. For example, users select music to automatically load when other people navigate to their page. Automatic loading of audio disrupts screenreaders when they attempt to navigate a page and breaks one of the simplest rules of creating an accessible page. While users are creating the inaccessibility, MySpace has a responsibility in establishing toolkits because the skill required to "pimp" a page is minimal:

> MySpace pages are designed by users of the service, so a very large proportion of pages do not satisfy the web accessibility standards stated by the W3C. Poorly formatted code can cause accessibility problems for those using software such as screen readers. According to Wikipedia, the MySpace homepage, as of 20 May 2009, fails HTML validation with around 101 errors using the W3C's validator. (Cahill and Hollier, 2009: 15)

MySpace's unwillingness to encourage accessibility features or release an accessibility policy has paralleled its declining popularity — it lost 54 percent of its market share in Australia between 2008 and 2009 with a similar decline in the United States (Cahill 2009). MySpace's Accessibility "fail" when compared to Facebook presents a formidable warning to sites such as Twitter that like MySpace, do not have an accessibility statement (Cahill, 2009). Accessibility features that coincidently improve the user experience for all could have a significant impact on the outcome of the competition to be the most popular social network.

At the height of its popularity in 2006, MySpace had become such an important communication interface that it had established a reputation for itself, whereby "if you're not on MySpace you don't exist" (boyd, 2007b). As MySpace has never released an accessibility policy, it would appear that disability does not exist in the world of MySpace. MySpace does not provide an accessible version of the site or explain accessibility workarounds on their help pages which in fact yield "no results" for an "accessibility" word search (Cahill and Hollier, 2009: 14).

Just as AbilityNet argued in 2008, Cahill and Hollier (2009) suggest the most problematic feature of MySpace is the use of Captcha at the login stage. Unlike Facebook, MySpace does not provide an audio option and this is the only way to log onto the site. In 2006, the AFB lobbied MySpace to provide an alternative to Captcha so that blind users could sign up independently (American Foundation for the Blind, 2006). They urged MySpace to adopt an audio Captcha option or to come up with another means of registration. Accessibility issues continue once users have got past the login stage in large part due to the dependence on advertising and the user-generated content:

> Cluttered web pages with many links can also complicate usage for a person who is blind. MySpace sometimes ha[s] more than 100 links on each page that loads — which makes for an overwhelming experience. While sighted users might quickly scan web pages for the most important information, screen reader users generally have to listen to web pages from start to finish, top to bottom, left to right. On MySpace ... this can mean going through a lot of content before finding the desired link. (American Foundation for the Blind, 2006)

By failing to provide an accessible version of MySpace or develop accessibility workarounds, or in fact build accessibility into the toolkit for user-generated content on MySpace, a large proportion of people with disability are prevented from becoming MySpace members.

Conclusion

The social networking sites Facebook and MySpace have been credited with changing the way social connections are made. They also perform an important function in the participation of people with disability. People with disability are embracing the mainstream social networking sites such as MySpace, Facebook, and Twitter. Following the AbilityNet (2008) research that criticized the overall lack of accessibility on the major social networking sites, many refused to comment, except for a representative from the social networking site Bebo who pointed toward their rather large deaf community — "Our site has been embraced by the deaf community. Accessibility hasn't been raised as an issue." (New Media Age, 2007). Accessibility is not a one-size-fits-all and users should be able to choose the way they access information. Many features of these sites' construction prevent access for people with a number of other impairments. The exclusion of people with disability from the most popular social networking sites is an example of the digital production of disability. Facebook and MySpace rely more on the development of the social side of their interfaces. As networks, they also become stronger, and more profitable, the more people that join.

This structural inaccessibility has continued across a number of social networking sites that have been created with a disabled audience and therefore marketing demographic in mind including disaboom.com, xable.com, disabled-passions.com. Following the trend of online dating and social networking, a number of disability internet dating sites have emerged such as Disabled Friends, Disabled Date, and Disabled United. AbilityNet (2007) rates these sites as only marginally better than other more mainstream social networking sites rating on average two stars and one star respectively, with the exception of Disabled Friends which rated three stars.

While Facebook, with its one star for accessibility, evolved as a continuation of social disablement, the potential for political mobilization within this site has increased the visibility of accessibility as an important issue. Only four months after the launch of Facebook to the wider community, political action appeared on the site calling for a more accessible interface. Eventually, following widespread criticism, Facebook was overhauled in consultation with the AFB. Alternatively, MySpace, already rapidly losing market share to Facebook continues to refuse to incorporate accessibility measures.

MySpace, by leaving the design of individual pages more open and not even providing accessibility guidelines, has a lot of user-generated content. This was initially an attraction, particularly in light of its predecessor Friendster's more prescriptive policies, and was driven by relatively simple and easy-to-use tools for people to do this customizing. However, there was no consideration given to universal design principles with these tools, or any advice given to users as to how to make their page accessible. This was perpetuated by the change in ownership to a large traditional media company perhaps more used to responding to legislation than user demand. In contrast, Facebook, by tightly controlling its layout was able to implement a more accessible template for users with disability to navigate, albeit one where there is still work that could be done.

Interestingly, while MySpace did not try to implement any accessibility policy or even recommendations for its users, Facebook is in a similar position in regard to its third-party developers. At the time of writing, there are no obvious successors to Facebook as the premier social networking site, although there has been much speculation on this in the face of heightened concerns about user privacy as Facebook seeks to spread its network across the websites that its users visit. We are glad to see that despite earlier problems, it is now belatedly focusing on accessibility for users with different impairments, and this is certainly a big step forward for people with disability to fully participate in this growing area of social interaction. Graeme Innes (2009) predicted that online social networking, and especially Facebook, would become increasingly important to participation in a democratic society — anyone not in the network would be disabled. When local government started using Facebook to communicate with their constituents in 2010, Innes' prediction was realized. The importance of online accessibility regulation was likewise highlighted and progressed as a result of this extension of Facebook's reach.

While predicting the future in this area is extremely difficult, we can imagine that ideally a social networking site would enable users to customize both what they put in, as well as how other people's information is displayed and accessed. Of course, to attract a mass market this also has to be done in a way that users find easy to customize and use. One of the other areas of potential development in this field is through the development of virtual worlds. This then is the focus of Chapter 7.

Part III
Where to Next?

7

Avatars with Wheelchairs, but No Virtual Guide Dogs

Disability and Second Life

"Virtual Reality n (1987): An artificial environment which is experienced through sensory stimuli (as sights and sounds) provided by a computer and in which one's actions partially determine what happens in the environment."

(Virtual reality, definition in the Miriam Webster online dictionary, 2010)

"the social codes by which we create values, the social mechanisms by which those values guide actions, and the ultimate uses we choose for the tools we create are questions about the future that [Virtual Reality] technologies are likely to force us to confront."

(Rheingold, 1991: 385)

When Jaron Lanier coined the term "virtual reality" in the 1980s, he predicted that by 2010 it would be accessible to consumers (Heiss, 2003). Online virtual worlds that made use of this concept were first depicted in novels such as *Neuromancer* (Gibson, 1984) and *Snow Crash* (Stephenson, 1992). Virtual reality and virtual worlds are no longer in the realm of far-off science fiction. Lainer was correct, although perhaps a little late, in his prediction. Perceptions of virtual reality have been a common feature of popular culture. In 1993, the Aerosmith music video for *Amazing* depicted two teenagers skydiving, making out, and riding a motorbike in a virtual environment using their personal computers from their separate bedrooms. More recently, the *Matrix* trilogy of films placed virtual worlds in a disturbing light. For some people with disability, virtual worlds such as Linden Lab's popular Second Life are enabling technologies. Yet, as the 1987 Webster definition suggests, sensory stimuli is a core aspect of one's navigation of those worlds. Virtual reality blurs the previously uncontroversial boundaries between technology and the body, by calling into question where bodies begin and end (Seymour, 1998: 6). These virtual worlds are accessed through a computer screen, keyboards, mouse, speakers, and microphone. The direct input into our brains envisaged in much of the fiction is yet to appear, however, these narratives demonstrate that the link between a person's physical body and the construction of their online persona can be a complex negotiation.

This chapter takes up this complex relationship in order to critically examine the intersection between disability and persistent online virtual worlds — specifically, Linden Lab's Second Life. The online three-dimensional world is similar in many respects to popular online games such as World of Warcraft, although unlike a game world, there is no specific objective for the players to achieve, and much of the world consists of user-generated buildings and landscapes. Avatars, or representations of online identities, are also an important feature of these worlds. In this chapter, we explore the importance of access to these increasingly popular virtual environments and the barriers to that access for people with disability. We also examine the construction of online identity and the ability and consequence of being able to "pass" as able-bodied in virtual worlds. Throughout these discussions, we explore how different individuals and groups are utilizing the environment in relation to disability and question the current role of disability studies in relation to these virtual worlds. We conclude by highlighting the importance of promoting a disability-rights agenda, as this increasingly important area of cyberspace develops.

Virtual worlds call into question the relevance of body appearance and hold much potential for the politicization of disability. Edward Castronova (2005) has claimed of virtual worlds:

> in synthetic worlds, we do not get a body, we pick one. Therefore our bodies will generally be just what we want them to be. Imagine the broad impact on human society of a world in which body appearance was completely fungible. Erase, at a stroke, every contribution to human inequality that stems from body difference.

A fungible body in these spaces, then, is one whose parts can be swapped or returned. However, a consideration of what Castronova does not say in his imagination of the potential of virtual reality, reveals that disability continues to occupy an otherness — a position of inequality. This otherness enforces a narrow version of normality (Goggin, 2009b). Despite the celebration of "choosing subjectivities" in the academic discourse surrounding virtual worlds, embodiment is central to the navigation of these online spaces. Interestingly, the online social revolution, which encompasses the creation of virtual worlds, is potentially of the most benefit to people with disability — yet they often have the most difficulty accessing it (Epstein, 2008). This difficulty can be due to impairment effects, and disabling design and attitudes, which fail to take these effects into consideration.

Virtual reality, specifically Second Life, is a very real component of the lives of its users. It has been predicted that over the next ten years, Second Life will both attract more users and have a greater effect on a larger number of these users in terms of work, play, and how they define themselves. Virtual reality is a performance of identity that does not eliminate the body but has the potential to mediate and influence relationships and ways of thinking about the self (Seymour and Lupton, 2004). The real world is not separate from the virtual world — they influence each other. Technology emerges through a broad social and cultural environment which influences how people then engage with it (Roulstone, 1998). Second Life provides both meaningful social identity and reflects older, analog, disabling values.

Virtual Worlds

Jaron Lanier spoke of virtual reality in the 1980s describing it as an effect that would "give people in disparate locations the feeling of being in the same room" (Heiss, 2003). Online virtual worlds add persistence to that room. Not only are people brought together through their avatars, but those avatars meet in a space that persists even when they are not there. If you create a building in Second Life, it will still be there for others to see while you are not online.

The first of these online worlds were the text-based environments, MUDs (multi-user dungeons) and MOOs (MUD, object-orientated). A virtual world was displayed as a text-based description of what participants could see and hear as they moved through them. Not unlike the early World Wide Web, these early types of virtual worlds remain relatively accessible. More recently, virtual worlds have developed into graphically rendered three-dimensional virtual spaces. The most popular of these are massive online games (MOGs) which involve particular objectives and stories that players engage with through their avatars. The most popular massive online game, World of Warcraft, has more than eleven-and-a-half million players (Blizzard Entertainment, 2008). While virtual gaming worlds have the most residents, other less-structured virtual spaces enabled through the internet are gaining in popularity. These worlds, such as Second Life, have less concrete goals, with residents performing the mundane rather than players achieving a goal. They enable a "virtual life" (Newton, 2010).

Virtual reality creates a context in which people construct and represent their bodies in varied ways. MUDs, as text-based games, are a powerful example of bodily performance for Seymour and Lupton because:

> The body is represented by one's own textual description; you can be what you want to be. Because other people can not see the body they are unable to judge the body in terms of its external characteristics. A site such as MUD is a powerful example of the potential of computer-mediated communication to reconstruct bodies in more auspicious ways. (Seymour and Lupton, 2004: 292)

Second Life, like MUDs before it, allows users to engage in anonymous social interaction and reconstruct the body in different performative ways. People are using Second Life to try on different identities or campaign for causes relevant in the real world.

Second Life

Second Life is a virtual world founded by former RealNetworks chief technology officer, Philip Rosedale. Inspired by Stephenson's novel from 1992, it first went live online in June 2003. Second Life initially charged a monthly access fee for people to use the world in line with the economic model established and adopted by the majority of MOGs. When this model was unsuccessful, the world was relaunched with free access for people to create avatars and visit the world. Linden Lab relied on the sale of virtual land and currency for their revenue.

Second Life has a significant population. At the end of June 2010, approximately 1.4 million different avatars had logged into Second Life in the previous 60 days. The Second Life Grid was the equivalent of 64 acres when the world was first launched, but by the beginning of 2009 it had grown to 65,000 acres (Bowers *et al.*, 2009). Daily trade of virtual goods in Second Life is estimated to be approximately $US 1 million (Richards, 2008). The Second Life currency, the Linden dollar (L$), trades against the $US at an exchange rate of approximately 250:1 depending on fluctuating demand.

However, it is not just the size, population or economy of the world alone that marks its significance, but rather the potential it represents. In response to the rapid growth of Second Life, de Pascale *et al.* (2008) predicts virtual reality will become vital to our connected society, with the potential to overthrow social networking and instant messaging as favored forms of communication. This potential has prompted a number of multinational companies to build a presence in Second Life as some speculate it may represent the next phase of the internet's development (Helmer, 2007). Second Life has similarly generated significant media interest, with Second Life identity Anshe Chung becoming a minor celebrity when she announced she had acquired sufficient assets in Second Life to be declared that world's first virtual millionaire (Anshe Chung Studios, 2006). The news agency Reuters assigned a reporter to Second Life in 2006. Disability groups initiated action within the world almost immediately.

While some of the earlier hype about the success of Second Life as a platform has subsided, including the subsequent withdrawal of the Reuters correspondent in 2008, the platform still has a great deal of attraction for many users and particularly people with disability. As noted in Chapter 3, educational institutions at the tertiary level have embraced Second Life at various levels of engagement (Jennings and Collins, 2008), as have people involved in medical research (Beard *et al.*, 2009; Bowers *et al.*, 2009; Yellowless and Cook 2006). The platform has also been used by a wide variety of groups dealing with different disability (see Norris 2009 ; Pajtas 2007; Schlender 2008). These virtual environments enable a variety of social interaction and experiences. However, if Second Life represents the three-dimensional future of the internet as some have suggested, then it will present a new set of challenges, particularly for those with perceptual and cognitive impairments.

In early 2007, Linden Lab released the source code for the Second Life Viewer client — the equivalent of the web browser for accessing Second Life. This made accessing the virtual world an open-source project and allowed people to develop their own specialized software to access the world (de Pascale *et al.*, 2008). IBM has since begun work on a virtual worlds user interface for the blind that produces a text description of the visual environment that can be accessed through a screenreader (IBM, 2008).

Linden Lab has been championing standards for virtual worlds, albeit for interoperability, rather than access, but this is leading to the development of technology that will enable access for users with disability. Universality and access regardless of disability are increasingly important as some predict the majority of internet users will be using virtual worlds within the next couple of years. For many people with disability, Second Life is already a vital internet platform:

> Because of the nature of my disabilities, a wheelchair is insufficient. However, [Second Life] permits me to do things without leaving the protected environment of my home where I have an ergonomic setup that allows for my disabilities. From my computer chair, I can teach, run a business, have an active social life, and be a functioning member of a community. Second Life is my wheelchair. (Seshat Czeret quoted in Epstein, 2008)

As this quote from the Second Life identity Seshat Czeret demonstrates, Second Life is used as an enabling technology by some people with disability. However, the development of web accessibility for others who may lack access requires that a consideration of impairment become a more important part of the discussion. Boulas and Burden (2007) recognize that people with disability face barriers in virtual worlds such as Second Life because:

> These worlds are essentially visually based environments, and as such the blind and visually impaired are excluded. However, researchers are currently working on spatialised audio interfaces for these worlds. Voice communication in 3-D virtual worlds, which can be seen as an accessibility enhancer for some people having difficulties dealing with/communicating with typed text, is a challenge for the hard of hearing and deaf. But again technologies are being developed that automatically convert the spoken word to sign language using speech recognition to animate an avatar. (Boulas and Burden, 2007)

Boulas and Burden's approach recognizes that different users require different adaptations, and these design aspects will benefit the non-disabled user as mobile technology is more broadly adopted. Different impairments will impact differently on a person's ability to present in a virtual world. Concerns of disability disclosure forced by the Second Life interface have been expressed in the context of higher education. For some students disclosure will be unavoidable (e.g. students with dyslexia), while for others it will no longer be necessary (e.g. wheelchair users):

> Some disabling real life conditions, e.g., paralysis or loss of legs, do not effect functioning in virtual worlds. Other conditions — print impairment, hearing impairment, and keyboard/mouse use impairment — may be more disabling in a virtual environment than real life. (Krueger *et al.*, 2009)

The world of Second Life — the parameters set by Linden Lab and the content placed there by its many users — consists of design decisions that impact differently on different impairments. Within Second Life, innovations that enhance digital accessibility for blind users can increase inaccessibility for those with hearing impairment. The introduction of voice communications between players in Second Life was controversial when it was introduced in 2007. Debates over its relative benefits highlighted some of the issues around disability that manifest in virtual worlds. People who had trouble typing were in favor of the change, while those with hearing impairments were not and the obvious impact on those with vision impairments were not even discussed (Boellstorff, 2008). However, in an example of putting users first through accessibility 2.0, there is potential for the virtual world to be accessed in different ways through different customized viewers that address the effects of different impairments. Similarly existing digital technology, both hardware and software can be used to help people interface with the existing viewers.

For those with impairments that specifically impact on their navigation of the physical interface through use of a mouse or keyboard, there are a number of existing technologies that are used to enable better access to computers which can be adapted for Second Life, particularly gaze or eye-tracking software. However, some of these potential aids are confounded by the design of the Second Life interface. If a person is using an onscreen keyboard with eye-tracking software and accidentally hits the "m" key, the program automatically shifts into "mouselook" mode where many of the controls disappear from the screen and the view of the world changes to as though a person is seeing through their avatar's eyes. Unfortunately, the only way to get out of this mode is through a physical keyboard. If a person does not have access to this, then they are locked in this mode and are forced to restart their computer. Antonelli (2008) observes:

> what makes it worse is that it would be such a simple matter for a programmer to add an option to the Second Life viewer to prevent accidentally going in to mouselook, or additional ways to exit mouselook that would be more accessible. (Antonelli, 2008)

Again, due to a lack of awareness, simple accessibility features are overlooked and users with vision impairments have particular difficulty navigating the platform. Aside from being an accessibility issue, this is inconvenient. Computer technology can improve the lives of people with disability and have the added benefit of convenience for non-disabled people. Innovative assistive technology, such as ergonomic keyboards, touch-sensitive pads and screens, eye-gaze control and predictive text software facilitates this convenience for everyone. Geoff Bubsy (quoted in Kavanagh, 2002) boldly describes this as "a manifestation of good design" rather than specialized technology.

Virtual worlds have great potential to address the effects of impairments without devaluing recognition of the way disability is created socially. As with other products of universal design, these features can act to enhance access for all users, not just those with specific impairments. The development of these different, accessible, viewers is still a relatively new process. Existing design, as seen by the problems with mouselook, still has a long way to come in terms of embracing accessible universal design and accessibility 2.0 principles.

Because impairments manifest disability differently, digital technologies could allow a culture whereby disability is considered within an ethics of diversity and becomes normalized as a different way of doing things to achieve the same goal. Krueger, Ludwig, and Ludwig's example highlights the crucial importance of accessibility 2.0, or putting the user at the center of the accessibility debate, as different impairments manifest digitally. Where non-disclosure is possible in the real world, it may not be online and vice versa. Accessibility 2.0 and the techniques described by Boulas and Burden (2007) earlier puts the user's differing requirements at the center.

It may well be that Second Life will be superseded by some as-yet-unthought-of platform before this type of online environment lives up to the current hype. However, if this does turn out to be the case, raising access issues at this relatively early stage of the platform's development is of great importance. Developing awareness of, and expectations for, accessible design for these environments as they develop — rather than retrofitting access — is crucial to allow people with disability a voice in this development.

In 2006, accessibility blogger Peter Abrahams suggested initiating a class action within Second Life to fix accessibility issues in order to ensure people with print impairments could navigate the largely visual interface as the platform developed:

> as we are still at the relatively earlier stages of SL [Second Life], ... accessibility issues should be fixed now. It is a new world and it should not debar anyone from it. Given that the interaction between the SL server and the user interface is a set of objects that define scenarios, it should not be that difficult to develop an alternative or extended interface that would provide the information in a format that would make it usable by people with various disabilities. (Abrahams, 2006)

Abrahams called for supporters to register their interest in the comments section of his blog. However, despite the at-the-time widespread media celebration of the inclusion of people with disability in the Second Life world, Abrahams was not able to garner much support and was ridiculed online with people suggesting accessibility measures would take away from the Second Life experience of non-disabled users (Hickey-Moody and Wood, 2008).

These debates and negotiations also take place in the more-directed virtual worlds of massive online games. The online group AbleGamers was able to negotiate with Mythic Entertainment, the developers of the massive online game Warhammer Online, to include access to an onscreen keyboard to increase the game's accessibility to people unable to use a traditional keyboard. This change, along with a number of other features included in the game to aid players with vision, hearing and physical impairments, was rewarded when AbleGamers named Warhammer the "Most Accessible Mainstream Game for 2008" (Gonzalez, 2009). In contrast to this, the group had less success at lobbying Blizzard Entertainment, the developers of World of Warcraft. Blizzard was concerned that if it allowed third-party applications to work with the game, it would provide potential for players to cheat and gain an unfair advantage. After three years of lobbying, Blizzard relented and allowed some third-party software to interface with its game, but only when faced with the threat of an AbleGamer group negative publicity campaign (Newton, 2010). With up to 20 percent of the gaming market made up of people with disability (Sinclair, 2008), and more than half a million players with a disability in World of Warcraft (Schramm, 2008), this reluctance to embrace accessibility, especially from a purely commercial perspective, is hard to understand.

A new set of legal and moral challenges emerge as Second Life and other virtual worlds exist outside standards-based designs and are assumed to be under no obligation to adopt accessibility measures to allow access for people with disability. However, Joshua Newton (2010) suggests the application of the Americans with Disabilities Act to virtual worlds may be more relevant under the wording of the ADA than the broader internet environment, because the service being provided is the virtual world itself. Newton sees third-party accessibility software as the way forward to make these worlds accessible. Again, accessibility 2.0, in conjunction with clear standards, enables the participation of people with disability, without taking away from the experience of users without disability or with different types of impairments. In this context, disability becomes part of the diversity of the human experience. Anna Hickey-Moody and Denise Wood (2009) suggest Second Life allows disability to be reframed as an articulation of difference which is central to broad concepts of humanity. In this context, disability as difference is no longer located in a single body and thus becomes a valuable expression of difference.

Disability and Second Life

When you first generate an account to join Second Life, you are asked to choose from a selection of starter avatars. They define your appearance in the world; your gender, skin color, and clothing style. You also choose a name, or rather your first name; your second name has to be chosen from a list of those available. In contrast to Facebook, Second Life expects you to present an alternate identity. Once your avatar first appears in the world, you cannot move, cannot turn your head to see or focus your vision, cannot hear, and cannot speak. At this level, Second Life is an inherently disabling technology for everyone regardless of impairment. Similarly you cannot fly or teleport, both of which are options for the other residents in Second Life, until an appropriate level of wetware is acquired.

The first task new users need to perform is to complete a brief training program that provides the basic literacy of movement and communication. With experience moving and communicating in the virtual world, many people are able to overcome this initial disability inherent in the world for the new user. Yet for people with impairments that affect their ability to work the interface with the virtual — to operate a standard keyboard and mouse or to receive the audio and visual feedback from a computer — this disabled position is perpetuated. Further, once this initial barrier to access at the interface of the virtual world is overcome, the actual construction of the virtual world may present its own disabling barriers to participation.

When access and participation within the world are available, there are a new set of issues to ponder. Many users report on the liberation they feel when participating in virtual worlds when they do not need to appear or identify as a person with a disability:

> Part of the pleasure in using SL is being able to transcend ... disability and interact "normally". I want to get away from the need for wheelchair accessible entrances, ramps, curb cuts, guide dogs, and all the other things we associate with physical limitations. After all, in SL I can fly. Why would I want to create another world in which I can't even get around without special accommodation? ("Eli" quoted in Friedkin, 2008)

However, if people with disability in this sense become invisible in virtual worlds, this could have implications for the visibility of people with disability in broader society. While Eli wishes to blend into the background of the Second Life community and reject the need for the accessible spaces which he sees as stigmatized, others recognize the importance of accessible spaces and use Second Life as a way to advocate for a more accessible world.

Those who wish to connect with their own avatar through displaying attributes of themselves in the real world may choose and desire to have a virtual wheelchair as part of their online identity. In Second Life, this initially proved unusually hard to achieve (Cassidy, 2008). Finally, we need to consider what people with disability are doing while in Second Life and how that relates to a disability rights agenda. The final issue relates to what type of organization is taking place and how the disability community organizes and expresses itself in virtual worlds.

Second Life is offering people with disability the opportunity for social power and represents a digital manifestation of Finkelstein's (1980) hypothetical and Groce's (1985) actual "disability island". There is a diversity of creativity and people are using Second Life to try on different identities or campaign for causes relevant in the real world. The Gimpgirl online community was established in 1998 as a place for women with disability to share their lives and experiences with people who have had similar experiences. As a result of web 2.0, Gimpgirl now traverses a number of online platforms including Twitter, Livejournal and, in 2008, Second Life. This online community for women with disability is a space where members discuss disabling language, questions over attractiveness, and whatever else is considered worthy for discussion by members. The group hold forums in Second Life which they make accessible to those not on Second Life via a text Chat Room. While Gimpgirl and other groups are able to use Second Life to raise consciousness and organize politically; for Second Life to reach its potential for social and political mobilization and inclusivity, accessibility issues must likewise be addressed.

Access is the first barrier to participation in Second Life for people with disability. A person's first moments in the virtual world are an inherently disabling experience. Access requires a level of skills and knowledge that is not immediately present in new users. However, before this can be addressed, a person has to be able to make that initial connection with the world. Regrettably, Second Life is not a particularly accessible platform. Second Life requires a high-speed internet connection which often serves to exclude people in regional or remote areas. While lacking this infrastructure, it is these people who could potentially benefit the most from being able to access this virtual world to ease their geographic isolation. The platform also uses a considerable amount of data, limiting potential for access from people in areas where bandwidth is metered. Second Life also requires a high-end computer to run the standard viewer software with high processing and graphic acceleration requirements that exclude many older inexpensive machines. As many people with disability are on the lower end of the economic scale, these barriers will act as the first point of exclusion.

The disregard for establishing access for people with print impairments extends back to the ways computers were developed as graphical user interfaces. The initial development of graphical user interfaces for computer operating systems simplified the use of computers, while paradoxically making them less accessible for blind people (de Pascale *et al.*, 2008). Hillis (1999) notes the Cartesian tradition that gives primacy to sight in a way that conceptually privileges the eye over the human body. These concerns are not unique to Second Life. Brendon Cole describes his experience trying to raise accessibility issues for people with vision impairments to Toy Head-Quarters (THQ) the developer of a number of interactive games and systems: "I wrote THQ a letter once suggesting things they could add to their WWE Smackdown games to make them more accessible to the blind ... I got a letter back thanking me for my appreciation of their cutting-edge graphics" (Peters, 2009). Clearly, the perspectives of blind people were not valued or even acknowledged in this situation. Second Life and other similar virtual worlds and games present a very rich visual environment. White, Fitzpatrick and McAllister (2008) have expressed concern that the growth of virtual worlds will lead to exclusion for people with vision impairments. However, there has been some work done specifically with Second Life to look at overcoming barriers to access that come from vision impairments using sound to provide feedback about an avatar's virtual surroundings (See de Pascale *et al.* 2008; White *et al.*, 2008; Boulos and Burden 2007).

These efforts have in part been facilitated by the decision in 2007 by Linden Lab to release the source code for their Second Life viewer to allow the software to become an open-source project. Since that time, a variety of different viewers and applications that provide access to the Second Life world have been developed. A number of these, such as the IBM Active World Project deal specifically with providing access for people with different types of impairments.

Making the source code open for the Second Life viewers highlights important questions about the role of Linden Lab in providing an accessible online environment. While it does open up the potential for outside developers to play a role in providing interfaces that address specific access issues, it should not let the company sidestep its obligations to provide accessibility features on its standard interface.

The new terms of service — that must be agreed to before accessing the Second Life grid — for the latest version of the Linden Lab Second Life viewer were not accessible to people using screenreaders. Fortunately, the Virtual Ability organization were able to provide an accessible copy of these terms and conditions available online for individuals, who rely on this type of technology for access. Accessibility needs to be more than a bandaid solution provided by third parties. It should be an integral part of the design process. This latest accessibility failure in Second Life essential documentation, along with the mouselook function — which is still a fault present in the new Linden Lab viewer — indicates that this process still has some way to go.

Virtual Identity

Social interactions in online virtual environments are governed by the same social norms that effect social interactions in the physical world. As Yee *et al.*

(2007) note: "Even as our identities became virtual, we insisted on embodiment. And in doing so, the rules that govern our physical bodies in the real world have come to govern our embodied identities in the virtual world" (Yee *et al.*, 2007). How much these rules governing our physical bodies stretch into virtual worlds, particularly in terms of disability, is contested. It also varies from person to person. Further complicating any analysis is the complex relationship between a particular avatar and the person or persons they represent. The Nine Souls of Wilde Cunningham are a group of nine adults with cerebral palsy, who are unable to individually operate the Second Life interface. They jointly decide on the actions of their avatar Wilde Cunningham, which is in turn controlled by an additional person who works with the collective.

> How did we decide on what we would look like, and our gender? We formed the man avatar first, because that day, we had more men in the group. We always wanted a female one, but we haven't taken the time to create her yet. Mary and Johanna would like that very much. We decided on how wilde would look first by starting with skin colors. We have both black and white in our real life group, and didn't want to have those because neither is better than the other. So we picked orange. (James quoted in Linden, 2004)

In this case, the construction of an avatar as a representation of "self" requires a far more nuanced understanding of what the self can be. The negotiation of virtual worlds involves a transformative process, whereby avatars are used to mediate an individual's course of adaptation (Jensen, 2009). The Nine Souls indicate that this mediation can be still more complex than when dealing with just one user. In other instances, one avatar is controlled sequentially by a number of different people with that avatar representing a particular position within an organization, such as a university librarian or a research team (see Beard *et al.*, 2009). Conversely, a single person might have several different avatars. Even one avatar can radically change its appearance at the click of a mouse. Castronova (2005) postulates the implications of a world where bodies don't matter:

> look at the contrast to social life as we experience it now: in our world, there are millions upon millions of human beings who live under crushing spiritual and even physical repression because of the bodies they inhabit. That pain can be relieved. That injustice can be undone. And once everyone gets used to the fact that bodies don't matter, they may cease to cause discrimination even on Earth. What a quantum improvement in human dignity that would be. (Castronova, 2005)

Avatars can allow people with disability to "pass" and not be forced to show their impairment in a virtual world. By contrast, others will feel that this is too much a part of their identity or self image to leave it behind in a virtual world: "Second Life becomes the ultimate game of dress-up. However, for some people, the avatar becomes an opportunity to express deeper personal identities that require radical reconfiguration of bodily space" (Jones, 2006). For some avatars, as indicated by Wilde Cunningham, this reconfiguration will necessarily be more radical than for others as they come to represent a fluid group identity in a single online persona.

Virtual reality and virtual worlds are rapidly changing areas that have been theorized about for over 20 years. Technology has now advanced to a point where we can respond to some of the early hypotheticals these theorists posit. The Rheingold (1991) quote at the beginning of the chapter demonstrates the impact virtual reality could have on social and cultural values which in turn actually determined the creation of these spaces. Heim (1991: 32) likewise posits three existential or "real world" features to anchor the virtual and the real including "morality/natality, carryover between past and future, and care". For Heim, these features are open to revision and it will be through a rejection of their reproduction that virtual reality will become truly imaginative. We are now in this "future" and the example of disability in Second Life suggests we are, in fact, reproducing the same cultural values of the "real world." Despite this, opportunities for confrontation do exist and Second Life is advancing a disability rights agenda.

There is some debate over whether people with disability should be disclosing their disabled status online. While some argue that it adds to the diversity of a world where avatars can fly and digitally represent humans as animals, others suggest it is an unnecessary disclosure. Simon Stevens (aka Simon Walsh) ran the nightclub Wheelies in Second Life and continues to use a wheelchair and helmet — similar to his real life self (Stevens):

> Because of the wide diversity of avatars, wheelchair-users are very much included within Second Life activities. There are, as anywhere, idiots who make offensive remarks. Within more private settings, there is a set questions people always ask, which include "are you disabled in real life?" and "why do you use a wheelchair?" which can always make for interesting chats. I personally changed Second Life's attitude toward disability when I set up "Wheelies", its first disability nightclub. This was one of those daft ideas which grew and grew. (Stevens quoted in Carter, 2007)

While Stevens is very vocal about disability and how the experience of disability translates in the Second Life world, other people with disability who use Second Life construct their avatars to reflect their real world impairment in more subtle ways such as Judy Brewer, the director of WAI the W3C's web accessibility arm:

> When I first came into Second Life, I found I had acquired some abilities. I could walk (I can't walk in real life); I could fly; I could even teleport. I felt more comfortable seated and so got a Segway [scooter] to move around in-world. (Brewer quoted in Wooley, 2007)

Finally many, like "Eli" cited earlier, prefer to pass as non-disabled and explore the situations Castronova imagines. Niles Sopor uses Second Life as an opportunity to see what life without an impairment is like and has found people treat him differently. In stark contrast to his "real life", in Second Life Niles is able to hold a camera and make short films. This allows him to run a media and communications consultancy within the virtual world (Cassidy, 2008). Second Life has been described as both inclusive (Cassidy, 2008) and exclusionary (Hickey-Moody and Wood, 2009). In any case, as Stevens "Wheelies" demonstrates, Second Life is proving to be integral in changing attitudes toward disability in a virtual and real sense and has given a number of people with disability a real sense of social power. As Stevens comments "you can even appear an as animal" (Hickey-Moody and Wood, 2009).

In order to pass as non-disabled in virtual worlds, people with disability will often need to use some form of assistive technology. This has led Vickers *et al.* (2008) to propose a type of Turing test for avatars. The original test proposed by Alan Turing determined if a computer could "pass" as a human. The avatar Turing test determines how well assistive technology works in enabling the avatar of a user with a disability pass as able-bodied in a virtual world. This also highlights the importance of accessibility in making the much celebrated online virtual social interaction possible.

While there is focus, on the one hand, at people's ability to pass as able-bodied in virtual worlds, others focus in almost the opposite direction. Fez Richardson is developing applications for use in Second Life so that the non-disabled can experience the effects of impairment in this virtual realm. He is recording his findings on the blog 2ndisability (Cassidy, 2008). Similarly, the University of California hosts a simulation in Second Life that seeks to mirror the experience of schizophrenia.

We approach this development within online worlds with some caution as computer applications that seek to replicate the experience of impairment to the non-disabled world have been heavily criticized within disability studies. Likewise, exercises where non-disabled people are encouraged to experience what it is like to be disabled by using a wheelchair for a half-an-hour or wear glasses that block out a certain portion of vision are similarly unwelcome within disability movements for social change. They are widely considered exploitative and neglect to consider adaptations initiated by people for whom this is reality. Second Life is offering a different and very important perspective by encouraging a certain diversity that half-an -hour in a wheelchair can't replicate. People can fly in Second Life or choose to manifest as an animal, or the opposite gender or perhaps even in orange. The ethics of diversity in Second Life allows disability to exist along a continuum of difference.

Simulated environments possible within Second Life may also prove vital in assisting people with disability navigate the "real world". For example, Suzanne

Conboy Hill (quoted in Funnell, 2009) is investigating whether introducing people with intellectual impairments to a virtual hospital environment in Second Life will give them a better understanding of medical procedures and make it easier for them to give "informed medical consent".

In this way, the virtual and the social overlap and when accessible, whether through an accessible interface or the support of another, can have positive implications on the way people with disability navigate the "real world". A number of support groups specific to particular impairments have also emerged. The disability rights agenda emerging on Second Life and other virtual worlds likewise has an important role in promoting disability advocacy and accessibility as this increasingly important area of cyberspace develops.

Conclusion

There is something very attractive about the idea of a world where "bodies no longer matter". However, individuals will continue to manifest on the analog side of the screen. As virtual worlds grow in popularity, the way in which disability is both portrayed and activated will necessarily evolve. Virtual worlds such as Second Life, despite operating on the internet rather than the World Wide Web, are often associated with web 2.0 technologies. In the case of Second Life, the user-generated content of the world operates in parallel to many of the web-based platforms seen as examples of these developments including YouTube, MySpace, and other social networking sites. Second Life shares with these web 2.0 platforms some of the challenges to universal design that can be reversed with more accessible user toolkits. However, these virtual worlds exist beyond the World Wide Web. With their predicted rapid expansion over the next few years both in terms of the number of people using them and their significance as online platforms, the importance of accessibility to these environments by people with different impairments will grow.

The link between a person's physical body and the construction of their online representation can be a complex negotiation, particularly when it relates to disability and identity. As the example of Second Life demonstrates, there is no one way to approach the complex negotiation of a disability identity in online and offline worlds. Different people have different perspectives, influenced by both the effects of their impairments and the social mediation of those impairments and an inaccessible world. While Eli and Niles Sopor gain social capital by manifesting online without disclosing their disability, others including Simon Stevens and Judy Brewer reproduce their offline advocacy within Second Life and the cultural artefacts of their disability is central to that. In addition, the Nine Souls demonstrate that sometimes an acknowledgment of the effects of impairment determines whether people with disability can participate in these worlds at all.

The importance of accessibility forms the other side of the discussion of Second Life and disability. If Second Life represents the three-dimensional future of the internet as some have suggested, then it will present a new set of challenges for those with perceptual and cognitive impairments. Accessibility 2.0 must be prioritized as people with different impairments participate in different ways. The new open source viewers being developed represent the possibilities that a disability culture could come to mean a celebration of diversity — another way of achieving the same goal. Second Life may provide meaningful social identity but care must be taken not to present it or technology broadly, unproblematically as a brave new world when it brings older, analog, world values with it.

We continue the discussion of challenges and opportunities around disability and the online realm in the next chapter, as we turn to chart the terrain ahead looking at the impact of potential developments such as 3D, augmented reality, and video captioning. Likewise, we will consider the evolving regulatory framework that could both enable and inhibit the fulfilment of Berners-Lee's understanding of the power of the web.

8

Challenges and Opportunities

The Road Ahead for Disability in a Digital World

"In the rush to implement Web 2.0, accessibility tends to get pushed back on the priority list."

Sharron Rush, Executive Director of Knowbility
(quoted in Hasson, 2009)

"New technologies, without accessibility, are being introduced. Only when their use becomes widespread do we require accessibility. However, by then, retrofitting accessibility is more complicated, more expensive (sometimes *much* more expensive), and often less effective than if accessibility had been included in the original design and specifications. The same pattern is being repeated in ... digital rights management in digital media, Web 2.0, Next Generation Network (NGN), and digital television."

(Vaughn, 2006)

We began this book with the often-cited Tim Berners-Lee quote regarding the importance of accessibility in order to create the most powerful web experience possible. Although a well-known quote that has been described as causing web developers' "eyelids to droop and their thoughts to turn to that cutie in Accounts with the tight jeans" (Lawson, 2006), it has not been similarly overused in disability, media, and cultural studies. While these disciplines and the cultural investigation of the web in the emerging field of internet studies have focused on the creation of a digital divide based on culturally specific yet arbitrary standards of humanness, a consideration of disability as it is socially created is conspicuously absent.

In their book *Digital Disability*, Goggin and Newell (2003) lamented the lack of disability theorization within the discipline of internet studies. In a later article they took the study of disability to task, suggesting that it should start interrogating digital technologies (2005a). We have sought to close these intersecting gaps throughout this book and consider the issue of web accessibility from a disability/media studies framework. Our focus has been specifically on web 2.0 technologies as these have posed both increased opportunities and greater challenges for people with disability. Web 2.0 is a more complex, graphic, multimedia-rich interface than the earlier text-intensive web experience. Although as Wood (2010) notes, there were no accessibility guidelines in place at the web's conception and it developed accordingly, specifications can be added to web 2.0 applications to ensure they allow adaptive technologies a way to interpret dynamic elements.

We begin this final chapter by drawing out Tim Berners-Lee's 1997 quote to give some further context on his goals for the web and what that means for the future. Berners-Lee's vision for accessibility included not only people with any kind of disability/impairment but also others who may be affected by other disabling elements including a digital divide along class and regional boundaries:

> The power of the Web is in its universality. Access by everyone regardless of disability is an essential aspect. The IPO [International Program Office] will ensure the Web can be accessed through different combinations of senses and physical capabilities just as other W3C activities ensure its operation across different hardware and software platforms, media, cultures and countries. (Berners-Lee, 1997)

Berners-Lee made this proclamation when he launched the International Program Office for WAI. Throughout this book we have addressed accessibility in its broadest sense, as a way to access the web regardless of impairment, browser, or device. The idea of web accessibility is to remove barriers. These barriers may be related to disability, however, increasingly, are also of concern to people attempting to access the web from other devices such as mobile phones or portable digital assistants as well as for those using slower internet connections or older equipment.

Berners-Lee has been called to task on the difficulty of applying his vision of universality to web 2.0. This chapter charts the terrain ahead, looking at the potential developments that could both enable and inhibit the fulfilment of Berners-Lee's perception of the power of the web. While forecasting the future of the internet is unreliable and has a tendency to create flame wars online, this chapter seeks to touch on the key areas that will impact on disability in the near-future digital environment. These include the evolving regulatory framework that supports the internet, specifically the issue of DRM and its legal ramifications of copyright enforcement, the issues surrounding video captioning, and a new legal discourse in the revised Rehabilitation Act. We consider evolving trends in digital design and online activity that will impact on this area such as three-dimensional virtual worlds, augmented reality, and mobile access, and we highlight the importance of mainstreaming access.

Digital Rights Management (DRM)

DRM software and hardware controls the way digital information is accessed and reproduced. It can encrypt time limits, lock content to a particular device, and disable certain accessibility functionalities (Schiller, 2010: 42). In an attempt by publishers to deal with the copyright issues that come with moving media such as music, video, and books onto digital platforms, DRM software imposes limitations on the way this content is used, for example to ensure a digital file can be used on only one device or technology. However, this has proved a contentious issue. Just as the early web browser wars prevented "access by everyone" by refusing to adopt a common form of communication across browsers, the increasing use of mobile and portable devices are again splitting the universal nature of the web. With the emergence of the iPhone, Kindle, BlackBerry, Droid, and iPad, web content has the potential to become "device specific" (Pepitone, 2010).

With the increasing popularity and choice of electronic book readers and online video content, companies are using DRM to force consumers to stay with a particular brand. The example introduced in Chapter 2 of DRM wrapped onto Apple iTunes music to ensure music could only be accessed using Apple hardware illustrates a highly successful implementation of DRM. Publishers trying to establish a viable ebook industry are using DRM to avoid such breaches in copyright that were rife during the formation of the downloadable music industry. DRM software was developed to protect copyright of music works, however, ten years on, the technology, or at least its intended application, has failed. Publishers are learning from this — the first MP3 players had no DRM installed; ebook readers have had it built in from the beginning.

Wrapping DRM onto electronic books protects the copyright of authors and publishers. However, unfortunately for consumers, and especially people with disability, there are competing ebook formats and DRM schemes. DRM is essentially a lock-and-key system — when consumers pick a particular brand, they are limiting what information they are able to access. For example, an ebook purchased from amazon.com can only be read on the Amazon-branded ebook reader — the Kindle.

For many users, this is frustrating. For users with disability, it can render the product next to useless. Drawing on the example of Adobe and DRM that we first introduced in Chapter 1 in relation to Dmitry Sklyarov's technology to circumvent it, accessibility issues specific to Adobe's use of DRM relate to the ability to change settings. Color and contrast settings cannot be changed according to individual tastes and screenreaders are blocked from accessing the information. There is also no in-built text-to-speech option. While a magnification range does exist, it is limited and a mouse must be used to copy text into screenreading programs as there are no keyboard shortcuts. These DRM measures disable those people with a number of impairments. As we outlined in Chapter 1, some basic accessibility measures include allowing exclusive use by either keyboard or mouse, as well as functionality to allow zoom function and text-to-speech (Techdis, 2010).

The increased digitization of information represents a fantastic potential for people with disability to access information in flexible ways, however, the use of DRM complicates this. Although allowing publishers to enforce copyright restrictions, DRM can also prevent lawful and fair use of the material such as accessing it in different formats using adaptive technologies. Many ebook readers come with a read-aloud voice output feature but publishers use DRM to disable this function in order to sell the print and audio rights of books separately. As the book is also DRM-protected to prevent it from being accessed on another device, a screenreader cannot read the content either. A study by TAP Information Services found that DRM on recorded books prevented access by the majority of people that they surveyed with both vision and physical impairments (Houghton-Jan, 2007: 54).

As DRM limits content to a narrow group of users and could potentially become increasingly restrictive, new measures are needed to impose accessibility. Ideally, access should be built in to players, such as the text-to-speech functionality. However, a better solution would be to make the interface accessible to allow people with disability to use their own tools of access. These assistive technologies are already individualized and allow for choice. This accessibility 2.0 strategy is more cost-effective for the producers — for example, including a Braille display on every e-reader is neither practical nor necessary.

Steve Jobs (Apple CEO) declared in *Thoughts on Music* (2007) that the future of DRM could take three different routes. First, DRM could continue on its current path with different organizations adopting different propriety features, in essence forcing consumers to do what the disparate companies wanted them to. In that environment, consumers would have to choose which content they would limit themselves to or find they needed to purchase multiple branded hardware. Alternatively, Apple could strive for interoperability by licensing its DRM "fairplay" technology to its competitors; however, Jobs saw security risks with this. Finally, DRM could be totally abolished (Jobs, 2007). In this article, Apple appeared to be speaking out against DRM, however, the suggestion of charging a DRM license fee to competitors — and likewise the extra cost invoked for consumers in purchasing higher-quality DRM-free music from iTunes — suggests otherwise. Interestingly, and to much criticism, Jobs did not suggest a collaborative development of a non-proprietary DRM schema (Houghton-Jan, 2007: 54). Such a schema could potentially satisfy the industry's requirements to protect their copyrighted material and also allow greater accessibility for people with disability.

Attempts by people seeking to transfer an ebook to a portable device such as a daisy reader or a refreshable Braille reader are complicated and often prevented by DRM. As such, the DAISY Consortium Board of Directors (2007) have passionately spoken out against the use of DRM because it prevents the legitimate access and manipulation of digital data by people seeking to access publications using assistive technology. Daisy is an audio format that is used by people with vision impairment to access text material. For example, newspapers are available daily via dedicated websites for people with vision impairments such as the RNIB or Vision Australia. Daisy audio is usually accessed using portable devices similar in appearance to the iPhone but designed specifically for use by people with vision impairment who can use large keys and audio to insert notes and jump from section to section.

The device-specific nature of DRM likewise poses problems for libraries who, by definition, seek to make their collections useable by the widest possible audience, including people with disability. It is not in any library's interest to offer device-specific material for loan, particularly when technological advancement is so rapid and uncertain. There is real danger that by selecting a specific device all of a library's digital collection could be unusable within ten years (Houghton-Jan, 2007: 54).

The Legal Ramifications of DRM

The very use of DRM in today's digital world is in many ways confounding — web 2.0 favors technology above the level of a single device. WCAG 2.0 likewise encourages robust technology that allows access in a number of ways. Under the Digital Discrimination Act (Australian Government (1992b) and other laws that mandate against disability discrimination, DRM could be unlawful as it limits access to information on the basis of a person's disability.

There is a widespread lack of understanding in relation to accessibility, adaptive technologies, and standards that mandate accessibility. While many web designers fail to put accessibility into place due to lack of awareness, publishers may actually circumvent accessibility in their attempt to protect digital files from piracy and copyright violation. Accessibility features may be available in the original software, however, DRM and the format of many ebooks allow publishers to disable these accessibility functions. Publishers are both suspicious of the disability community and their demands for accessibility and uninterested in this potential market.

There is also confusion over whether audio rights are needed for text converted to speech (Huddy and Swan, 2006). Uncertain publishers will often turn text-to-speech options off just in case (Kerscher and Fruchterman, 2002). Amazon famously disabled the text-to-speech function on the Kindle following (false) claims from the Authors Guild that this function violated copyright law. In recognition of the benefits new technologies have on the lives of people with disability, a coalition of people with disability protested, urging Amazon not to "disable the Kindle" (Jones, 2009). With less than 4 percent of books being produced in an accessible format (World Blind Union, 2008), preventing the ability of people with disability to lawfully access written material goes against the interests of authors, publishers, and booksellers — not to mention people with disability. DRM limits the usefulness, convenience, and engagement of existing legal rights (Clark, 2003). It is not just an accessibility issue, it confuses all customers. Musicload, a European online music store, claims that three out of four calls to their customer service line are about DRM (Fisher, 2007).

The ramifications from the implementation of DRM represent one of the most obvious examples of ableist assumptions generating disability for people with different impairments. While the rights of the owners of copyright are already enshrined in law, as are the penalties for breaching these rights, the addition of these technical complements to existing legal structures as a side-effect render the now "protected" content inaccessible for people who make use of additional assistive technologies. This situation is then made worse by the addition of laws that criminalize attempts to circumvent these restrictions, such as those used to prosecute Dmitry Sklyarov, and threaten legal sanction on others who would try to overcome these socially constructed impediments to access.

The ongoing tightening of this preventative legal framework, particularly the adoption of the "three strikes" policies recently embraced in France and New Zealand (and under discussion in the United Kingdom and Australia) is particularly troubling. Under this type of legislation, a household accused three times of breaching copyright through the internet can have their internet connection severed. Leaving aside the obvious issues of natural justice and collective household punishment, these laws will have a disproportionate impact on people with disability who may have a much higher reliance on the internet than their non-disabled peers. These types of regulations also serve as a disincentive to attempts to make content more accessible.

DRM stifles innovation and digital creativity. It also has the potential to prevent the notion of community accessibility that we introduced in Chapter 3. Community accessibility allows the network of web users to initiate accessibility options as a way to contribute to the creation of content. Accessibility measures such as the third-party Twitter platform Accessible Twitter or Virtual Ability on Second Life would not be possible, if Twitter and Second Life had restricted access to their content with DRM.

It seems strange that such advantage is given to large corporations to further enforce their existing copyright holdings, particularly in light of the negative consequences, while the enforcement of laws and regulations relating to accessibility and the human rights of people with disability relies on the diligence of individuals and organizations outside of formal law enforcement to bring complaints and civil actions. This hierarchy is clearly illustrated in the muted effect of the DDA on the implementation of different DRM processes.

Video Captioning

AbilityNet's (2008) accessibility review of social networking sites found that all of the five websites reviewed allowed users to upload video content. However, none outlined the importance of including captions and only one had an option to upload a transcript. The video file-sharing site YouTube failed a basic level of accessibility, with problems occurring in relation to hardcoded text size, ajax (Asynchronous JavaScript and XML) during the registration stages, thumbnail images without alt text and Captcha (AbilityNet, 2008). However, as we mentioned in Chapter 3, YouTube has more recently made their content accessible with the inclusion of captioning as part of the standard toolkit. These captions are another example of technology introduced to aid people with disability that have been seen to have wide-ranging and unanticipated benefits for the wider community. The advanced search capabilities linked to captioning are increasingly important in the development of video technology. They also allow translation into other languages and make it easy to jump straight to the required section of a video.

However, who should be responsible for the creation of captions in online videos — the site such as YouTube which provides the platform or the average user generating content? When Berners-Lee was questioned by video bloggers as to whether they needed to provide captions in order to make their content accessible, he suggested "community captioning" in the spirit of web 2.0 where the web community provides captions after the video-blogger makes a posting (Outlaw, 2006). This solution embraces the collaboration that underscores web 2.0 and highlights the importance of corporate leaders and television networks in setting the example by broadcasting online captions.

While the major television networks currently provide inaccessible online video content, some independent content creators and television networks include closed captions in their online videos. In addition to the obvious benefits for viewers with hearing impairment, there are also economic benefits as captions mean a video is more likely to show up in a search result. As a result of this technology, textual search in video is likely to become a standard feature (Joyner, 2010). There is also the option of including a "Closed captioning is brought to you by … " message within the video in a similar way to TV closed captioning advertising opportunities (Whitney, 2009).

Again, while most beneficial to people designated "disabled", closed captions can potentially assist other groups. The Australian Government's (2008) review of *Access to Electronic Media for the Hearing And Vision Impaired* found that captions were used by viewers of television, DVD, and cinema who: are deaf; have a hearing impairment; are learning English; are developing literacy skills; and/ or are viewing content in a noisy environment, such as a club or gym. The review was prompted by changes in media consumption and access. While independent media outlets and communities of bloggers are embracing video captioning online, networked television has not been as quick to adopt this feature of accessibility and the potential benefits. The online realm — although being revolutionized by network television in many ways — is exempt from closed captioning laws that mandate captions be available on television.

Closed captions were not widely embraced by television producers nor audiences until they became required by law. The United States' Television Decoder Circuitry Act 1990 mandated that every television set made or sold in America had to have an in-built closed caption decoder chip unless the screen was smaller than 13 inches (Robson, 2004: 47). This law was designed to work in conjunction with the ADA to drive the uptake of captioning on television. Prior to the Act, captioning was an expensive process for both the networks and for deaf people who had to pay for more specialized technology. In Australia, closed captioning was mandated for free-to-air television under the Broadcasting Services Act 1992; this worked in conjunction with the DDA as it promoted equal opportunity and made disability discrimination unlawful.

While the Broadcasting Services Act mandates that national broadcasters must provide captions for television programs aired during prime time (6 p.m.– 10:30 p.m.), some programs are exempt, including: programs not in English or mainly not in English; non-vocal music-only programs; incidental or background music; live sport coverage with unscheduled extended coverage that displaces a news program; and programs broadcast on digital channels during the simulcast period.

Thus, again, new technology (specifically digital television) is being introduced without accessibility measures in place. Online video platforms utilized by television networks are likewise exempt. Attempts to reverse these exemptions are underway — the Twenty-first Century Communications and Video Accessibility Act of 2009 is before Congress in the United States at the time of writing. Introduced in 26 June 2009, the bill seeks to ensure that people with disability are able to access the full range of communication and video programming available as a result of advances in internet-based technology (Library of Congress, 2010). The bill recommends that a schedule be set up to establish a deadline for the provision of closed captioning of online video content. However, in the context of television, the deadline was ten years — even if the bill were to pass, closed captions will not be widely available immediately. Further, exemptions will likely include user-generated content. Again this demonstrates the ways new technology fails to embrace accessibility, even when regulation is in place.

Several issues have emerged in relation to the wording of the actual bill and the impact this will have on the quality of captioning in the near future. The bill itself deals with a number of issues including timelines, schedules, exemptions, and pre-programmed and live video. If passed, all online video, with the exception of user-generated video, will be required to include closed captions. It is anticipated, however, that if the networks lead the way with captioned video then the importance of this accessibility issue will be recognized by the average video blogger. The bill is progressing and has been referred to the House Committee on Energy and Commerce.

However, the following example demonstrates how confounding it actually is that all networks and programs do not offer online video captions. The network PBS Kids caption all of their online video content. As captions are required on broadcast tapes, PBS Kids use these program tapes that already have embedded captions in their online video player. This proves their claim that children with disability are an important part of their audience (Whitney, 2009).

When Netflix aired *The Wizard of Oz* online to celebrate its seventieth anniversary, they did not include closed captions. Captions for this film are widely available on both DVD and television versions of the film. The Director of Communications at Netflix was also alerted to the potential problem of uncaptioned video by the National Association of the Deaf (NAD). The NAD describe the lack of response from Netflix as evidence that people who are deaf or hard of hearing are not valued members of the Netflix audience (Haller, 2009a).

It must be argued that there comes a point where "lack of awareness" can no longer be a viable excuse, particularly when accessibility measures are already available but simply not used for any justifiable reason. If a more accessible version of the film was already widely available to Netflix then, just as PBS Kids do for their audience of deaf children, it should have been used. Likewise in Australia, a large portion of television shows are offered for download after they have aired on television. Despite the availability of captioning, already created for the television broadcast, none of the downloadable programs have captions. Yet several of these, including the popular programs *Sea Patrol*, *Kath and Kim*, and *Thank God You're Here* are later released on DVD with both captions and audio descriptions (Media Access Australia, 2008).

Marlee Matlin, Hollywood actress and caption patron has used Twitter to raise awareness of the issue of captions on internet videos. Heavily involved in the momentum that led to the development of the Television Decoder Circuitry Act in the 1980s and 1990s, Matlin maintains that the achievements of that Act are being undone by the dearth of uncaptioned online video content available by means of Apple's iTunes amongst other online avenues. Although iTunes was the first to offer digital downloads of captioned movies, they are not mandatory (Haller, 2009b). As this mode of dissemination gains in popularity, then captions need to be mandated to enable accessibility for all.

In a welcome recent move, YouTube has announced all videos uploaded to its service since April 2010 are now available with captions provided by its voice-recognition software (Stelter, 2010). While this service is currently limited to videos in English with a clear soundtrack, it is nonetheless an encouraging step in the right direction.

A New Legal Discourse: The Revised Rehabilitation Act

Along with these calls for an accessibility standardization of DRM and a mandatory online video captioning bill before the Senate, Section 508 of the Rehabilitation Act 1973 is also under review at the time of writing. The Rehabilitation Act was established in 1973 to prevent discrimination on the basis of disability within federal agencies or programs receiving federal funding. Section 508 was established to update the Act in 1998 in response to changing technology to require federal agencies to make their electronic and information technology accessible to people with disability. Section 508 was again updated in 2002 to include User Agent Accessibility Guidelines for web browser developers following the rife inaccessibility issues during the browser wars. Evaluation and update at regular intervals is written into the Act. The most recent review seeks to reconsider these regulations in light of a fundamental shift in the way the web is used. While Section 508 does not require private companies to make their sites accessible to people with disability, it is hoped that the federal government represents such a large potential customer base that private companies will likewise embrace accessibility.

The current refresh proposes to combine Section 508 of the Rehabilitation Act and Section 255 of the Telecommunications Act which, as mentioned in Chapter 1, are two separate guidelines. The refresh is an attempt to encourage web developers to keep disability/accessibility in mind from the design phase rather than go about retrofits and looks at the ways technology are used rather than delineating between types of products:

> Requirements have been reorganized according to functionality instead of product type since many devices now feature an array of capabilities and applications. The released draft includes proposed revisions to various performance criteria and technical specifications that are designed to improve accessibility, add clarity to facilitate compliance, address market trends, and promote harmonization with other guidelines and standards. (Access Board, 2010a)

A committee has been established by the United States' independent federal agency Access Board to oversee the review process. This committee has recommended changes to the structure and the content of both Sections 508 and 255 in response to technological innovation and market changes (Boswell, 2008: 23). The update has followed a rigorous review process consisting of public discussions (via public forums and a discussion paper), focus groups, as well as corporate consultation. The process began in 2006 when the Access Board established a 41-member crosssection of stakeholders to comment on the guidelines as part of a Telecommunications and Electronic and Information Technology Advisory Committee (TEITAC). In 2007, the American Foundation for the Blind (AFB) joined the process through which consumers, industry, and government agencies prepared recommendations to the Access Board. A range of interest groups were consulted including representatives from industry, disability interest groups, academia, as well as national and international accessibility consultants from both public and non-profit agencies.

In 2009, the Access Board received the report prepared by the AFB as a result of the consultation process with these stakeholders. On 25 March 2010, the California State University Northridge (CSUN) Conference on Technology and Persons with Disabilities gave positive feedback to the Access Board and highlighted the urgency of updating the regulations in light of the changes in the way the web and telecommunications are used. As a result of convergence, groupings initially established in Section 508 (and outlined in Chapter 1) are no longer relevant. Telephones are no longer exclusively used to make a telephone call to another person; they are now also a device used to access email or participate in social networking. Instead of separating software and web applications, the feedback was to look at how products are actually used:

> Several new categories were recommended including:
> General Technical Requirements.
> Requirements for Hardware Aspects of Products.
> Requirements for User Interfaces and Electronic Content.
> Additional Requirements for Audio-Visual Players or Displays.
> Requirements for Audio and/or Video Content.
> Additional Requirements for Real-time Voice Conversation Functionality.
> Additional Requirements for Authoring Tools. (TEITAC, 2008)

These new categories recognize convergence and the overlap that now exists between Sections 508 and 255. Although checklists can potentially stifle innovation within a rapidly advancing area, clear standards for compliance remain important. The committee recommends the provisions address specific technical approaches in the vein of accessibility 2.0:

> All of these provisions ... describe the required types of accessibility features. Some refer to specific accessibility features that are known to be both feasible and effective. Federal agency compliance with the procurement process will encourage and give incentives to manufactures [sic] and providers to meet and hopefully exceed these requirements, and will help foster innovation and improvement in accessibility. (TEITAC, 2008)

It is anticipated that the updated guidelines will provide practical information regarding accessibility as well as foster the potential for innovation and new technology. The significant changes in the way the web and other telecommunications are used could not have been accurately predicted ten years ago and so any changes to the guidelines must, like WCAG 2.0 and accessibility 2.0, allow for previously unthought-of and exciting new technologies as they will undoubtedly have an impact on the ways people with disability access the web. Current trends such as mobile access and augmented reality also suggest accessibility will become mainstreamed.

Trends In Digital Design and Online Activity

Predicting what will happen with rapidly evolving internet technologies, portals, and platforms is notoriously unreliable. However, there are several emerging design trends gaining increasing currency that we predict will be central to the web's development in the mainstream as well as in virtual reality as a way to social network. These include mobile access, augmented reality, the increasing use of keyboard shortcuts, and other accessibility features such as voice commands and zoom.

While accessibility in web 2.0 is of most benefit to people with disability, especially those with vision impairments, to older people and to people in the developing world, the recent trend toward mobile applications and internet usage suggests the majority of internet users would benefit from accessibility options (Zajicek, 2007). The mobile versions of the Facebook and Amazon pages provide better accessibility and allow a greater ease of use when viewed in conjunction with screenreading software. They are less cluttered and more intuitive for users with print impairments and people using smaller mobile screens.

These accessibility features will become increasingly important as the general population moves toward adopting mobile media. The importance of web 2.0 platforms to our daily lives can't be denied; however, increasingly, new media theorists argue we have actually moved past web 2.0. We see an interesting link between the predicted future of the web and accessibility options for people with disability as text-to-speech and text-recognition software, virtual worlds and avatars dominate most people's perceptions about the way forward (Pegrum, 2010).

We also predict a future web where accessibility is important and adds to optimum functioning. Standards and accessibility will become increasingly important to the mainstream as the web continues to change the relationship between our bodies and the way we navigate the world. The mobile web, in particular, has been credited with changing the relationship between the body and the world it inhabits by allowing ever-present interaction within both the actual and virtual world (Richardson, 2007: 205). The mobile phone has become a kind of prosthesis, a way of being in the world (Richardson, 2007: 206); the same is true for mobile internet connections. Mainstreaming accessibility initiatives to enable a greater and more constant web connection relies on disability as a narrative prosthesis. While Mitchell and Snyder (2000) use this concept to demonstrate the importance of disability to the development of western literature, its relevance can also be applied to the internet and web technologies as more accessibility features are mainstreamed for the convenience of all.

In the previous chapter, we suggested that persistent online three-dimensional virtual worlds represented the future of the web. If web 2.0 relates to user-generated content, software as a platform, and users acting as co-developers, then the future will expand the emphasis on multimedia to initiate a new level of collaboration. Advances in three-dimensional processing will give rise to innovative applications such as massive multiplayer mobile games. In virtual worlds, there will be new types of traffic demands and network constraints.

Most people are attracted to the blending of the virtual and the real — possible on three-dimensional virtual worlds. These worlds are especially important to people with disability as they have the potential to decrease their isolation by means of immersive virtual communities. They facilitate social interaction, information-sharing, and allow a collaborative, experiential learning environment for students with disability. Indeed, it could be argued that they could be of most benefit to people with disability yet, ironically, inaccessibility often prevents access (Wood, 2010).

Where virtual reality overlays the real onto the virtual, augmented reality adds another layer to the real by providing more information regarding the environment that the person is in. Augmented reality applications have been developed for mobile phones that allow people an historical insight into how an environment that they are currently inhabiting used to look, for example an image of London during the 1800s overlayed on the present city, which can be "seen" on a mobile phone. These types of applications can also provide people with disability with an insight into the sense or experience that they do not perceive as a result of their impairment. It is now possible for people with vision impairments to "see with sound" as visual information is decoded by mobile phone applications and communicated audibly to users.

Recent developments on computer console games are allowing people to interface with games by virtue of their own movement, doing away with the use of traditional gaming interfaces long associated with platforms such as Sony's PlayStation and the Wii. Whether these will be adapted by more general computers — recreating the technology foreseen in *Minority Report* — remains to be seen, however, the medium-term potential for the integration of this technology alongside a further developed augmented reality platform, within a mobile telephone handset, paints a picture of both the challenges and opportunities that lie ahead for access for people with disability.

Mainstreaming Accessibility

Comments like "why would a blind person want to read" and the "troublesome" reputation (Wood, 2010) of accessibility measures that seem to only benefit a few people, suggest accessibility is somehow separate from web design and neither important for business reasons nor for all customers. However, what is considered an accessible retrofit in today's web environment will become increasingly important for the average user of the future as people become progressively more mobile in their web use. This has important implications for the way disability is framed and understood in both the broader community and amongst web developers. As John Foliot suggests:

> That the moment you start to ghettoize or sort of hold accessibility out at something special or different, sometimes you lose traction, you lose interest. But the reality is that accessibility and accessible web development, needs to be part and parcel of everything you do. It just needs to be part of the whole process. (Lembree, 2010)

Many technologies developed to enable greater participation of people with disability have become mainstreamed, for example predictive text, the telephone, and the phonograph (Reena, 2009). More recently, text-to-speech software, initially developed for screenreading use by people who are blind or have vision impairments, is being mainstreamed through the iPhone and GPS navigation devices. Kindle uses Nuance screenreading technology — Nuance was the first company to develop screenreaders for people with print impairments (Reena, 2009). Likewise, dictation software, having long been used by people with disability, has been appropriated by motorists seeking to speak commands to their mobile rather than use their hands. Text-to-speech and speech input are the hands-free of the future.

In another example, people with vision impairments who are unable to see a mouse onscreen use keyboard shortcuts or hot keys exclusively. However, many other software users are also adopting built-in keyboard hot keys for convenience and speed — it's faster as you do not have to remove your fingers from the keyboard. Audio web surfing often features in predications regarding both the future of the web and mobile media; this is a vital feature of accessibility software as utilized by screenreaders. However, McBlain (2009) suggests audio web surfing will become utilized by the mainstream as people again seek to multitask while web browsing:

> people on the train with headphones attached to their mobile device while Text-to-Speech reads them the latest articles from their favorite sites. HTML5 is a step in an awesome direction with regards to easy reference points; header, footer, nav, section, and article could be logical jump-to points by audible instruction. Rather than reading and clicking, the audience can tell the browser where they want to go with spoken commands. (McBlain, 2009)

These technologies, considered innovative and convenient by the non-disabled population, are only available to the mass market because people with disability push software and hardware companies to improve their products (Reena, 2009).

However, there are still potential threats to accessibility ahead. Google released its increasingly popular web browser Chrome for the Mac operating system in mid 2010. As noted in Chapter 2, the latest versions of this operating system have given priority to accessibility functions. Unfortunately, none of these features are available when using the Chrome browser. When this was raised in the Mac-cessibility Network blog (Lioncourt, 2010), a comment was posted by someone claiming to be from the Google Chrome development team:

> I'm a developer on the Google Chrome team. I agree with you that accessibility is important. In fact, I don't think you'd find anyone on the team who disagrees. When you say that Google "broke, disabled, or chose to remove" accessibility support, you're not correct; the truth is more complicated ... Doing this in a secure, performant way that still makes both the browser and the screen reader work properly is a very difficult task. Someone is currently working on precisely this task, but we didn't want to delay the release of milestone 5 for the Mac (or other OSes) until this was done. (Pkasting posting quoted in Lioncourt, 2010)

This reads like the response to the decline in accessibility in Internet Explorer 4.0 when it was launched back in 1997. Since the end of the browser wars in the 1990s, the increased competition from browsers such as Firefox, Safari, and now Chrome have challenged Explorer's dominance — this rivalry may encourage further innovation, but may also turn out to be to the detriment of an accessible web environment.

Conclusion

Berners-Lee's vision for accessibility included both people with any kind of disability/impairment and other people experiencing social disablement, a group now known as the digital divide. While the importance of accessibility is gaining currency within web design and the future of the internet, disability studies still have much work to do in considering how technologies are designed to reflect the ableist oppression of the analog word. Digital information — and the flexible way it is accessed — should not block out people with disability. In many ways, digital technologies should be the answer to a number of access issues — as Finkelstein suggested, it should become a third stage of disability and precipitate a change in practices and ideas.

However, the same old challenges have followed alongside the opportunities for participation made possible in the digital era. As web design has moved away from the promise of access by anyone regardless of disability, the medium itself has come to play a more prominent role as part of participation in broader society. The digital world is at a crossroads. It can continue to move away from universal design principles, while at the same time increasing the social and economic costs to those who are then excluded. Or it can move back toward universal design and access by encouraging the work done by people with disability to develop better, more flexible, and customizable technology which can be mainstreamed to benefit everyone.

There has been a paradigm shift in the way accessibility is valued in the general community. Perhaps the greatest awareness can be attributed to the well-publicized accessibility overhaul by Apple, Microsoft, and Google in relation to their most recent products, the latest version of Chrome hopefully being only an exception to this trend. Social networking sites and communities of accessibility advocates, such as the movement to make Twitter more accessible as we discussed in Chapter 3, have helped to raise the level of accessibility awareness in the general community.

While community and large corporations are important in raising the visibility of accessibility, a regulatory framework must also exist and evolve alongside these rapid advances in technology. The updates to Section 508 of the Rehabilitation Act and Section 255 of the Telecommunications Act underway in the United States at the time of writing seek to guide the implementation of accessibility within a paradigm of use rather than technology. Calls to abolish, or at least significantly curtail, DRM and to caption online video will benefit a large number of groups and should not be thought of as something specific for the disabled.

In a semiotic sense, the fact that accessibility allows greater "mobile" access provides an interesting moment of contemplation — civil rights discourses of disability have long aimed to reduce inaccessible environments and allow greater flexibility. As more people both with and without disability seek flexible and mobile access, accessibility will become a universal goal, not a disability-specific one. Accessibility can potentially hold a central position, with mainstream benefits, as the web moves beyond web 2.0.

In addition to the move toward a mobile web with greater integration between the analog and virtual worlds highlighted in this chapter, many also talk about the growth of the semantic web, long championed by Tim Berners-Lee, as the potential future direction for the World Wide Web and new media. This potential new architecture can provide the technological framework to open up further accessibility possibilities for people with disability and the broader community (Kouroupetroglou *et al.*, 2006). This approach is also closely tied to the processes advocated as part of accessibility 2.0 (Kelly *et al.*, 2007).

In the concluding chapter of this book, we look to the future with more hope than trepidation. While the online environment continues to evolve, it is the use of agreed standards that have facilitated this growth. These in turn, if applied to universal design, will facilitate the participation in this environment for both people with disability and also for those without who are turning to newer technologies, such as mobile internet devices. The standards developed by the W3C in terms of internet accessibility for people with disability now form the basis of the standards being developed to optimize usability of the internet for mobile users. There is enormous potential for the online environment to mitigate for different impairments; however, questions must be asked as to how much of this potential will be realized and whether the existing position in relation to universal design will deteriorate further.

Conclusion

Once a piece of information or content is digitized, its form is significantly transformed. Whereas a work written on a page is locked in that format, once a work is a digital file it can be transformed to suit any person trying to access it. It can appear as the written word, it can be automatically translated into another language, it can be interpreted as an image, it can be shown in sign language, and it can be displayed on a Braille tablet. Once that file is connected to the internet, all these different modes of access can take place simultaneously, all over the world. This information can be requested through a traditional keyboard, by speech, through eye-tracking software or by moving any of a number of different mouse devices. Making that content accessible is a choice. Making it inaccessible is also a choice. These choices are often informed by decisions relating to copyright and preventing authorized access, but also often they are made without thought, to display a particular piece of information in a way that cannot be accessed by people with disability for no other reason than a lack of awareness or perceived conflicting priorities with aesthetics and convenience. These choices are often portrayed as merely technical decisions but they are highly political and can betray a disturbing trend of ableist assumption that serve to exclude people with disability.

Throughout this book, we have followed the work of Tim Berners-Lee. He was the driving force behind the development of the World Wide Web and had the prescience to release its code to the world for free, thus allowing the internet to evolve into the staple of everyday life that it has since become. Berners-Lee also had the foresight to see that an agreed set of common standards was essential for the web to continue to grow for the benefit of everyone. Fundamental to this vision was accessibility for all people, regardless of disability. Crucially, this concern came from the inception of the idea. As we outlined in the introductory chapter, it is easy to observe three stages in the development of new media. Often the first stage is when a medium is relatively unknown, yet accessible, At this point, the access to the digital file noted previously is less-mediated, and paradoxically more accessible. All too often the next phase consists of a more regulated medium that is not accessible to many people with disability. This is most often seen as a case of oversight rather than active discrimination; however, the assumption of what it is to be human and the requirements of access to a technology, are at the very heart of discrimination. The final phase is thankfully when a platform has reached a level of popular success where any lack of access begins to attract political agitation from those excluded and their allies, and accessibility measures are brought into play.

We have argued throughout this book that it would be best for accessibility to be considered from the very inception of a new media platform, as they were for the World Wide Web. Having made this point, we are happy to see that there has been so much movement from stage two to stage three of this model by the different platforms and networks we have covered here as examples. While in an ideal world, we would like awareness of accessibility for people with disability to be inherent in all technology, we are still pleased to see so much progress being made in previously hard-to-access technology.

We have been writing about and researching accessibility in the applications explored in this book for about three years now, initially collaborating online from two different hemispheres, now in the same city. It is certainly true that five years in internet history is like a millennia in other disciples. In that time, we have seen both radical advances in accessibility and a continuation of disappointing trends. While Apple, YouTube, Facebook, and World of Warcraft made major improvements and the third-party Twitter application Accessible Twitter was made available, Second Life released an inaccessible version of its terms and conditions and *Wired* launched an inaccessible edition on the iPad. Our first publication on this topic was an earlier version of chapter 2. Twenty-four hours before we published this paper in 2008, T&T consultancy announced J-tunes. Although concerned about the relevance of our argument in this rapidly changing area, we felt the move proved that accessibility is important. Then, one week before our first conference paper on the topic, Apple announced that people who are blind or vision impaired would be able to use iTunes through greater compatibility with screenreaders for both Mac and Windows operating systems, and the new generation of iPod nanos supporting spoken menus. That was relatively easy to incorporate into the paper. Then as we were wrapping up the draft of Chapter 6 which was initially intended as an expose of Facebook's inaccessibility agenda, we discovered that Facebook was now ranking as the most accessible social media site!

While for writers on a deadline, these changes were pretty terrifying, they truly illustrate the crossroads at which we now sit. As the online environment continues to evolve, it is the use of agreed standards that facilitated this growth and these in turn, if applied to universal design will facilitate the participation in this environment for people with disability and also those without who are turning to newer technologies such as mobile internet devices. The standards developed by W3C in terms of internet accessibility for people with disability now form the basis of the standards being developed to optimize usability of the

internet for mobile users. There is enormous potential for the online environment to mitigate for different impairments, although questions must be asked as
to how much of this potential will be realized, and the danger that the existing
position in relation to universal design will deteriorate further.

People with different types of impairments will experience different disabling
elements in terms of interfacing with a computer. Recognition of the intersection
between self, society, impairment, and the navigation of online spaces is crucial
to extending the theorization of disability as a cultural identity. From this point
of view, disability has been described as a "complex relationship" between the
body and the environment in which it exists (Marks, 1999: 611). This complex
relationship is evident in the different ways people interact on online worlds.
People have different experiences in terms of how disability is represented within
the virtual world itself and in the interactions between its varied inhabitants and
the construction of an online identity.

The social model of disability that has served as a point of political motivation
for disability activists deliberately conflates different impairments. This serves
a useful role in creating consciousness and political solidarity amongst the disability community. However, implementing universal design online requires an
acknowledgment of, and accommodations for, different types of impairments.
The possibilities that ICTs can offer people with disability for independence,
and self- empowerment are much celebrated in the popular press and within
academia. However, these celebrations tend to focus on disability in terms of
mobility impairment and reveal a wider tendency to focus on ability in discussions around the internet and disability. While an important discussion, such a
focus potentially crowds out discussions of impairments that prevent initial and
continued access. Like curb cuts, modifications to accessibility in new media
technologies that help some impairments create different problems for others.
Fortunately, unlike the side of the road, we do not have to make a choice between
one or another assistive technology. In a digital environment, they can all be
implemented simultaneously. The ability to bridge this gap between acknowledging difference and maintaining solidarity and awareness is crucial to the
project to make the digital environment accessible to all people with disability,
and more accessible to the wider community. Because accessibility is a choice,
it is inherently a political decision. While this may be covered by discrimination
that manifests in a lack of awareness, it is a contested position where attitudes
can be changed. There is an important place in this change for activists and academics to make their voices heard. Before this can happen, existing paradigms
and theories need to evolve.

We have approached this book from a disability, media studies, and internet
studies perspective. All these fields are inherently crossdisciplinary and political in their outlook, with a particular concern for social justice that betrays their
common cultural studies background. Yet in this area of obvious overlap there

is relative silence, and even less interaction between these areas of scholarship. We have repeatedly acknowledged our debt in this project to Christopher Newell and Gerard Goggin and their work in *Digital Disability*. While we see this book as an extension of that project, we hope that it will lead to further needed debate and awareness in this important field.

We do look to the future with more hope than trepidation. There have been great strides made recently in terms of accessibility to new media for people with disability. While it would obviously be preferable that these changes were not necessary, we hope that a threshold of awareness is being reached in this area that will inform future developments with an awareness of the importance of accessibility to this important area for people with disability. We hope that this book is a step in that process.

Bibliography

AAP (2010). "iPad is the new iAid." *Brisbane Times*, 19 *April, 2010*. Retrieved 21 June, 2010, fromhttp://www.brisbanetimes.com.au/digital-life/digital-life-news/ipad-is-the-new-iaid-20100419-sn43.html

Abberly, P. (1999). "The Significance of Work for the Citizenship of Disabled People." *Disability Studies Archive*. Retrieved 19 June, 2010, from http://www.leeds.ac.uk/disability-studies/archiveuk/Abberley/sigofwork.pdf

AbilityNet (2005). "December 2005—Favourite Websites of Disabled People." *State of the eNation Reports*. Retrieved 19 June, 2010, from http://www.abilitynet.org.uk/content/oneoffs/eNation%20report%20-%20favourites.pdf

—— (2007). "February 2007—Dating Websites." *State of the eNation Reports*. Retrieved 19 June, 2010, from http://www.abilitynet.org.uk/docs/enation/2007datingSites.pdf

—— (2008). "State of the eNation web accessibility reports: Social Networking Websites." *State of the eNation Reports*. Retrieved 19 June, 2010, from http://www.abilitynet.org.uk/docs/enation/2008SocialNetworkingSites.pdf

Abrahams, P. (2006). "Second Life Class Action." *IT Analysis*. Retrieved 26 June, 2010, from http://www.it-analysis.com/blogs/Abrahams_Accessibility/2006/11/second_life_class_action.html

Accessify (2009). "Interview with Accessible Twitter creator Dennis Lembree." *Accessify: Verb to Make Accessible*. Retrieved 19 June, 2010, from http://accessify.com/news/2009/04/interview-with-accessible-twitter-creator-dennis-lembree/

Adams-Spink, G. (2004). "Web Opens Up for Learning Disabled." *BBC News*. Retrieved 18 June, 2010, from http://news.bbc.co.uk/2/hi/technology/3379547.stm

—— "Virtual World Opens up to Blind." *BBC News*. Retrieved 18 June, 2010, from http://news.bbc.co.uk/2/hi/technology/6993739.stm

Alexander, D. and S. Rippon (2007). "University Website Accessibility Revisited." *Southern Cross University*. Retrieved 5 June, 2010, from http://ausweb.scu.edu.au/aw07/papers/refereed/alexander/paper.html

Allen, M. (2010). "The Experience of Connectivity." *Information, Communication & Society* 13(3): 350–74.

Alltree, J. and N. Quadri (2007). "Flexible Study—What Students Do and What They Want." *Second International Blended Learning Conference*. University of Hertfordshire, 14 June, 2007. Retrieved 21 June, 2010, from https://uhra.herts.ac.uk/dspace/bitstream/2299/1689/2291/901872.pdf

American Foundation for the Blind (2006). "Are Social Networking Sites Accessible to People with Vision Loss?" *American Foundation For the Blind*. Retrieved 21 April, 2010, from http://www.afb.org/Section.asp?SectionID=57&TopicID=167&DocumentID=3153

Andersen, A. (2010). "Future Web Accessibility: HTML5 Semantic Elements" *Webaim*. Retrieved 26 June, 2010, from http://webaim.org/blog/future-web-accessibility-html5-semantic-tags/

Anshe Chung Studios (2006). "Anshe Chung Becomes First Virtual World Millionaire." *Press Release*. Retrieved 24 March, 2008, from http://www.anshechung.com/include/press/press_release251106.html

Antonelli, J. (2008). "Improving Accessibility." *The Imprudence Blog*.Retrieved 14 June, 2010, from http://imprudenceviewer.org/2008/09/14/improving-accessibility/

Apple (2010a). "Apple's Commitment to Accessibility." *Apple Inc.* Retrieved 21 June, 2010, from http://www.apple.com/accessibility/

—— (2010b). "iPhone 3G." *Apple Inc.* Retrieved 20 June, 2010, from http://www.apple.com/iphone/iphone-3gs/

—— (2010c). "What is iPod Touch?" *Apple Inc.* Retrieved 20 June, 2010, from http://www.apple.com/ipodtouch/what-is/ipod.html

Arnold, B. (2008). "Other Accessibility Cases." *Caslon Analytics Accessibility Guide.* Retrieved 25 June, 2010, from http://www.caslon.com.au/accessibilityguide10.htm

Asakawa, C. (2005). "Keynote Speech: What's the Web iLke if You Can't See It?" *International Cross-Disciplinary Workshop on Web Accessibility (W4a)*. Chiba, Japan, 10 May, 2005.

Australian Government (1992a). "Broadcasting Services Act." *Commonwealth Consolidated Acts*. Retrieved 26 June, 2010, from http://www.austlii.edu.au/au/legis/cth/consol_act/bsa1992214/

—— (1992b). "Disability Discrimination Act." *Commonwealth Consolidated Acts.* Retrieved 25 June, 2010, from http://www.austlii.edu.au/au/legis/cth/consol_act/dda1992264/

—— (2008a). "Access to Electronic Media for the Hearing And Vision Impaired." Department of Broadband, Communications and the Digital Economy. Retrieved 21 June, 2010, from http://www.dbcde.gov.au/television/television_captioning/media_access_review/?a=126580

—— (2008b). "Captioning." Department of Broadband, Communications and the Digital Economy. Retrieved 13 June, 2010, from http://www.archive.dbcde.gov.au/2008/03/captioning

Australian Human Rights Commission (2009). "Virgin Blue Becomes More Accessible." *Media Releases*. Retrieved 25 June, 2010, from http://www.humanrights.gov.au/about/media/media_releases/2009/86_09.html

Aviv, R. (2009). "Listening to Braille" *New York Times*. Retrieved 19 June, 2010, from http://www.nytimes.com/2010/01/03/magazine/03Braille-t.html?sudsredirect=true

Barnes, C. (1999). "A Working Social Model? Disability and Work in the 21st Century." *Disability Studies Archive*. Retrieved 19 June, 2010, from http://www.leeds.ac.uk/disability-studies/archiveuk/Barnes/Edinbrg2.pdf

Barr, T. (2002). "The Internet and Online Communication." *The Media and Communications in Australia*. Stuart Cunningham and G. Turner. Crows Nest, Allen & Unwin.

Beard, L., K. Wilson, D. Morra, and J. Keelan (2009). "A Survey of Health-Related Activities on Second Life." *Journal of Medical Internet Research* 11(2): Retrieved 26 June, 2010, from http://www.jmir.org/2009/2002/e2017

Berners-Lee, T. (1997). "World Wide Web Consortium (W3C) Launches International Web Accessibility Initiative" *Web Accessibility Initiative (WAI)*. Retrieved 19 June, 2010, from http://www.w3.org/Press/WAI-Launch.html

—— (1998). "The World Wide Web: A Very Short Personal History." *Short History.* Retrieved 19 June, 2010, from http://www.w3.org/People/Berners-Lee/ShortHistory

—— (1999). *Weaving the Web: The Original Design and Ultimate Destiny of the World Wide Web.* San Francisco, HarperSanFrancisco.

—— (2006). "Isn't it Semantic?" *BCS: The Chartered Institute for IT.* Retrieved 26 June, 2010, from http://www.bcs.org/server.php?show=ConWebDoc.3337

Bernhart Walker, M. (2010). "Prepare Now for 508 Web-Compliance Changes." *Fierce Government IT.* Retrieved 25 June, 2010, from http://www.fiercegovernmentit.com/story/prepare-now-508-web-compliance-changes/2010-04-29?utm_medium=nl&utm_source=internal

Bigham, J. P., C. M. Prince, and R. E. Ladner (2008). "WebAnywhere: A Screen Reader On-the-Go." *17th International World Wide Web Conference.* Beijing. Retrieved 25 June, 2010, from http://webinsight.cs.washington.edu/papers/webanywhere-html/

Blansett, J. (2008). "Digital Discrimination." *Library Journal* 133(13): 26.

Blizzard Entertainment (2008). "World of Warcraft Subscriber Base Reaches 11.5 Million Worldwide." *Press Release.* Retrieved 29 June, 2010, from http://us.blizzard.com/en-us/company/press/pressreleases.html?081121

Bloustein, G. (2007). "'Wigging People Out': Youth Music Practice and Mediated Communities." *Journal of Community and Applied Social Psychology* 17(6): 446–62.

Boellstorff, T. (2008). *Coming of Age in Second Life: An Anthropologist Explores the Virtually Human.* Princeton, Princeton University Press.

Boswell, S. (2008). "Access Board Updates Guidelines: Standards Revised on Communication Technologies for People with Disabilities." *The Asha Leader*: 23, 17 June 2008.

Boulos, M. N. K. and D. Burden (2007). "Web GIS in Practice V: 3-D Interactive and Real Time Mapping in Second Life." *International Journal of Health Geographics* 6(51): Retrieved 3 September, 2010, from http://www.ij-healthgeographics.com/content/6/1/51

Bourke, P. (2008). "Evaluating Second Life as a Tool for Collaborative Scientific Visualisation." Computer Games and Allied Technology. Singapore.

Bowers, K. W., M. W. Ragas, and J. C. Neely (2009). "Assessing the Value of Virtual Worlds for Post-Secondary Instructors: A Survey of Innovators, Early Adaptors and the Early Majority in Second Life." *International Journal of Humanities and Social Sciences* 4(5): 327–37. Retrieved 3 September, 2010, from http://www.waset.org/journals/ijhss/v4/v4-5-45.pdf

boyd, d. (2006). "Friends, Friendsters and Top 8: Writing Community into Being on Social Network Sites." *First Monday* 11(12), December. Retrieved 3 September, 2010 from http://firstmonday.org/htbin/cgiwrap/bin/ojs/index.php/fm/article/view/1418/1336

—— (2007a). "Viewing American Class Divisions through Facebook and MySpace." Retrieved 25 February, 2008, from http://www.danah.org/papers/essays/ClassDivisions.html

—— (2007b). "Why Youth (Heart) Social Network Sites: The Role of Networked Publics in Teenage Social Life." *McArthur Foundation Series on Digital Learning—Youth, Identity, and Digital Media Volume.* D. Buckingham. Cambridge, MIT Press.

boyd, d. and N. Ellison (2007). "Social Network Sites: Definition, History, and Scholarship." *Journal of Computer-Mediated Communication* 13(1): 210–30. Retrieved 25 June, 2010, from http://jcmc.indiana.edu/vol13/issue1/boyd.ellison.html

Brabazon, T. (2006). "Socrates in Earpods: The iPodification of Education." *Fast Capitalism* 2(1). Retrieved 8 June, 2008, from http://www.uta.edu/huma/agger/fast capitalism/2_1/brabazon.htm

Buckley, K. (2009). "Accessibility For iPhone And iPod touch: A Blind User's Review" *Nillabyte*. Retrieved 24 June, 2010, from http://www.nillabyte.com/entry.php?280-Accessibility-For-iPhone-And-iPod-touch-A-Blind-User-s-Review&bt=952

Burnett, R. and D. Marshall (2003). *Web Theory: An Introduction*. London and New York, Routledge.

Bush, V. (1945). "As We May Think." *The Atlantic*. Retrieved 26 June, 2010, from http://www.theatlantic.com/magazine/print/1969/12/as-we-may-think/3881/

Cahill, M. (2009). "A Wake-Up Call For Twitter." *New Matilda*. Retrieved 24 June, 2010, from http://newmatilda.com/2009/12/01/wakeup-call-twitter

Cahill, M. and S. Hollier (2009). "Social Media Accessibility Review — Version 1.0." *Media Access Australia*. Retrieved 13 October, 2009, from http://www.mediaaccess.org.au/index.php?option=com_content&view=article&id=682&Itemid=10

Calvo, M. (2008). "iTunes and iPod Now Accessible to the Blind!" *Serotek*. Retrieved 23 June, 2010, from http://blog.serotek.com/2008/09/ipod-and-itunes-are-now-accessible-to.html

Campbell, F. (2001). "Inciting Legal Fictions: 'Disability's' Date with Ontology and the Ableist Body of the Law." *Griffith Law Review* 2, 10.2 (2001): 42–62.

——— (2009). *Contours of Ableism: The Production of Disability and Abledness*. New York, Palgrave Macmillan.

Carroll, J. M. (2009). "Encyclopedia Entry on Human Computer Interaction (HCI)." *Interaction Design org*. Retrieved 24 June, 2010, from http://www.interaction-design.org/encyclopedia/human computer_interaction_hci.html

Carter, P. (2007). "Virtually the Same." *Disability Now*, May 2007.

Cassidy, M. (2008). "Flying with Disability in Second Life." *Eureka Street*.Retrieved 15 June, 2008, from http://www.eurekastreet.com.au/article.aspx?aeid=4849

Castro, E. (2003). *HTML for the World Wide Web*. Berkeley, Peachpit Press.

Castronova, E. (2005). *Synthetic Worlds: The Business and Culture of Online Games*. Chicago, The University of Chicago Press.

Caverly, D. (2009). "Mobile Internet Growth Tied To Facebook, Twitter." *WebPro News*. Retrieved 12 June, 2010, from http://www.webpronews.com/topnews/2009/07/14/mobile-internet-growth-tied-to-facebook-twitter

Centre for Universal Design. (1997). "The Principles of Universal Design." *Centre for Universal Design*. Retrieved 19 June, 2010, from http://www.design.ncsu.edu/cud/pubs_p/docs/poster.pdf

Chong, C. (2007). "America Online: An Internet Service That the Blind Can Use." *Braille Monitor*. Retrieved 26 June, 2010, from http://www.nfb.org/images/nfb/publications/bm/bm07/bm0701/bm070105.htm

Christopherson, K. M. (2007). "The Positive and Negative Implications of Anonymity in Internet Social Interactions: 'On the Internet, Nobody Knows You're a Dog'." *Computers in Human Behavior* 23(6), November: 3038–56.

Clark, J. (2002). "Accessibility and the Law." *Building Accessible Websites*. Retrieved 20 June, 2010, from http://joeclark.org/book/sashay/serialization/AppendixA.html

——— (2003). "Accessibility implications of digital rights management." *Media Access*. Retrieved 26 June, 2010, from http://joeclark.org/access/resources/DRM.html

——— (2010). "Smart Designer Exports Dumb Pictures of Text." *Daring Fawnyball*. Retrieved 20 June, 2010, from http://daringfawnyball.wordpress.com/2010/06/02/wiredapp/

Cole, P. (2007). "The Body Politic: Theorising Disability and Impairment." *Journal of Applied Philosophy* 24(21): 169–76.

Coombs, N. (2007). "Interview: Jennison Asuncion." *EASI: Equal Access to Software and Information.* Retrieved 21 June, 2010, from http://easi.cc/podcasts/itnews/itnews-tr/jennison01.htm

Craven, J. (2008). *Web Accessibility: What We Have Achieved and Challenges Ahead.* World Library and Information Congress: 74th IFLA General Conference and Council, Québec, Canada.

Crichton, P. (2007). "More on the iPhone. … " *Access 2.0.* Retrieved 12 April, 2008 from http://www.bbc.co.uk/blogs/access20/2007/01/more_on_the_iphone.shtml

Daily, M. (2008). "AC/DC turns off iTunes for 'Black Ice'" *Reuters.* Retrieved 22 June, 2010, from http://www.reuters.com/article/idUSTRE49C4BH20081013

Daily Paulson, L. (2009). "W3C Adopts Web-Accessibility Specifications." *Computer* 42(2): 23–26.

DAISY Consortium Board of Directors. (2007). "DAISY Board of Directors Position Statement on Digital Rights Management (DRM)." *DAISY Consortium.* Retrieved 18 June, 2010, from http://data.daisy.org/publications/docs/positionpapers/position_paper_protecting_content.html?q=publications/docs/positionpapers/position_paper_protecting_content.html

Davis, L. (1995). *Enforcing Normalcy: Disability, Deafness, and the Body.* London, Verso.

de Pascale, M., S. Mulatto, and D. Prattichizzo (2008). *Bringing Haptics to Second Life for Visually Impaired People.* Proceedings of the 6th international conference on Haptics: Perception, Devices and Scenarios, Madrid, Spain, Springer Verlag, 10–13 June, 2008.

Dewsbury, G., K. Clarke, D. Randall, M. Rouncefield, and I. Sommerville (2004). "The Anti-social Model of Disability." *Disability & Society,* 19(2): 145–58.

Disability Bitch (2008). "Disability Bitch vs Flat Shoes." *Ouch! Its a Disability Thing.* Retrieved 26 June, 2010, from http://www.bbc.co.uk/ouch/opinion/bltch/disability_bitch_vs_flat_shoes.shtml

Disability Rights Advocates (2010). "National Federation of the Blind v. Target." *Disability Rights Advocates.* Retrieved 25 June, 2010, from http://www.dralegal.org/cases/private_business/nfb_v_target.php

Dolson, J. (2010). "Accessibility Review: Target.com." *Practical ecommerce insights for online merchants.* Retrieved 25 June, 2010, from http://www.practicalecommerce.com/articles/1717-Accessibility-Review-Target-com

Ecker, K. D. (2008). "Mobile Phones as a Social Medium for the Deaf: A Uses and Gratifications Study." Department of Communication, The Rochester Institute of Technology. Master of Science Degree in Communication and Media Technologies.

Edwards, J. (2007). "Technology Is the Last, Best Hope for Accessibility." *Brothercake.* Retrieved 1 May, 2008, from http://www.brothercake.com/site/resources/reference/hope

———— (2008). "Stop Using Ajax." *Brothercake.* Retrieved 1 May, 2008, from http://dev.opera.com/articles/view/stop-using-ajax

Ellcessor, E. (2010). "Bridging Disability Divides." *Information, Communication & Society* 13(3): 289–308.

Ellis, K. (2008). *Disabling Diversity: The Social Construction of Disability in 1990s Australian National Cinema.* Saarbrücken, VDM-Verlag.

———— (2010). "A Purposeful Rebuilding: YouTube, Representation, Accessibility and the socio-political space of Disability." *Telecommunications Journal of Australia* 60(2): 21.1–21.12.

Ellis, K. and M. Kent (2010). "Community Accessibility: Tweeters take responsibility for an accessible Web 2.0." *Fast Capitalism* 6(2).

Epstein, F. (2008). "Second Life is my Wheelchair." *The Metaverse Journal*. Retrieved 12 August, 2009, from http://www.metaversejournal.com/2008/09/19/second-life-is-my-wheelchair

Facebook (2010). "Statistics." *Facebook*. Retrieved 19 June, 2010, from http://www.facebook.com/press/info.php?statistics

Fine, A. (2006) "A New Bargain: YouTube politics." *San Francisco Chronicle*, 31 October, 2006.

Finkelstein, V. (1975). "To Deny or Not to Deny Disability." *Magic Carpet* 27(1): 31–38.

———— (1980). "Attitudes and Disabled People: Issues For Discussion." *Disability Archive UK*. Retrieved 5 June, 2010, from http://www.leeds.ac.uk/disability-studies/archiveuk/finkelstein/attitudes.pdf

———— (1981). "Disability and the Helper/Helped relationship: A Historical View." *Disability Archive UK*. Retrieved 5 June, 2010, from http://www.leeds.ac.uk/disability-studies/archiveuk/finkelstein/Helper-Helped%20Relationship.pdf

Fisher, K. (2007). "Musicload: 75% of Customer Service Problems Caused by DRM." *Ars technica*. Retrieved 17 June, 2010, from http://arstechnica.com/tech-policy/news/2007/03/75-percent-customer-problems-caused-by-drm.ars

Fletcher, D. (2009). "What Happens to Your Facebook After You Die." *Time*. Retrieved 10 June, 2010, from http://www.time.com/time/business/article/0,8599,1932803,00.html

Foley, A. and R. Voithofer (2008). *Social Networking Technology, NetGen Learners, and Emerging Technology: Democratic Claims and the Mythology of Equality*. American Educational Research Association (AERA) national conference, New York, 25–27 March. Retrieved 18 June, 2010, from http://flynnfoley.typepad.com/FoleyVoithofer.pdf

Ford, K. (2010). "The Web More Accessible, Really?" *Kelly's Corner*. Retrieved 19 June, 2010, from http://blog.kellyford.org/archives/2010/01/the_web_more_ac.html

French, S. (1993). "Disability, Impairment or Something in Between." *Disabling Barriers—Enabling Environments*. John Swain, Sally French, Colin Barnes, and Carol Thomas. London, Sage Publications with the Open University Press: 17–25.

Friedkin, K. (2008). "Accessibility & Second Life." *Grid Life*. Retrieved 26 June, 2010, from http://www.kippiefriedkin.com/2008/09/11/accessibility-second-life/

Funnell, A. (2009). "Second Life's other life." *ABC Future Tense*. Retrieved 15 October, 2009, from http://www.abc.net.au/rn/futuretense/stories/2009/2711237.htm

Furendal, D. (2007). "Downloading Music and Videos from the Internet: A Study of the Accessibility of The Pirate Bay and iTunes store." *Presentation at Uneå University*. Retrieved 13 April, 2008, from http://www.david.furendal.com/Accessibility.aspx

Garland-Thompson, R. (2000). "Incorporating Disability Studies into American Studies." *Georgetown University*. Retrieved 2 July, 2001, from www.georgetown.edu/crossroads/interests/ds-hum/thompson.html

Gibson, B. (2007). "Keynote Speech: Enabling An Accessible Web 2.0." *16th International World Wide Web Conference*. Banff, Canada: http://www.w4a.info/2007/prog/k2001-gibson.pdf

Gibson, W. (1984). *Neuromancer*. New York, Ace.

Giroux, H. (2009). "The Iranian Uprisings and the Challenge of the New Media: Rethinking the Politics of Representation." *Fast Capitalism* 5(1): Retrieved 26 October, 2009, from http://www.uta.edu/huma/agger/fastcapitalism/5_2/Giroux5_2.html

Goffman, E. (1963, republished 1997). "The Stigmatized Self: Stigma: Notes on the Management of Spoiled Identity." *The Goffman Reader.* Charles Lemert and A. Branaman. Oxford, Blackwell Publishers Inc.: 73–80.

Goggin, G. (2005). "The Internet, Online and Mobile Cultures." *Media and Communications in Australia.* Stuart Cunningham and G. Turner. Sydney, Allen & Unwin.

—— (2008). "Innovation and Disability." *Media Culture* 11(3): Retrieved 25 July, 2008, from http://journal.media-culture.org.au/index.php/mcjournal/article/view Article/56

—— (2009a). "Adapting the Mobile Phone: The iphone and its Consumption." *Continuum: Journal of Media and Cultural Studies* 23(2): 231–44.

—— (2009b). "Disability and the Ethics of Listening." *Continuum: Journal of Media and Cultural Studies* 23(4): 489–502.

Goggin, G. and C. Newell (2003). *Digital Disability: The Social Construction of Disability in New Media.* Lanham, Rowman and Littlefield Publishers Inc.

—— (2005a). *Disability in Australia: Exposing a Social Apartheid.* Sydney, University of New South Wales.

—— (2005b). "Introduction: The Intimate Relations between Technology and Disability." *Disability Studies Quarterly* 25(2): Retrieved 17 June, 2010, from http://www.dsq-sds.org/article/view/547/724

Goggin, G. and T. Noonan (2006). "Blogging Disability: The Interface between New Cultural Movements and Internet Technology." *Use of Blogs.* Axel Burns and J. Jacobs. New York, Lang: 161–72.

Gonzalez, A. (2009). "AbleGamers Gives Warhammer 'Most Accessible Mainstream Game' of 2008." *AbleGamer.* Retrieved 29 June, 2010, from http://www.ablegamers.com/game-news/ablegamers-gives-warhammer-game-of-2008.html

Goodwin, M. S. (2008). "Enhancing and Accelerating the Pace of Autism Research and Treatment: The Promise of Developing Innovative Technology." *Focus on Autism and Other Developmental Disabilities* 23(2): 125–28.

Gordon, J. (2009). "How to Create Your First iPhone Application." *Smashing Magazine.* Retrieved 17 June, 2010, from http://www.smashingmagazine.com/2009/08/11/how-to-create-your-first-iphone-application/

Gracy, K. F. (2007). "Moving Image Preservation and Cultural Capital." *Library Trends* 56(1): 183–97.

Griffey, J. (2010). "Electronic Book Readers." *Library Technology Reports*, April: 7–19.

Groce, N. (1985). *Everyone Here Spoke Sign Language: Hereditary Deafness on Martha's Vineyard.* Cambridge, Harvard University Press.

Habermas, J. (1962). *The Structural Transformation of the Public Sphere: An Inquiry into a Category of Bourgeois Society.* Cambridge, Polity.

Haller, B. (2009a). "National Association of the Deaf calls out Netflix for lack of captioned 'Wizard of Oz'." *Disability Dis & Dat.* Retrieved 25 June, 2010, from http://media-dis-n-dat.blogspot.com/2009/10/national-association-of-deaf-calls-out.html

—— (2009b). "Join Marlee Matlin in demanding captioning of online video content." *Disability Dis & Dat.* Retrieved 27 October, 2009, from http://media-dis-n-dat.blogspot.com/2009/10/join-marlee-matlin-in-demanding.html

—— (2010). *Representing Disability in an Ableist World: Essays on Mass Media.* Louisville, Louisville Avocado Press.

Harper, P. (2003). "Networking the Deaf Nation." *Australian Journal of Communication* 30(3): 153–66.

Harrenstien, K. (2009). "Automatic Captions in Google." *The Official Google Blog.* Retrieved 18 June, 2010, from http://googleblog.blogspot.com/2009/11/automatic-captions-in-youtube.html?utm_source=feedburner&utm_medium=feed&utm_campaign=Feed:+blogspot/MKuf+%28Official+Google+Blog%29

Hartley, J. (2002). *Communication, Cultural and Media Studies: The Key Concepts.* London and New York, Routledge.

Hasselbring, T. S. and C. H. Williams Glaser (2000). "Use of Computer Technology to Help Students with Special Needs." *Children and Computer Technology* 10(2): 102–22.

Hasson, J. (2009). "It's a Challenge to Make Gov 2.0 Accessible to Disabled." *Fierce Government IT: The Government IT news briefing.* Retrieved 19 June, 2010, from http://www.fiercegovernmentit.com/story/its-challenge-make-gov-2-0-accessible-disabled/2009-11-15#ixzz0p5w5bjCc

Hawkins, L. (2007). "STOP Facebook Discriminating Against Disabled Users." *Facebook.* Retrieved 29 June, 2010, from http://www.facebook.com/?ref=home#!/group.php?gid=5922943061&ref=ts

Haynes, C. A. and J. R. Holmevik (2001). *High Wired: On the Design, Use, and Theory of Educational MOOs.* Michigan, University of Michigan Press.

Heim, M. (1991). "The Metaphysics of Virtual Reality." *Virtual Reality.* Sandra K. Helsel and J. P. Roth. Westport, Meckler.

Heiss, J. J. (2003). "Coding from Scratch: A Conversation with Virtual Reality Pioneer Jaron Lanier." *JavaOne Magazine*, 23 January.

Helmer, J. (2007). "Second Life and Virtual Worlds." *Learning Light.* Retrieved 26 June, 2010, from http://www.norfolkelearningforum.co.uk/wp-content/uploads/2009/04/virtual-worlds_ll_oct_2007.pdf

Hesseldahl, A. (2009). "Apple's iDecade." *Bloomberg Business Week*, 31 December.

Hevey, D. (1997). "Controlling Interests." *Framed: Interrogating Disability in the Media.* A. Pointon and C. Davies. London, British Film Institute: 209–13.

Hickey-Moody, A. and D. Wood (2008). "Imagining Otherwise: Deleuze, disability & Second Life.", conference paper presented at the ANZCA08 Conference *Power and Place.* Wellington New Zealand, July 2008.

——— (2009). "Ethics in Second Life: Difference, Desire and the Production of Subjectivity." *Emerging Ethical Issues of Life in Virtual Worlds.* Charles Wankel and S. Malleck. USA, IAP: 153–75.

Hillis, K. (1999). *Digital Sensations: Space Identity and Embodiment in Virtual Reality.* Minneapolis, University of Minnesota Press.

Holloway, D. (2007). "Gender, Telework and the Reconfiguration of the Australian Family Home." *Continuum: Journal of Media and Cultural Studies* 21(1): 33–44.

Houghton-Jan, S. (2007). "Imagine No Restrictions." *School Library Journal* 53(6) (June): 52–54.

Howe, W. (2010, 24 March). "An Anecdotal History of the People and Communities that Brought about the Internet and the Web." *A Brief History of the Internet.* Retrieved 25 June, 2010, from http://www.walthowe.com/navnet/history.html

Huang, J. and B. Guo (2005). "Building Social Capital: A Study of the Online Disability Community." *Disability Studies Quarterly* 25(2): Retrieved 25 June, 2010, from http://www.dsq-sds.org/article/view/554/731

Huddy, H. and H. Swan. (2006). "Disability Rights and Digital Rights Management: Lock out pirates not disabled people." *Human Factors of DRM.* Retrieved 25 June, 2010, from http://www.indicare.org/tiki-download_file.php?fileId = 182

Hudson, R. (2009). "Refreshable Braille and the Web." *Dingo Access.* Retrieved 25 June, 2010, from http://www.dingoaccess.com/accessibility/refreshable-braille-and-the-web/

Human Rights and Equal Opportunities Commission (2000). "Accessibility of Electronic Commerce and New Service and Information Technologies for Older Australians and People with a Disability." *Report of the Human Rights and Equal Opportunity Commission on a reference from the Attorney-General.* Retrieved 30 April, 2008, from http://www.hreoc.gov.au/disability_rights/inquiries/ecom/ecomrep.htm#BM2_1

———— (2003). "Don't Judge What I Can Do by What you Think I Can't: Ten years of Achievements using Australia's Disability Discrimination Act" *HREOC.*Retrieved 25 June, 2010, from http://www.hreoc.gov.au/disability_rights/dont_judge.htm

———— (2009). "Virgin Blue Becomes more Accessible." *HREOC media release.* Retrieved 25 June, 2010, from http://www.humanrights.gov.au/about/media/media_releases/2009/86_09.html

IBM (2008). "Virtual Worlds User Interface for the Blind." Retrieved 29 June, 2010, from http://services.alphaworks.ibm.com/virtualworlds/

Iheni (2008). "A Brief History of Web Standards in Greek." *Iheni: Making the Web World Wide.* Retrieved 26 June, 2010, from http://www.iheni.com/a-brief-history-of-web-standards-in-greek/

Innes, G. (2009a). "Creating Welcoming School Communities." *More Than Gadgets.* Fremantle Western Australia, 24–25 August ,2009.

———— (2009b). "Presentation to State and Local Government CEO's."*Australian Human Rights Commission.* Retrieved 2 June, 2010, from http://www.humanrights.gov.au/disability_rights/speeches/2009/waceo.htm

Instance, H., R. Bates, A. Hyrskykari, and S. Vickers (2008). *Snap Clutch, a Moded Approach to solving the Midas Touch Problem.* Symposium on Eye tracking research & applications, Savannah, Georgia.

Jackson, N. M., M. A. Maede, P. Ellenbogen, and K. Barrett (2006). "Perspectives on Networking, Cultural Values, and Skills among African American men with Spinal Cord Injury: A Reconsideration of Social Capital Theory." *Journal of Vocational Rehabilitation* 25(2006): 21–33.

James, D. and J. Drennan (2005). "Exploring Addicative Consumption of Mobile Phone Technology." *ANZMAC 2005: Electronic Marketing.*

Jennings, N. and C. Collins (2008). "Virtual or Virtually U: Educational Institutions in Second Life." *International Journal of Social Sciences* 2(3)**:** 180–86.

Jensen, S. S. (2009). "Avatar-Based Sense-Making and Communication Practices in the Metaverse—An Empirical Study of Actors and their Use of Avatars as Personal Mediators in the Virtual Worlds of EverQuest and Second Life." *MedieKultur. Journal of Media and Communication Research* 47. Retrieved 29 June, 2010, from http://ojs.statsbiblioteket.dk/index.php/mediekultur/article/viewArticle/1403

Jobs, S. (2007). "Thoughts on Music." *Apple Inc.* Retrieved 25 June, 2010, from http://www.apple.com/hotnews/thoughtsonmusic/

Johnson, S. (2009). "How Twitter Will Change the Way We Live." *Time in partnership with CNN.* Retrieved 29 March, 2010, from http://www.time.com/time/printout/0,8816,1902604,00.html

Jones, D., E. (2006). "I, Avatar: Construction of Self and Place in Second Life and Technological Innovation." *Gnovis.* Retrieved 8 August, 2009, from http://gnovisjournal.org/journal/i-avatar-constructions-self-and-place-second-life

Jones, T. (2009). "Disability Access Activists Gather to Protest Kindle DRM." *Electronic Frontier Foundation.* Retrieved 19 June, 2010, from http://www.eff.org/deeplinks/2009/04/protest-kindle-drm

Jordan, T. (1999). *Cyberpower: The Culture and Politics of Cyberspace and the Internet.* London, Routledge.

Joyner, A. (2010). "Speaker text adds transcripts to YouTube Videos. Can it get investors to write a big check. *Inc.*"Katalov, V. (2001). "Press-release: Advanced Acrobat eBooks are NOT Really Secure." *Planet ebook.* Retrieved 19 June, 2010, from http://www.planetebook.com/mainpage.asp?webpageid=169

Kavanagh, J. (2002). "Bulletin Interview: Geoff Busby." *Computer Bulletin.* 44(2): 18–19.

Keen, A. and M. Laskoff (2007). "What to Do About Web 2.0." *Brandweek.* 48(28): 24–24.

Keizer, G. (2007). "Hearing Loss Group Complains to FCC about iPhone." *Computerworld.* Retrieved 12 April, 2008, from http://www.computerworld.com/action/article.do?command=viewArticleBasic&articleId=9037999

Kelly, B. (2008). "Is Accessibility 2.0 Becoming Mainstream?" *UK Web Focus.* Retrieved 25 June, 2010, from http://ukwebfocus.wordpress.com/2008/05/01/is-accessibility-20-becoming-mainstream/

Kelly, B., D. Sloan,S. Brown, J. Seale, H. Petrie, P. Lauke, and S. Ball(2007). *Accessibility 2.0: People, Policies and Processes.* 16th International World Wide Web Conference, Banff, Canada, 7–8 May. Retrieved 3 September, 2010, from http://www.ukoln.ac.uk/web-focus/papers/w4a-2007/w4a-2007-kelly.pdf

Kent, M. (2008). "Cultware: Constructing the matrix of internet access." *The Revolution Will Not be Downloaded: Dissent in the Digital Age.* T. Brabazon. Oxford, Chandos: 89–99.

Kerscher, G. and J. Fruchterman (2002). "The Soundproof Book: Exploration of Rights Conflict and Access to Commercial EBooks for People with Disabilities." *First Monday* 7(6): Retrieved 3 September, 2010, from http://131.193.153.231/www/issues/issue7_6/kerscher/

Kouroupetroglou, C., M. Salampasis, and A. Manitsanis (2006). *"A Semantic-web Based Framework for Developing Applications to Improve Accessibility in the WWW."* International Cross-disciplinary Workshop on Web Accessibility (W4A): Building the Mobile Web: Rediscovering Accessibility? Edinburgh, UK.

Kraynak, J. (2004). *The Complete Idiot's Guide to Computer Basics.* London, Alpha Books.

Krazit, T. (2009). "Web Accessibility no Longer an Afterthought." Retrieved 25 June, 2010, from http://edition.cnn.com/2009/TECH/12/15/cnet.web.accessibility/index.html

Krueger, A., A. Ludwig, and D. Ludwig (2009). "Universal Design for Virtual Worlds." *Journal of Virtual Worlds Research* 2(3). Retrieved 29 June, 2010, from http://journals.tdl.org/jvwr/article/view/674/524

Lake, E. (2009). "Iran Prepared to Track Dissent on Social Networks." *The Washington Times*: http://www.washingtontimes.com/news/2009/jun/2020/iran-has-tech-to-track-tweets-texts/

Laker, S. (2010). "Survey Finds the Internet is a Lifeline for People with Disabilities." *Freedom Disability.* Retrieved 18 June, 2010, from http://www.freedomdisability.com/survey-finds-the-internet-is-a-lifeline-for-people-with-disabilities/

Landro, L. (2006). "The Informed Patient: Social Networking Comes to Health Care; Online Tools Give Patients Better Access to Information and Help Build Communities." *Wall Street Journal (Eastern Edition).* New York, 12 July, 2006, Page D1.

Lawson, B. (2006). "Tim Berners-Lee Accessibility Quotes." *Bruce Lawson.* Retrieved 19 June, 2010, from http://www.brucelawson.co.uk/2006/tim-berners-lee-accessibility-quotes/

Lembree, D. (2010). "Transcription: Web Axe Episode 81 (HTML5 and John Foliot)." *WebAxe*. Retrieved 25 June, 2010, from http://weboverhauls.com/web_axe_pod cast/transcripts/81.htm

Li, H. and C. Hamel (2003). "Writing Issues in College Students with Learning Disabilities: A Synthesis of the Literature from 1990 to 2000." *Learning Disability Quarterly* 26(1): 29–46.

Library of Congress. (2010). "Thomas." Retrieved 30 May, 2010, from http://www.thomas.gov/

Liccardi, I., A. Ounnas, R. Pau, E. Massey, P. Kimunnen, S. Lewthwaite, M. Midy, and C. Sarkar (2007). "The Role of Social Networks in Students' Learning Experiences." *Working Group Reports on ITiCSE on Innovation and Technology in Computer Science Education*. Retrieved 23 June, 2010, from http://eprints.ecs.soton.ac.uk/14907/2/ITiCSE2007_WG4.pdf

Licklider, J. (1960). "Man-Computer Symbiosis." *IRE Transactions on Human Factors in Electronics*. Retrieved 26 June, 2010, from http://groups.csail.mit.edu/medg/people/psz/Licklider.html

Linden, H. (2004). "The Nine Souls of Wilde Cunningham." *New World Notes*. Retrieved 26 June, 2010, from http://secondlife.blogs.com/nwn/2004/12/the_nine_souls_.html

Linden, P. (2007). "Embracing the Inevitable." *Second Life Blogs*. Retrieved 26 June, 2010, from http://blogs.secondlife.com/community/features/blog/2007/01/08/embracing-the-inevitable

Linton, S. (1996). *Claiming Disability: Knowledge and Identity*. New York, New York University Press.

Lioncourt (2010). "Google Chrome for Mac Disregards Accessibility." *Mac-cessibility Network*. Retrieved 25 June, 2010, from http://www.lioncourt.com/2010/06/01/google-chrome-for-mac-disregards-accessibility/

Lobez, S. (1999). "SOCOG and HREOC; Jaidyn Leske-Justice Denied?" *The Law Report*. Retrieved 25 June, 2010, from http://www.abc.net.au/rn/talks/8.30/lawrpt/stories/s57027.htm

Lunat, Z. (2008). "The Internet and the Public Sphere: Evidence from civil Society in Developing Countries." *EJISDC*. Retrieved 15 March, 2010, from http://www.ejisdc.org/ojs2/index.php/ejisdc/article/viewFile/501/253

Madden, M. and L. Raine. (2003). "America's Online Pursuits: The Changing Picture of Who's Online and What they Do." *Pew Internet & American Life Project*. Retrieved 29 April, 2004, from http://www.pewinternet.org/reports/reports.asp?Report=106&Section=ReportLevel1&Field=Level1ID&ID=463

Male, M. (2003). *Technology for Inclusion: Meeting the Special Needs of All Students*. Boston, Allyn and Bacon.

Marks, D. (1999). "Dimensions of Oppression: theorising the embodied subject." *Disability & Society* 14(5): 611–26.

Martínez-Cabrera, A. (2010) "Web More Accessible to Those With Disabilities." *San Francisco Chronicle,* 1 January.

Mason, B. (2008). "Why AOL Is Web 2.0." *AOL Developer Network*. Retrieved 26 June, 2010, from http://dev.aol.com/article/2008/why_aol_is_web20

McBlain, A. (2009). "6 Predictions for the Future of the Internet." *Six Revisions*. Retrieved 19 June, 2010, from http://sixrevisions.com/web-technology/6-predictions-for-the-future-of-the-internet/

McConnaughey, J., D.W. Everette, T. Reynolds, and W. Lader (1999). "Falling Through the Net: Defining the Digital Divide." Washington: U.S. Department of Commerce.

McCullagh, D. (2001). "Why Dmitry Sklyarov belongs in jail, by inside.com's R. Parloff (resend)." *Politech: Politics and Technology.* Retrieved 25 June, 2010, from http://www.politechbot.com/p-02360.html

—— (2002). "Judge: Disabilities Act doesn't cover Web." *cnet News.* Retrieved 25 June, 2010, from http://news.cnet.com/2100-1023-962761.html?tag = fd_top_1

McGee, P. and V. Diaz (2007). "Wikis and Podcasts and Blogs! Oh, My! What is a Faculty Member Supposed to Do?" *Educause Review.* 42(5) September/October: 28–41.

McKay, A. (2007). "The Official Petition for a More Accessible Facebook." *Facebook.* Retrieved 17 May, 2010, from http://www.facebook.com/?ref=home#!/group.php?gid=2384051749&ref=ts

Media Access Australia (2008). "Streaming Video." *Media Access Australia.* Retrieved 25 June, 2010, from http://www.mediaaccess.org.au/index.php?option=com_content&view = article&id = 602&Itemid = 104

Microsoft (1998). "Greg Lowney: Microsoft's Director of Accessibility is Motivated by the Millions of People His Work Will Benefit." *Microsoft News Centre.* Retrieved 26 June, 2010, from http://www.microsoft.com/presspass/features/1998/10–22-lowney.mspx

Miller, P., S. Parker, and S. Gillinson (2004). "Disableism: How to tackle the last prejudice." *Demos.* Retrieved 16 June, 2010, from http://www.demos.co.uk/files/disablism.pdf

Mitchell, D. and S. Snyder (2000). *Narrative Prosthesis: Disability and the Dependencies of Discourse.* Ann Arbor, The University of Michigan Press.

Morgan Stanley & Co. (2009). "The Mobile Internet Report." Retrieved 13 June, 2010, from http://www.morganstanley.com/institutional/techresearch/mobile_internet_report122009.html

Morrissey, B. (2007). "Social Networks: The Power of Many." *Billboard.* Retrieved 29 June, 2010, from http://www.billboard.com/news/ask-billboard-1003685494.story#/news/ask-billboard-1003685494.story

Mullen, L., J. Beilke, and N. Brooks (2007). "Redefining Field Experiences: Virtual Environments in Teacher Education." *International Journal of Social Sciences* 2(1): 22–28. Retrieved 29 June, 2010, from http://www.waset.org/journals/ijss/v2/v2-1-4.pdf

Munro, N. (2001). "When the Dot-Com Bubble Burst." *National Journal* 33(6): February 10.

National Disability Officer Coordination Program (2010). "Sourcing Alternative Formats." *Australian Government Department of Education Employment and Workplace Relations.* Retrieved 15 June, 2010, from http://www.ndcovictoria.net.au/Information–Resources/Student-Transition–Participation/Sourcing-Alternative-Formats.aspx

New Media Age (2007).' Disability Experts Slam Social Sites'. *New Media Age.* London, Centaur Communications Limited: 1.

Newton, J. (2010). "Virtually Enabled: How Title III of the Americans with Disabilities Act might be Applied to Online Virtual Worlds." *Federal Communications Law Journal* 62(1): 183–205.

Next Generation Technologies Incorporated. (2010). "What is J-Tunes?" *Next Generation Technologies Incorporated.* Retrieved 5 June, 2010, from http://www.ngtvoice.com/products/software/tandt/j-tunes/

Norris, J. (2009). "The Growth and Direction of Healthcare Support Groups in Virtual Worlds." *Journal of Virtual Worlds Research* 2(2). Retrieved 30 June, 2010, from http://journals.tdl.org/jvwr/article/view/658/500

NTIA (1999). "Falling Through the Net: Defining the Digital Divide." *United States Department of Commerce.* Retrieved 26 June, 2010, from http://www.ntia.doc.gov/ntiahome/fttn99/fttn.pdf

O'Reilly, T. (2005). "What Is Web 2.0: Design Patterns and Business Models for the Next Generation of Software." *O'Reilly* 30 September, 2005. Retrieved 18 June, 2010, from http://oreilly.com/web2/archive/what-is-web-20.html

—— (2006). "Web 2.0 Compact Definition: Trying Again" *O'Reilly*, 10 December 2006. Retrieved 18 June, 2010, from http://radar.oreilly.com/2006/12/web-20-compact-definition-tryi.html

O'Reilly, T. and J. Battelle (2009). "Web Squared: Web 2.0 Five Years On." *Web 2.0 Summit.* Retrieved 18 June, 2010, from http://assets.en.oreilly.com/1/event/28/web2009_websquared-whitepaper.pdf

Oliver, M. (1978). "The Misuse of Technology: Walking Appliances for Paraplegics." *Journal of Medical Engineering & Technology* 2(2): 69–70.

—— (1996). *Understanding Disability: From Theory to Practice.* Hampshire, Palgrave.

Ondrejka, C. (2010). "'Big Brother' versus 'Little Brother': Two Possible Media Futures." *The Futurist.* March–April, 2010: 33–34.

OS iPhone Reference Library (2010). "Making Your iPhone Application Accessible." *Apple Developer.* Retrieved 18 June, 2010, from http://developer.apple.com/iphone/library/documentation/UserExperience/Conceptual/iPhoneAccessibility/Making_Application_Accessible/Making_Application_Accessible.html#//apple_ref/doc/uid/TP40008785-CH102-SW5

Ostrow, A. (2009). "Facebook Overtakes MySpace (Again)." *Mashable.* Retrieved 12 June, 2010, from http://mashable.com/2009/02/19/facebook-bigger-than-myspace-in-us/

Ouch! (2010). "About Ouch! An Introduction to the BBC's Disability Site." *Ouch!.* Retrieved 30 June, 2010, from http://www.bbc.co.uk/ouch/about.shtml

Outlaw (2006). "Berners-Lee Applies Web 2.0 to Improve Accessibility." *Outlaw News.* Retrieved 25 June, 2010, from http://www.out-law.com/page-6946

Pajtas, P. E. (2007). "Navigating Virtual Reality Platforms: Virtual World as Niche for Support Groups and Philanthropy." *Harvard Brain* 14 May 2007: 12–14.

Pearlman, L. (2007). "The Gift Shop is Now Open … for Everyone." *Facebook.* Retrieved 25 October, 2009, from http://blog.facebook.com/blog.php?post=2341917130

Pegrum, M. (2010). "Web 3.0 in Education." *E-Language Wikispaces.* Retrieved 25 June, 2010, from http://e-language.wikispaces.com/web3.0

Pepitone, J. (2010). "End of the Web as we know it, thanks to iPad and others." *CNN-Money.com.* Retrieved 25 June, 2010, from http://money.cnn.com/2010/02/03/technology/Web_splintering/index.htm?postversion=2010020313

Peters, M. (2009). "Spot On: The blind Gaming the Blind." *Game Spot.* Retrieved 29 June, 2010, from http://au.gamespot.com/news/6215457.html

Pierce, B. (1999). "NFB Sues AOL." *Braille Monitor.* Retrieved 26 June, 2010, from http://nfb.org/legacy/bm/bm99/bm991201.htm

Pinder, C. (2005). "Customers with Disabilities: The Academic Library Response." *Library Review* 54(8): 464–71.

Popov, V. (2006). "Can WCAG 2.0 be Simpler?" *evolt.org.* Retrieved 25 June, 2010, from http://www.evolt.org/can_wcag_2_be_simpler

Power, M. R. and D. Power (2004). "Everyone Here Speaks Text: Deaf People Using SMS in Australia and the rest of the World." *Journal of Deaf Studies and Deaf Education* 9(3): 333–43.

Power, D., M. R. Power, and Horstmanshof (2007). "German Deaf People Using Text Communication: Short Message Service, TTY, Relay Services, Fax, and E-mail." *American Anals of the Deaf* 152(3): 291–301.

Power, M. R., D. Power, and B. Rehling (2006). "Deaf People Communicationg via SMS, TTY, Relay Service, Fax, and Computers in Australia." *Journal Deaf Studies and Deaf Education* 12(1): 80–92.

Praveen. (2009). "Stroller (& handicap) Accessibility iPhone and Web Apps." *Mass-DotDevelopers.* Retrieved 18 June, 2010, from http://groups.google.com/group/massdotdevelopers/browse_thread/thread/dfeff09b4f79bce4?pli=1

Price, M. E (1995). *Television, the Public Sphere, and National Identity.* Oxford, Clarendon Press.

Putnam, S. (2007). "Folmer Believes a Virtual World Doesn't Have to Be a Visual One." *Axistive.* Retrieved 18 June, 2010, from http://www.axistive.com/folmer-believes-a-virtual-world-doesn%E2%80%99t-have-to-be-a-visual-one.html

Raskind, M., K. Stanberry, and M. Margalit (2007). "Social Networking on the Internet for Youth with Learning Disabilities." *Perspectives on Language and Literacy,* Summer: 25–30.

Raynes-Goldie, K. (2010). "Aliases, Creeping, and Wall-Cleaning: Understanding Privacy in the Age of Facebook." *First Monday* 15(1): Retrieved 17 June, 2010, from http://firstmonday.org/htbin/cgiwrap/bin/ojs/index.php/fm/article/view/2775/2432

Reena, J. (2009). "How Tech for the Disabled is Going Mainstream." *Business Week,* McGraw Hill Companies Inc, published 24 September, 2009.

Regan, B. (2004). *Accessibility and Design: A Failure of the Imagination.* International Cross-disciplinary Workshop on Web Accessibility (W4A), 17–22 May, 2004.

Rheingold, H. (1991). *Virtual Reality.* London, Secker & Warburg.

Richards, J. (2008). "McKinsey: Ignore Second Life at Your Peril." *Times Online:* Retrieved 17 June, 2010, from http://technology.timesonline.co.uk/tol/news/tech_and_web/article3803056.ece

Richardson, I. (2007). "Pocket Technospaces: The Bodily Incorporation of Mobile Media." *Continuum: Journal of Media and Cultural Studies* 21(2): 205–16.

Rimmer, M. (2003). "Virtual Countries: Internet Domain Names and Geographical Terms." *Media International Australia, Incorporating Culture and Policy* (106): 125–36.

Robinson, S. (2002). "Human or Computer? Take This Test." *New York Times.* Retrieved 25 October, 2009, from http://www.msri.org/people/members/sara/articles/ai.html

Robson, G. D. (2004). *The Closed Captioning Handbook.* Amsterdam, Gulf Professional Publishing.

Rose, F. (2005) "Battle for the Soul of the MP3 Phone." *Wired Magazine* 13(11): Retrived 25 June, 2010, from http://www.wired.com/wired/archive/13.11/phone.html

Roulstone, A. (1998). *Enabling Technology: Disabled People, Work, and New Technology.* Buckingham, Open University Press.

Salman, S. (2006). "Autism Community Forges Virtual Haven." *The Guardian.* Retrieved 30 June, 2010, from http://www.guardian.co.uk/society/2006/mar/08/guardiansocietysupplement1

Sapey, B. (2000). "Disablement in the Information Age." *Disability & Society* 15(4): 619–37.

Schiller, K. (2010). "A Happy Medium: Ebooks, Licensing, and DRM." *Information Today* 27(2): 1, 42, 44.

Schlender, S. (2008). "Second Life Frees Disabled from Restrictions on Everyday Life." *Voice of America News.* Retrieved 12 September, 2008, from http://www.voanews. com/english/archive/2008–{09/2008}-09-17-voa24.cfm?CFID=265239176&CFT OKEN=68172091&jessionid=88305599426cc3bdc715019b4c1429144d24

Schramm, M. (2008). "Blizzard and the Hidden Population of Disabled Players." *WOW. Com.* Retrieved 29 June, 2010, from http://www.wow.com/2008/09/05/blizzard-and-the-hidden-population-of-disabled-players/

Schultz, J. (2002). "The Press." *The Media & Communications in Australia.* Stuart Cunningham and G. Turner. Crows Nest, Allen & Unwin: 101–16.

Sen, K. and D. T. Hill (2000). "The Internet: Virtual Politics." *Media, Culture and Politics in Indonesia.* Krishna Sen and D. T. Hill. Melbourne, Oxford University Press: 194–217.

Seymour, W. (1998). *Remaking the Body: Rehabilitation and Change.* London and New York, Routledge.

Seymour, W. and D. Lupton (2004). "Holding the Line Online: Exploring Wired Relationships for People with Disabilities." *Disability & Society* 19(4): 291–305.

Shakespeare, T. (2006). *Disability Rights and Wrongs.* New York, Routledge.

——— (2009). "Not Just a Pretty Facebook." *Ouch!* Retrieved 28 July, 2009, from http://www.bbc.co.uk/ouch/opinion/not_just_a_pretty_facebook.shtml

Shakespeare, T. and N. Watson (1997). "Defending the Social Model." *Disability Studies: Past Present and Future.* Len Barton and M. Oliver. Leeds, The Disability Press. Retrieved 29 June, 2010, from http://www.leeds.ac.uk/disability-studies/archiveuk/Shakespeare/chapter18.pdf

——— (2002). "The Social Model of Disability: An Outdated Ideology?" *Research in Social Science and Disability* 2: 9–28. Retrived 29 June, 2010, from http://www. leeds.ac.uk/disability-studies/archiveuk/Shakespeare/social %20model%20of%20 disability.pdf

Sheldon, A. (2003). "Changing Technology." *Disability Studies Archive.* Retrieved 18 June, 2010, from http://www.leeds.ac.uk/disability-studies/archiveuk/Sheldon/ chapter%20for%20alison.pdf

Shrestha, M., S. Wilson, and M. Singh (2008). "Knowledge Networking: A Dilemma in Building Social Capital Through Nonformal Education." *Adult Education Quarterly* 58(2): 129–50.

Sims, G. (2008). "iTunes 8 + Jaws 10 = Accessibility: Hearing is Believing." *oz: the blog of glenda sims (the goodwtch).* Retrieved 25 June, 2010, from http://www.glendathe-good.com/blog/?p=319

Sinclair, B. (2008). "Survey: Casual Gamers Disproportionately Disabled." *GameSpotAu.* Retrieved 29 June, 2010, from http://au.gamespot.com/news/6192402.html

Sinclair, L. (2010). "Facebook targets $2bn as it overtakes Google." *The Australian.* Retrieved 22 March, 2010, from http://www.theaustralian.com.au/business/media/ facebook-targets-2bn-as-it-overtakes-google/story-e6frg996–1225843478239

Smith, J. (2008). "WebAim Blog Target lawsuit settled ." *Webaim Blog.* Retrieved 25 June, 2010, from http://webaim.org/blog/target-lawsuit-settled/

——— (2009). "Fastest Growing Demographic on Facebook: Women Over 55." *Inside Facebook.* Retrieved 25 October, 2009, from http://www.insidefacebook. com/2009/02/02/fastest-growing-demographic-on-facebook-women-over-55/

Smith, T. (2008). "Ten Years Old: The World's First MP3 Player." *Register Hardware.* Retrieved 12 April, 2008, from http://www.reghardware.co.uk/2008/03/10/ ft_first_mp3_player/

Snyder, S. (2006). "About the Encyclopedia Covers: Visualizing Variation." *Encyclopedia of Disability*. G. Albrecht. Thousand Oaks, Sage. 1: xx–xxv.

Solove, D. (2007). *The Future of Reputation: Gossip, Rumor, and Privacy on the Internet.* New Haven, Yale University Press.

Stelter, B. (2010)." On Web Video, Captions Are Coming Slowly." *New York Times*. Retrieved 20 June, 2010, from http://www.nytimes.com/2010/06/21/business/media/21captions.html

Stephenson, N. (1992). *Snow Crash New York*. New York, Bantam/Spectra.

Stienstra, D. and L. Troschuk (2005). "Engaging Citizens with Disabilities in eDemocracy." *Disability Studies Quarterly* 25(2): online. Retrieved 24 June, 2010, from http://www.dsq-sds.org/article/view/550/727 .

Suarez-Balcazar, Y., F. E. Balcazar, and T. Taylor-Ritzler (2009). "Using the Internet to Conduct Research with Culturally Diverse Populations: Challenges and Opportunities." *Cultural Diversity and Ethnic Minority Psychology* 15(1): 96–1074.

Sylvie. (2009). "Disability and iPhone apps." *Population of One*. Retrieved 18 June, 2010, from http://www.sylvienoel.ca/blog/?p=1195

Symington, L. (2004). "Creating a Vision: Why Do I Need a Plan?" *Computer Resources for People with Disabilities: A Guide to Assistive Technologies, Tools and Resources for People of All Ages*. A. Mummery. Berkeley, Hunter House Publishers: 8–26.

Taylor, C. (2008). "The Disability Boom." *FSB: Fortune Small Business*: 58–60.

Techdis (2010). "e-Books and Accessibility—a briefing for education libraries" *JISC Advance*. Retrieved 25 June, 2010, from http://www.techdis.ac.uk/index.php?p=9_33_2

TEITAC (2008). "Report to the Access Board: Refreshed Accessibility Standards and Guidelines in Telecommunications and Electronic and Information Technology." *Access Board*. Retrieved 25 June, 2010, from http://www.access-board.gov/sec508/refresh/report/#a2

Terzi, L. (2004). "The Social Model of Disability: A Philosophical Critique." *Journal of Applied Philosophy* 21(2): 141–57.

Thomas, B. (1997). *The Internet for Scientists and Engineers: Online Tools and Resources.* Oxford and New York, Oxford University Press.

Thomas, C. (1999). *Female Forms: Experiencing and Understanding Disability*. Buckingham and Philadelphia, Open University Press.

Towns, S. (2010). "Will Facebook Replace Traditional Government Web Sites?" *Government Technology*. Retrieved 25 June, 2010, from http://www.govtech.com/gt/747140

Turkle, S. (2001). "Foreword: All MOOs are Educational—the Experience of "Walking Through the Self." *High Wired: On the Design, Use, and Theory of Educational MOOs*. Cynthia A. Haynes and J. R. Holmevik. Michigan, University of Michigan Press: ix–xix.

Twitter (2010). "About Us." Retrieved 29 March, 2010, from http://twitter.com/about#about

Udell, J. (2006). "The iTunes U Agenda." *InfoWorld*. Retrieved 12 April, 2008, from http://weblog.infoworld.com/udell/2006/02/22.html

United Nations (2006). "Convention on the Rights of Persons with Disabilities." *Department of Public Information © United Nations*. Retrieved 25 June, 2010, from http://www.un.org/disabilities/convention/conventionfull.shtml

United States Access Board (1998). "Preamble to the Telecommunications Act Accessibility Guidelines." *Federal Register.* Retrieved 25 June, 2010, from http://www.access-board.gov/telecomm/preamble.htm

—— (2010a). "Board Releases Draft Refresh of Section 508 Standards and Section 255 Guidelines." *Access Board.* Retrieved 25 June, 2010, from http://www.access-board.gov/news/ict-draft-rule.htm

—— (2010b). "The Telecommunications Act (Section 255)." *Frequently Asked Questions.* Retrieved 25 June, 2010, from http://www.access-board.gov/telecomm/FAQ.htm

Van Gove, J. (2009). "John Mayer Releases Augmented Reality Music Video." *Mashable.* Retrieved 2010, from http://mashable.com/2009/10/19/augmented-reality-music-video/

Vaughn, J. R. (2006). "Over the Horizon: Potential Impact of Emerging Trends in Information and Communication Technology on Disability Policy and Practice." *National Council on Disability.* Retrieved 19 June, 2010, from http://eric.ed.gov/ERICDocs/data/ericdocs2sql/content_storage_01/0000019b/80/28/09/7b.pdf

Vickers, S., R. Bates, and H. O. Istance (2008). "Gazing into a Second Life: Gaze-Driven Adventures, Control Barriers, and the Need for Disability Privacy Online. *"7th International Conference on Disability, Virtual Reality and Associated Technology.* Maia, Portugal, ArtAbilitation.

Virtual Reality (2010). "Merriam-Webster Online Dictionary." *Merriam-Webster Online.* Retrieved 30 June, 2010, from http://www.merriam-webster.com/dictionary/virtual%20reality

Vogelstein, F. (2008) "The Untold Story: How the iPhone Blew Up the Wireless Industry." *Wired Magazine* 16.

—— (2009). "The Wired Interview: Facebook's Mark Zuckerberg." *Wired Magazine.* Retrieved 20 June, 2010, from http://www.wired.com/epicenter/2009/06/mark-zuckerberg-speaks/

W3C (1999). "Web Content Accessibility Guidelines 1.0." *W3C Recommendation.* Retrieved 25 June, 2010, from http://www.w3.org/TR/WCAG10/

Walker, T. (2010). "Welcome to FarmVille: Population 80 Million." *The Independent.* Retrieved 13 June, 2010, from http://www.independent.co.uk/life-style/gadgets-and-tech/features/welcome-to-farmville-population-80-million-1906260.html

Watson Hyatt, G. (2008). "Social Networking: Including or Excluding People with Disabilities?" *Disaboom live forward.* Retrieved 19 June, 2010, from http://www.disaboomlive.com/Blogs/left_thumb_blogger/archive/2008/01/18/social-networking-including-or-excluding-people-with-disabilities.aspx

—— (2009). "How POUR is Your Blog? Tips for Increasing Your Blog's Accessibility." Retrieved 19 June, 2010, from http://www.blogaccessibility.com/resources/how-pour-is-your-blog.pdf

Watters, A. (2010). "Majority of Tech Experts Think Work Will Be Cloud-Based by 2020, Finds Pew Research Center." *Read Write Cloud.* Retrieved 26 June, 2010, from http://www.readwriteweb.com/cloud/2010/06/majority-of-tech-experts-think.php?utm_source = feedburner&utm_medium = feed&utm_campaign = Feed%3A+readwriteweb+%28ReadWriteWeb%29&utm_content = Twitter

Waunters, R. (2009). "China's Social Network QZone Is Big, But Is It Really The Biggest?" *Techcrunch.* Retrieved 12 May, 2010, from http://techcrunch.com/2009/02/24/chinas-social-network-qzone-is-big-but-is-it-really-the-biggest/

WebAIM (2010a). "Constructing a POUR Website." Retrieved 25 June, 2010, from http://www.webaim.org/articles/pour/

—— (2010b). "Creating Accessible JavaScript." Retrieved 29 June, 2010, from http://www.webaim.org/techniques/javascript/

—— (2010c). "WebAIM Distractibility Simulation." Retrieved 29 June, 2010, from http://www.webaim.org/simulations/distractability.php

Weisen, M., H. Petrie, N. King, and F. Hamilton (2005) "Web Accessibility Revealed: The Museums, Libraries and Archives Council Audit." *Ariadne.*

Wendell, S. (1996). *The Rejected Body: Feminist Philosophical Reflections on Disability.* London and New York, Routledge.

Westin, S. (2005). "Cutting Curbs on the Information highway: Embracing Adaptive technology to Broaden the Web." *Journal of Organizational and End User Computing* 17(3): i–ix.

White, G., R, G. Fitzpatrick, and. G. McAllister, (2008). "Towards Accessible 3DVirtual Environments for the Blind and Visually Impaired. "*3rd International Conference on Digital Interactive Media in Entertainment Arts.* Athens.

Whitney, D. (2008). "Web Search Engines Lead Way to Video." *Television Week,* 3 March, 2008, 27(7): 4–14.

—— (2009). "Captioning Expands Audience." *Television Week,* Crain Communications Inc. 28(4): 12–26.

Wilkinson, J. (2001). "Copyright Law Pits Disability Access against Intellectual Property Rights." *Disability World* 11. Retrieved 19 June, 2010, from http://www.disability-world.org/11–12_01/access/copyright.shtml

Williams, J. and M. Fardon (2007). *Perpetual Connectivity: Lecture Recordings and Portable Media Players.* Proceedings of the conference: Ascilite Singapore 2007, 1084–92. Retrieved 13 April, 2008, from http://www.ascilite.org.au/conferences/singapore07/procs/williams-jo.pdf

Wilson, P. (2010). "iPhone and iPod Touch Apps—Childhood Disability." *Bella Online: The Voice of Women.* Retrieved 19 June, 2010, from http://www.bellaonline.com/articles/art62136.asp

Wolman, D. (2008). "The Truth About Autism: Scientists Reconsider What They Think They Know." *Wired Magazine.* Retrieved 30 June, 2010, from http://www.wired.com/medtech/health/magazine/16–03/ff_autism?currentPage=all#ixzz0sJgGFgAW

Wood, A. and M. Smith (2005). *Online Communication: Linking Technology, Identity, and Culture.* New York and London, Routledge.

Wood, D. (2010). "Communicating in Virtual Worlds Through an accessible Web 2.0 Solution." *Telecommunications Journal of Australia* 60(2): 19.11–19.16.

Wood, L. (2008). "Blind Users Still Struggle with 'Maddening' Computing Obstacles." Computerworld. Retrieved 27 April, 2008, from http://www.computerworld.com/action/article.do?command=viewArticleBasic&articleId=9077118&source=NLT_AM&nlid = 1

Wooley, P. (2007). "Second Life and the Voluntary Sector." Second Life News Network. Retrieved 30 September, 2009, from http://www.slnn.com/article/accessibility-in-a-3d-world/

World Blind Union (2008). "International Right to Read campaign homepage." World Blind Union. Retrieved 12 June, 2010, from http://www.worldblindunion.org/en/right-to-read.html

Worthington, T. (2000). "Olympic Failure: A Case for Making the Web Accessible." Oxford University Computing Laboratory. Retrieved 25 June, 2010, from http://www.tomw.net.au/2000/bat.html

Yee, N., J. N. Bailenson, M. Urbanek, F. Chang, and D. Merget (2007). "The Unbearable Likeness of Being Digital: The Persistance of Nonverbal Social Norms in Online Virtual Environments." *Cyberpsychology and Behaviour* 10(1): 115–21.
Yellowless, P. and M. Cook (2006). "Education About Hallucinations Using an Internet Virtual Reality System: A Qualitative Survey." *Academic Psychiatry* 30(6): 534–40.
Zajicek, M. (2007). "Keynote address: Web 2.0: Hype or Happiness?", *16th International World Wide Web Conference*, Banff, Canada, 7–8 May 2007.
Zeff, R. (2007). "Universal Design across the Curriculum." *New Directions for Higher Education* 137(Spring): 27–44.
Zuckerberg, M. (2009). "Governing the Facebook Service in an Open and Transparent Way." *The Facebook Blog*. Retrieved 29 June, 2010, from http://blog.facebook.com/blog.php?post=56566967130

Bibliography for films

Logan's Run. Dir. Michael Anderson. MGM. 1976.
The Net. Dir. Irwin Winkler. Columbia Pictures Corporation. 1995.
The Matrix. Dir. Andy Wachowski and Lana Wachowski. Groucho II Film Partnership.1999.
Minority Report. Dir. Steven Spielberg. Twentieth Century Fox Film Corporation. 2002.
Tron: The Electronic Gladiator. Dir. Steven Lisberger. Walt Disney Productions. 1982.
The Terminator . Dir. James Cameron. Hemdale Film. 1984.
Terminator 2: Judgment Day. Dir. James Cameron. Carloco Pictures. 1991.
Terminator 3: Rise of the Machines. Dir. Jonathan Mostow. C-2 Pictures. 2003.
Terminator Salvation. Dir. McG. The Halcyon Company. 2009.

Index